W9-CUT-906

Mixed Bag

ARTIFACTS FROM THE CONTEMPORARY CULTURE

Helene D. Hutchinson

Kendall College

Scott, Foresman and Company

FOR BILL, LAURA, AND ROB

Library of Congress Catalog Card No. 73-116774
Copyright © 1970 by Scott, Foresman and Company. Glenview, Illinois 60025.
Philippines Copyright 1970 by Scott, Foresman and Company.
All Rights Reserved.
Printed in the United States of America.
Regional offices of Scott, Foresman and Company are located in
Atlanta, Dallas, Glenview, Palo Alto, Oakland, N.J., and
London, England.

ACKNOWLEDGMENTS

"The Enemy's Testament" by Etel Adnan. Reprinted from *Where Is Vietnam*, ed. Walter Lowenfels (New York: Doubleday & Co., 1967), by permission of Etel Adnan.

"We Burned Every Hut" (Letter to the Editor). Reprinted from the *Akron Beacon Journal*, March 27, 1967, by permission of the *Akron Beacon Journal*.

"The Lion" and "The Tiger" by Hilaire Belloc. From *Cautionary Verses*, by Hilaire Belloc. Published 1941 by Alfred A. Knopf, Inc. Reprinted by permission of the publisher.

From "Violence: A Neglected Mode of Behavior" by Bruno Bettelheim. Reprinted from the *Annals of the American Academy of Political and Social Science*, vol. 364, March 1966, by permission of The American Academy of Political and Social Science and the author.

"Atomic War Now" and "Brotherhood" (graffiti). From "The Golden Age of Graffiti" by Warren Boroson, *Fact*, July-August 1966. Reprinted by permission of *Avant Garde*.

"The Scapegoat" by J. Bronowski. Reprinted by permission of World Publishing Company from *The Face of Violence* by J. Bronowski. Copyright © 1967 by J. Bronowski.

"Heaven" by Rupert Brooke. Reprinted by permission of Dodd, Mead & Company, Inc. from *The Collected Poems of Rupert Brooke*. Copyright 1915 by Dodd, Mead & Company. Copyright 1943 by Edward Marsh.

From "An Introduction to Soul" by Claude Brown. Reprinted from *Esquire* Magazine, April 1968. Copyright © 1968 by Claude Brown. Reprinted by permission of The Sterling Lord Agency.

"Just How Do You Relax Colored People at Parties?" by Lennie Bruce. Reprinted from *The Essential Lenny Bruce* (New York: Ballantine Books, 1967). Permission granted by Douglas Corporation, 145 West 55th Street, New York, New York.

"God Is Mr. Big, Real Big" and "The Rich Creep Has It Hard" by Carl F. Burke. Reprinted from *God Is For Real, Man* by Carl F. Burke (New York: Association Press, 1966) by permission of the publisher.

From "An Introduction to Soul" by Al Calloway. Reprinted from *Esquire* Magazine, April 1968. Reprinted by permission of *Esquire* Magazine. © 1968 by Esquire, Inc.

"Torch Song" by John Cheever. From *The Enormous Radio and Other Stories* by John Cheever. Reprinted by permission of the publisher, Funk & Wagnalls.

"Golden Falcon" by Robert Tristram Coffin. Reprinted with permission of The Macmillan Company from *Collected Poems* by Robert P. Tristram Coffin. Copyright 1929 by The Macmillan Company, renewed 1957 by Robert P. T. Coffin, Jr.

"The Secret Heart" by Robert Tristram Coffin. Reprinted with permission of The Macmillan Company from *Collected Poems* by Robert P. Tristram Coffin. Copyright 1935 by The Macmillan Company, renewed 1963 by Margaret Coffin Halvosa.

Forward

The purpose of this book is to excite interest and elicit emotional response by bringing into the classroom the colors and forms of the world outside. Advertisements, buttons, cartoons, photographs, paintings, graffiti, and song lyrics are carefully integrated with provocative written materials such as poems, stories, and essays to provide an idea explosion in a mixed bag. The book is a fabric of intellectual relationships—cause, effect, similarity, antithesis, example, and qualification—innumerable modulations of thought for the student to discover and explore, unhindered by any editorial apparatus.

One assumption underlying this book is that involvement precedes thought, and thought precedes writing. For, as Sydney Harris argues, "You don't learn with the mind alone." Accepting this premise, I've tried to select materials that will involve students emotionally. Students write best under such conditions. Their grammar improves; their fluency increases; independent thought emerges. And even if emotional involvement isn't an automatic cure for all learning problems, we can make the modest assumption that students don't learn anything when they're asleep; if we can keep them awake, at least the learning process has a chance to begin.

Learning is progression, not stasis. In order to help our students to evolve from what they are to what they may become, we must begin where they are, not where we want them to be. That is why each section of this book contains artifacts from the student's own culture, ranging from graffiti to pop songs. Students are most likely to grow if they can move from the familiar to the unfamiliar, from the particular to the general, from the concrete to the theoretical, from the emotionally-charged to the impersonal. But emotion is just the beginning. Once excitement has been generated, the classroom must itself become a forum for exchange of ideas, a place of intellectual interplay between the students, the teacher, and the text. It is in this interplay that, if we are lucky, learning and writing and original thinking begin. In other words, I hope that both teachers and students will consider this book as incomplete, as theirs to finish.

Mixed Bag obviously includes strong statements and biased positions, controversy, and anger. The divergent attitudes reflected in the selections are included because they exist and because reality cannot be interpreted and survived unless it is examined. However, on no condition should any of the materials be taken to necessarily represent the views of the publisher, nor should this book be regarded as an attempt to promulgate any one social, religious, or political bias. The vigorous statement has been included before the bland, safe, and equivocal, not to proselytize, but to seize attention and demand thought.

Because this book owes its existence to Kendall College, I would like to express my gratitude not only for two research grants, unlimited clerical aid, and xeroxing privileges, but for an environment of high intellectual stimulation and untrammeled freedom that made experimentation with previously untried materials possible. I owe more than I can say to the encouragement of President Wesley Westerberg whose support of the concept of a humane writing program provided a context for my work. My deepest appreciation is also due our former dean, Durrett Wagner, for his initial belief in the book and his unstinting efforts on its behalf. To Dr. Robert Thompson, Dean of Faculty, I extend sincere thanks for his willingness to make scheduling adaptations that made my work possible, while our registrar, Doretta Fuhs, miraculously implemented any schedule at last minute notice. I owe warmest thanks to Noel McInnis, Director of the Kendall College Center for Curriculum Design; the Center's files of newspaper clippings, back-issue magazines, cartoons, advertisements, song lyrics, and out-of-print books were invaluable. The germinal idea for the chapter on "Tigers" also came from Noel, along with uninterrupted moral support. My colleagues Dr. Lewis Hopfe, Reverend Richard Heiss, Jerry Stone, Dr. Leon Aufdemberger, Mrs. Josephine Hayford, and Mrs. Eileen Cooper all suggested materials for inclusion in the book, answered innumerable scholarly and bibliographical questions, and, above all, provided an environment in which thought flourishes.

To my former students Linda Skolnick, Ray Helmers, Ben Olds, and Helen Fisch go my thanks for photographs and back-issue magazines. The children's street songs came from many young friends, among whom were Evelyn Asch, Thomas Asch, Caroline Willens, and my own Rob and Laura Hutchinson. For popular song lyrics and innumerable record albums I offer thanks to Jamie and David Young, Ricky Moses, Debbie Willens, Kathy Starr, and Ray Helmers; though I couldn't include most of their favorite songs, it was through them that my introduction to the music of the young was launched.

Very special thanks are due my dear friend and former librarian, Mrs. Gloria Simmons, who not only helped me with selection of materials but adapted library procedures to the rather peculiar needs of my classes as these materials evolved through the process of classroom use.

Above all, I wish to thank Verne Reaves for his keen sense of the superfluous, John Reuter-Pacyna for his loving design, and Carol Gee and Jenny Gilbertson for their endless patience. Without their assistance, this book could not have existed.

HELENE D. HUTCHINSON

CONTENTS

Family 1

Photograph: by Ben Olds 2
Photograph: by Manuel Alveraz Bravo 3
Poem: "With Child" by Genevieve Taggard 3
Poem: "The Secret Heart" by Robert Tristram Coffin 4
Photograph: by N. R. Farbman 5
Poem: "When I Am a Man" (Kwakiutl Indian) 5
Advertisement: "Buy the Oedipus Cycle" 6
Myth: "Oedipus" by Edith Hamilton 7
Button: "Oedipus Loved His Mother" 10
Story: "My Oedipus Complex" by Frank O'Connor 10
Button: "Incest Is Relative" 16
Poem: "Daddy" (Student) 17
Essay: "The Blood Jet Is Poetry" (*Time*) 18
Poem: "Daddy" by Sylvia Plath 20
Painting: "Woman With Flowered Hat" by Roy Lichtenstein 22
Story: "Everything That Rises Must Converge" by Flannery O'Connor 23
Poem: "The Last Echo" by Walter Lowenfels 35
Photograph: by Horst Faas 36
Poem: "Children's Elegy" by Muriel Rukeyser 37
Photograph: by Fred Eng 37
Photograph: by Russell Lee 38
Poem: "Young Woman" by Howard Nemerov 38
Poem: "Marriage" by Gregory Corso 40
Poem: "How Do I Love Thee?" by Elizabeth Barrett Browning 43
Poem: "Three" by Rod McKuen 44
Poem: "A Young Wife" by D. H. Lawrence 45
Poem: "Item" by E. E. Cummings 47
Cartoon: by Jules Feiffer 48
Cartoon: by James Thurber 50
Essay: "The Crisis of American Masculinity" by Arthur Schlesinger, Jr. 51
Comic Strips: "Dotty" by Buford Tune and "The Berrys" by Carl Grubert 59
Comic Strip: "Blondie" by Chic Young 60
Comic Strips: "Dotty" by Buford Tune and "The Berrys" by Carl Grubert 61
Story: "The Unicorn in the Garden" by James Thurber 62
Cartoon: by Gahan Wilson 63
Poem: "A Marriage" by Robert Creeley 64
Poem: "Divorce" by Anna Wickham 64
Photograph: by Kosti Ruohomaa 66
Song: "When You Are Old and Gray" by Tom Lehrer 67

Violence 69

Painting: "Pistol" by Roy Lichtenstein 70
Graffiti: Selected 73
Cartoon: by Jules Feiffer 74
News Item: "37 Who Saw Murder Didn't Call Police" 75
Buttons: Various 75

Cartoon: by Jim Crane **76**
Story: ''The Large Ant'' by Howard Fast **77**
Advertisement: Canada Dry **84**
Cartoon: by Charles Addams **86**
Story: ''The Snake'' by John Steinbeck **87**
Poem: from ''Stella Figura'' by Arthur Symons **94**
Photograph: by W. Eugene Smith **95**
Songs: Children's Street Songs **96**
News Items: Various **100**
Photograph: by UPI **102**
Essay: ''Arsenal in Action'' (*Time*) **102**
Poem: ''The Enemy's Testament'' by Etel Adnan **103**
Quotation: ''Who Is the Slayer?'' by Sophocles **104**
Letter: ''We Burned Every Hut'' by a GI **105**
Poem: from ''Confession'' by Morton Marcus **107**
Song: ''Ballad of the Green Berets'' by Barry Sadler **107**
Cartoon: by Siné **108**
Poem: ''Death of the Ball Turret Gunner'' by Randall Jarrell **108**
Poem: ''Mother, the wardrobe is full of infantrymen'' by Roger McGough **109**
Photo: by James L. Ballard **110**
Caption: ''Three people are enjoying . . .'' (*Esquire*) **111**
Essay: ''The Mass Perversion Called Porno-Violence'' by Tom Wolfe **112**
Painting: ''Varoom!'' by Roy Lichtenstein **117**
Essay: ''The Revolt of Leo Held'' (*Time*) **118**
Essay: from ''Violence: A Neglected Mode of Behavior'' by Bruno Bettelheim . . . **120**
Bible: ''Song of the Suffering Servant'' **122**
Essay: ''The Scapegoat'' by J. Bronowski **123**
Cartoon: by Jim Crane **124**
Essay: ''Whose Face Is That in the Mirror?'' by Sydney Harris **126**
Poem: ''A Marine's Creed'' by John E. Dovale **128**
Poem: ''A Lullaby'' by Randall Jarrell **128**
Bulletin: ''Why We Are in Vietnam'' **129**

Race **131**

Photograph: by Onofrio Paccione **132**
Poem: ''Nigger'' by Karl Shapiro **134**
Photograph: by DeClan Haun **136**
Song: ''Trouble Every Day'' by Frank Zappa **138**
Painting: ''Liberation of the Peon'' by Diego Rivera **140**
Poem: ''Middle Passage'' by Robert Hayden **141**
Folktale: ''The Mojo'' by Abraham Taylor **144**
Poem: ''Two Worlds of One: Black and White'' (Student) **145**
Cartoon: by Jim Crane **146**
Satire: ''Just How Do You Relax Colored People at Parties?'' by Lenny Bruce **148**
Photograph: by Art Kane **152**
Definition: ''Soul'' by Claude Brown **152**
Definition: ''Soul'' by Al Calloway **152**
Photograph: by Art Kane **153**

Essay: "The Style of Soul" (*Esquire*) **153**
Essay: from *Crisis in Black and White* by Charles E. Silberman **154**
Poem: "Government Injunction Restraining Harlem Cosmetic Co." by Josephine Miles **156**
Advertisement: Nadinola **157**
Poem: "I Hate Black" by Susan Drobac **158**
Cartoon: by John Dempsey **158**
Poem: "Wonders Never Cease" by Don Lee **159**
Photograph: by Phillipe Halsman **161**
Essay: "The Psychobiology of Racial Violence" by Louis Jolyon West **162**
Cartoon: by Malone **172**
Song: "Society's Child" by Janis Ian **173**
Photograph: by Hal A. Franklin **174**
Caption: "Soul Heroes" (*Esquire*) **176**
Poem: "Back Home Again" by Don Lee **177**
Poem: "Awareness" by Don Lee **177**
Advertisement: Epic Hair Straightener **178**
Story: "Winds of Change" by Loyle Hairston **179**
Song: "Yowzah" by Shel Silverstein **187**

DEATH **189**

Painting: by Robert Amft **190**
Poem: "Golden Falcon" by Robert Tristram Coffin **190**
Poem: "Communion" by Eugene McCarthy **191**
Essay: "Day of the Hunter" by Fred Myers **192**
Poem: "The Groundhog" by Richard Eberhart **196**
Photograph: by May Mirin **197**
Quotation: "As the generation . . ." by Homer **197**
Poem: "Spring and Fall: To a Young Child" by Gerard Manley Hopkins **198**
Painting: "The Triumph of Death" by Giovanni di Paolo **199**
Poem: "Dirge" by Kenneth Fearing **200**
Photograph: by UPI **201**
Poem: from *The Rubaiyat of Omar Khayyam* by Edward FitzGerald **202**
Poem: "Ozymandias" by Percy Bysshe Shelley **202**
Painting: "Sleepers" by George Tooker **203**
Cartoon: by Charles Addams **204**
Poem: "Richard Cory" by Edwin Arlington Robinson **205**
Poem: "Utopian Journey" by Randall Jarrell **206**
Painting: "That Which I Should Have Done . . ." by Ivan Albright **207**
Poem: "A Refusal to Mourn" by Dylan Thomas **208**
Photograph: by H. Armstrong Roberts **209**
Poem: "Heaven" by Rupert Brooke **210**
Drawing: from *Believe It Or Not!* by Ripley **211**
Commercial: Chambers' Caskets **211**
Essay: from *The American Way of Death* by Jessica Mitford **212**
Painting: "Coq Guerrier" by Jean Lurcat **219**
Poem: "Janet Waking" by John Crowe Ransom **220**
Story: "Torch Song" by John Cheever **221**

RELIGION **235**

Drawing: "God Besieged by Demons" (*Fact*) 236
Parody: "God Is Dead in Georgia" by Anthony Towne 237
Button: "Jean Paul Sartre Isn't" 239
Painting: "God Separating Land and Water" by Raphael 240
Essay: "Toward a Hidden God" (*Time*) 241
Poem: from *A Coney Island of the Mind* by Lawrence Ferlinghetti 254
Cartoon: by Jim Crane 256
Painting: "Christ on the Cross" by Peter Paul Rubens 258
Song: "New Christ Cardiac Hero" by Janis Ian 259
Story: "The Art of Pain" by Robert Burdette Sweet 260
Definition: from *The Devil's Dictionary* by Ambrose Bierce 269
News Item: "Actor Shot" 269
Song: "Crucifixion" by Phil Ochs 270
Photograph and Caption: from *Better Homes and Gardens* 272
Poem: "Christ Climbed Down" by Lawrence Ferlinghetti 273
Story: from *Opus 21* by Philip Wylie 274
Cartoon: by Handelsman 283
Button: "Nail a Commie for Christ" 284
Letter: "Remembrance Tribute" by Evelyn L. Gill 284
Cartoon: by Charles Addams 285
Bible: Mark 10:17–31 286
Poem: "The Rich Creep Has It Hard" by Carl F. Burke 287
Bible: Exodus 20:1–17 288
Poem: "God Is Mr. Big, Real Big" by Carl F. Burke 289

TIGERS **293**

Photograph: by Sid Avery 294
Advertisement: Fabergé 295
Advertisement: Bengal Gin 296
Advertisement: Westclox 297
Advertisement: Volkswagen 298
Poem: "The Tiger" by William Blake 299
Cartoon: by Alain 300
Poem: "For the One Who Would Take Man's Life in His Hands" by Delmore Schwartz 301
Poem: from "Triumph of Sensibility" by Sylvia Townsend Warner 301
Photograph: by Stan Wayman 302
Essay: "My Year With the Tigers" by George Schaller 303
Poem: "The Lion" by Hilaire Belloc 311
Poem: "The Tiger" by Hilaire Belloc 311
Story: "The Lady or the Tiger?" by Frank Stockton 312
Drawing: from *Believe It Or Not!* by Ripley 317
Definition: "Tiger" 318
Painting: "Tiger Attacking a Buffalo" by Henri Rousseau 319

A Note on the Type 321

Family

Photograph by Ben Olds, E.P.S. Studios Inc.

Photograph by Manuel Alveraz Bravo.

"WITH CHILD"

Now I am slow and placid, fond of sun,
Like a sleek beast, or a worn one:
No slim and languid girl—not glad
With the windy trip I once had,
But velvet-footed, mising of my own,
Torpid, mellow, stupid as a stone.

You cleft me with your beauty's pulse, and now
Your pulse has taken body. Care not how
The old grace goes, how heavy I am grown,
Big with this loneliness, how you alone
Ponder our love. Touch my feet and feel
How earth tingles, teeming at my heel!
Earth's urge, not mine—my little death, not hers;
And the pure beauty yearns and stirs.

It does not heed our ecstasies, it turns
With secrets of its own, its own concerns
Toward a windy world of its own, toward stark
And solitary places. In the dark,
Defiant even now, it tugs and moans
To be untangled from these mother's bones.

Genevieve Taggard

THE SECRET HEART

Across the years he could recall
His father one way best of all.

In the stillest hour of night
The boy awakened to a light.

Half in dreams he saw his sire
With his great hands full of fire.

The man had struck a match to see
If his son slept peacefully.

He held his palms each side the spark
His love had kindled in the dark.

 4

His two hands were curved apart
In the semblance of a heart.

He wore, it seemed to his small son,
A bare heart on his hidden one.

A heart that gave out such a glow
No son awake could bear to know.

It showed a look upon a face
Too tender for the day to trace.

One instant, it lit all about,
And then the secret heart went out.

But it shone long enough for one
To know that hands held up the sun.

Robert Tristram Coffin

When I am a man, then I shall be a hunter
When I am a man, then I shall be a harpooner
When I am a man, then I shall be a canoe-builder
When I am a man, then I shall be a carpenter
When I am a man, then I shall be an artisan
Oh father! ya ha ha ha

Kwakiutl Indian

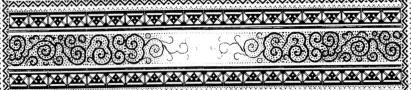

6

King Laius of Thebes was the third in descent from Cadmus. He married a distant cousin, Jocasta. With their reign Apollo's oracle at Delphi began to play a leading part in the family's fortunes.

Apollo was the God of Truth. Whatever the priestess at Delphi said would happen infallibly came to pass. To attempt to act in such a way that the prophecy would be made void was as futile as to set oneself against the decrees of fate. Nevertheless, when the oracle warned Laius that he would die at the hands of his son he determined that this should not be. When the child was born he bound its feet together and had it exposed on a lonely mountain where it must soon die. He felt no more fear; he was sure that on this point he could foretell the future better than the god. His folly was not brought home to him. He was killed, indeed, but he thought the man who attacked him was a stranger. He never knew that in his death he had proved Apollo's truth.

When he died he was away from home and many years had passed since the baby had been left on the mountain. It was reported that a band of robbers had slain him together with his attendants, all except one, who brought the news home. The matter was not carefully investigated because Thebes was in sore straits at the time. The country around was beset by a frightful monster, the Sphinx, a creature shaped like a winged lion, but with the breast and face of a woman. She lay in wait for the wayfarers along the roads to the city and whomever she seized she put a riddle to, telling him if he could answer it, she would let him go. No one could, and the horrible creature devoured man after man until the city was in a state of siege. The seven great gates which were the Thebans' pride remained closed, and famine drew near to the citizens.

So matters stood when there came into the stricken country a stranger, a man of great courage and great intelligence, whose name was Oedipus. He had left his home, Corinth, where he was held to be the son of the King, Polybus, and the reason for his self-exile was another Delphic oracle. Apollo had declared that he was fated to kill his father. He, too, like Laius, thought to make it impossible for the oracle to come true; he resolved never to see Polybus again. In his lonely wanderings he came into the country around Thebes and he heard what was happening there. He was a homeless, friendless man to whom life meant little and he determined to seek the Sphinx out and try to solve the riddle. "What creature," the Sphinx asked him, "goes on four feet in the morning, on two at noonday, on three in the evening?" "Man," answered Oedipus. "In childhood he creeps on hands and feet; in manhood he walks erect; in old age he helps himself with a staff." It was the right answer. The Sphinx, inexplicably, but most fortunately, killed herself; the Thebans were saved. Oedipus gained all and more than he had left. The grateful citizens made him their King and he married the dead King's wife, Jocasta. For many years they lived happily. It seemed that in this case Apollo's words had been proved to be false.

But when their two sons had grown to manhood Thebes was visited by a terrible plague. A blight fell upon everything. Not only were men dying throughout the country, the flocks and herds and the fruits of the field were blasted as well. Those who were spared death by disease faced death by famine. No one suffered more than Oedipus.

He regarded himself as the father of the whole state; the people in it were his children; the misery of each one was his too. He dispatched Jocasta's brother Creon to Delphi to implore the god's help.

Creon returned with good news. Apollo had declared that the plague would be stayed upon one condition: whoever had murdered King Laius must be punished. Oedipus was enormously relieved. Surely the men or the man could be found even after all these years, and they would know well how to punish him. He proclaimed to the people gathered to hear the message Creon brought back:—

> . . . *Let no one of this land*
> *Give shelter to him. Bar him from your homes,*
> *As one defiled, companioned by pollution.*
> *And solemnly I pray, may he who killed*
> *Wear out his life in evil, being evil.*

Oedipus took the matter in hand with energy. He sent for Teiresias, the old blind prophet, the most revered of Thebans. Had he any means of finding out, he asked him, who the guilty were? To his amazement and indignation the seer at first refused to answer. "For the love of God," Oedipus implored him. "If you have knowledge—" "Fools," Teiresias said. "Fools all of you. I will not answer." But when Oedipus went so far as to accuse him of keeping silence because he had himself taken part in the murder, the prophet in his turn was angered and words he had meant never to speak fell heavily from his lips: "You are yourself the murderer you seek." To Oedipus the old man's mind was wandering; what he said was sheer madness. He ordered him out of his sight and never again to appear before him.

Jocasta too treated the assertion with scorn. "Neither prophets nor oracles have any sure knowledge," she said. She told her husband how the priestess at Delphi had prophesied that Laius should die at the hand of his son and how he and she together had seen to it that this should not happen by having the child killed. "And Laius was murdered by robbers, where three roads meet on the way to Delphi," she concluded triumphantly. Oedipus gave her a strange look. "When did this happen?" he asked slowly. "Just before you came to Thebes," she said.

"How many were with him?" Oedipus asked. "They were five in all," Jocasta spoke quickly, "all killed but one." "I must see that man," he told her. "Send for him." "I will," she said. "At once. But I have a right to know what is in your mind." "You shall know all that I know," he answered. "I went to Delphi just before I came here because a man had flung it in my face that I was not the son of Polybus. I went to ask the god. He did not answer me, but he told me horrible things—that I should kill my father, marry my mother, and have children men would shudder to look upon. I never went back to Corinth. On my way from Delphi, at a place where three roads met, I came upon a man with four attendants. He tried to force me from the path; he struck me

 8

with his stick. Angered I fell upon them and I killed them. Could it be the leader was Laius?" "The one man left alive brought back a tale of robbers," Jocasta said. "Laius was killed by robbers, not by his son—the poor innocent who died upon the mountain."

As they talked a further proof seemed given them that Apollo could speak falsely. A messenger came from Corinth to announce to Oedipus the death of Polybus. "O oracle of the god," Jocasta cried, "where are you now? The man died, but not by his son's hand." The messenger smiled wisely. "Did the fear of killing your father drive you from Corinth?" he asked. "Ah, King, you were in error. You never had reason to fear—for you were not the son of Polybus. He brought you up as though you were his, but he took you from my hands." "Where did you get me?" Oedipus asked. "Who were my father and mother?" "I know nothing of them," the messenger said. "A wandering shepherd gave you to me, a servant of Laius."

Jocasta turned white; a look of horror was on her face. "Why waste a thought upon what such a fellow says?" she cried. "Nothing he says can matter." She spoke hurriedly, yet fiercely. Oedipus could not understand her. "My birth does not matter?" he asked. "For God's sake, go no further," she said. "My misery is enough." She broke away and rushed into the palace.

At that moment an old man entered. He and the messenger eyed each other curiously. "The very man, O King," the messenger cried. "The shepherd who gave you to me." "And you," Oedipus asked the other, "do you know him as he knows you?" The old man did not answer, but the messenger insisted. "You must remember. You gave me once a little child you had found—and the King here is that child." "Curse you," the other muttered. "Hold your tongue." "What!" Oedipus said angrily. "You would conspire with him to hide from me what I desire to know? There are ways, be sure, to make you speak."

The old man wailed, "Oh, do not hurt me. I did give him the child, but do not ask more, master, for the love of God." "If I have to order you a second time to tell me where you got him, you are lost," Oedipus said. "Ask your lady," the old man cried. "She can tell you best." "She gave him to you?" asked Oedipus. "Oh, yes, oh, yes," the other groaned. "I was to kill the child. There was a prophecy—" "A prophecy!" Oedipus repeated. "That he should kill his father?" "Yes," the old man whispered.

A cry of agony came from the King. At last he understood. "All true! Now shall my light be changed to darkness. I am accursed." He had murdered his father, he had married his father's wife, his own mother. There was no help for him, for her, for their children. All were accursed.

Within the palace Oedipus wildly sought for his wife that was his mother. He found her in her chamber. She was dead. When the truth broke upon her she had killed herself. Standing beside her he too turned his hand against himself, but not to end his life. He changed his light to darkness. He put out his eyes. The black world of blindness was a refuge; better to be there than to see with strange shamed eyes the old world that had been so bright.

Edith Hamilton

OEDIPUS
LOVED
HIS MOTHER

𝔉𝔯𝔞𝔫𝔨 𝔒'𝔆𝔬𝔫𝔫𝔬𝔯

𝔐𝔶 𝔒𝔢𝔡𝔦𝔭𝔲𝔰 𝔆𝔬𝔪𝔭𝔩𝔢𝔵

 10

Father was in the army all through the war—the first war, I mean—so, up to the age of five, I never saw much of him, and what I saw did not worry me. Sometimes I woke and there was a big figure in khaki peering down at me in the candlelight. Sometimes in the early morning I heard the slamming of the front door and the clatter of nailed boots down the cobbles of the lane. These were Father's entrances and exits. Like Santa Claus he came and went mysteriously.

In fact, I rather liked his visits, though it was an uncomfortable squeeze between Mother and him when I got into the big bed in the early morning. He smoked, which gave him a pleasant musty smell, and shaved, an operation of astounding interest. Each time he left a trail of souvenirs—model tanks and Gurkha knives with handles made of bullet cases, and German helmets and cap badges and button-sticks, and all sorts of military equipment—carefully stowed away in a long box on top of the wardrobe, in case they ever came in handy. There was a bit of the magpie about Father; he expected everything to come in handy. When his back was turned, Mother let me get a chair and rummage through his treasures. She didn't seem to think so highly of them as he did.

The war was the most peaceful period of my life. The window of my attic faced southeast. My mother had curtained it, but that had small effect. I always woke with the first light and, with all the responsibilities of the previous day melted, feeling myself rather like the sun, ready to illumine and rejoice. Life never seemed so simple and clear and full of possibilities as then. I put my feet out from under the clothes—I called them Mrs. Left and Mrs. Right—and invented dramatic situations for them in which they discussed the problems of the day. At least Mrs. Right did; she was very demonstrative, but I hadn't the same control of Mrs. Left, so she mostly contented herself with nodding agreement.

They discussed what Mother and I should do during the day, what Santa Claus should give a fellow for Christmas, and what steps should be taken to brighten the home. There was that little matter of the baby, for instance. Mother and I could never agree about that. Ours was the only house in the terrace without a new baby, and Mother said we couldn't afford one till Father came back from the war because they cost seventeen and six. That showed how simple she was. The Geneys up the road had a baby, and everyone knew they couldn't afford seventeen and six. It was probably a cheap baby, and Mother wanted something really good, but I felt she was too exclusive. The Geneys' baby would have done us fine.

Having settled my plans for the day, I got up, put a chair under the attic window, and lifted the frame high enough to stick out my head. The window overlooked the front gardens of the terrace behind ours, and beyond these it looked over a deep valley to the tall, red-brick houses terraced up the opposite hillside, which were all still in shadow, while those at our side of the valley were all lit up, though with long strange shadows that made them seem unfamiliar; rigid and painted.

After that I went into Mother's room and climbed into the big bed. She woke and I began to tell her of my schemes. By this time, though I never seem to have noticed it, I was petrified in my nightshirt, and I thawed as I talked until, the last frost melted, I fell asleep beside her and woke again only when I heard her below in the kitchen, making the breakfast.

After breakfast we went into town; heard Mass at St. Augustine's and said a prayer for Father, and did the shopping. If the afternoon was fine we either went for a walk in the country or a visit to Mother's great friend in the convent, Mother St. Dominic. Mother had them all praying for Father, and every night, going to bed, I asked God to send him back safe from the war to us. Little, indeed, did I know what I was praying for!

One morning, I got into the big bed, and there, sure enough, was Father in his usual Santa Claus manner, but later, instead of uniform, he put on his best blue suit, and Mother was as pleased as anything. I saw nothing to be pleased about, because, out of uniform, Father was altogether less interesting, but she only beamed, and explained that our prayers had been answered, and off we went to Mass to thank God for having brought Father safely home.

The irony of it! That very day when he came in to dinner he took off his boots and put on his slippers, donned the dirty old cap he wore about the house to save him from colds, crossed his legs, and began to talk gravely to Mother, who looked anxious. Naturally, I disliked her looking anxious, because it destroyed her good looks, so I interrupted him.

"Just a moment, Larry!" she said gently.

This was only what she said when we had boring visitors, so I attached no importance to it and went on talking.

"Do be quiet, Larry!" she said impatiently. "Don't you hear me talking to Daddy?"

This was the first time I had heard those ominous words, "talking to Daddy," and I couldn't help feeling that if this was how God answered prayers, he couldn't listen to them very attentively.

"Why are you talking to Daddy?" I asked with as great a show of indifference as I could muster.

"Because Daddy and I have business to discuss. Now, don't interrupt again!"

In the afternoon, at Mother's request, Father took me for a walk. This time we went into town instead of out in the country, and I thought at first, in my usual optimistic way, that it might be an improvement. It was nothing of the sort. Father and I had quite different notions of a walk in town. He had no proper interest in trams, ships, and horses, and the only thing that seemed to divert him was talking to fellows as old as himself. When I wanted to stop he simply went on, dragging me behind him by the hand; when he wanted to stop I had no alternative but to do the same. I noticed that it seemed to be a sign that he wanted to stop for a long time whenever he leaned against a wall. The second time I saw him do it I got wild. He seemed to be settling himself forever. I pulled him by the coat and trousers, but, unlike Mother who, if you were too persistent, got into a wax and said: "Larry, if you don't behave yourself, I'll give you a good slap," Father had an extraordinary capacity for amiable inattention. I sized him up and wondered would I cry, but he seemed to be too remote to be annoyed even by that. Really, it was like going for a walk with a mountain! He either ignored the wrenching and pummeling entirely, or else glanced down with a grin of amusement from his peak. I had never met anyone so absorbed in himself as he seemed.

At teatime, "talking to Daddy" began again, complicated this time by the fact that he had an evening paper, and every few minutes he put it down and told Mother something new out of it. I felt this was foul play. Man for man, I was prepared to compete with him any time for Mother's attention, but when he had it all made up for him by other people it left me no chance. Several times I tried to change the subject without success.

"You must be quiet while Daddy is reading, Larry," Mother said impatiently.

It was clear that she either genuinely liked talking to Father better than talking to me, or else that he had some terrible hold on her which made her afraid to admit the truth.

"Mummy," I said that night when she was tucking me up, "do you think if I prayed hard God would send Daddy back to the war?"

She seemed to think about that for a moment.

"No, dear," she said with a smile. "I don't think he would."

"Why wouldn't he, Mummy?"

"Because there isn't a war any longer, dear."

"But, Mummy, couldn't God make another war, if he liked?"

"He wouldn't like to, dear. It's not God who makes wars, but bad people."

"Oh!" I said.

I was disappointed about that. I began to think that God wasn't quite what he was cracked up to be.

Next morning I woke at my usual hour, feeling like a bottle of champagne. I put out my feet and invented a long conversation in which Mrs. Right talked of the trouble she had with her own father till she put him in the Home. I didn't quite know what the Home was but it sounded

like the right place for Father. Then I got my chair and stuck my head out of the attic window. Dawn was just breaking, with a guilty air that made me feel I had caught it in the act. My head bursting with stories and schemes, I stumbled in next door, and in the half-darkness scrambled into the big bed. There was no room at Mother's side so I had to get between her and Father. For the time being I had forgotten about him, and for several minutes I sat bolt upright, racking my brains to know what I could do with him. He was taking up more than his fair share of the bed, and I couldn't get comfortable, so I gave him several kicks that made him grunt and stretch. He made room all right, though. Mother waked and felt for me. I settled back comfortably in the warmth of the bed with my thumb in my mouth.

"Mummy!" I hummed, loudly and contentedly.

"Sssh! dear," she whispered. "Don't wake Daddy!"

This was a new development, which threatened to be even more serious than "talking to Daddy." Life without my early-morning conferences was unthinkable.

"Why?" I asked severely.

"Because poor Daddy is tired."

This seemed to me a quite inadequate reason, and I was sickened by the sentimentality of her "poor Daddy." I never liked that sort of gush; it always struck me as insincere.

"Oh!" I said lightly. Then in my most winning tone: "Do you know where I want to go with you today, Mummy?"

"No, dear," she sighed.

"I want to go down the Glen and fish for thornybacks with my new net, and then I want to go out to the Fox and Hounds, and—"

"Don't-wake-Daddy!" she hissed angrily, clapping her hand across my mouth.

But it was too late. He was awake, or nearly so. He grunted and reached for the matches. Then he stared incredulously at his watch.

"Like a cup of tea, dear?" asked Mother in a meek, hushed voice I had never heard her use before. It sounded almost as though she were afraid.

"Tea?" he exclaimed indignantly. "Do you know what the time is?"

"And after that I want to go up the Rathcooney Road," I said loudly, afraid I'd forget something in all those interruptions.

"Go to sleep at once, Larry!" she said sharply.

I began to snivel. I couldn't concentrate, the way that pair went on, and smothering my early-morning schemes was like burying a family from the cradle.

Father said nothing, but lit his pipe and sucked it, looking out into the shadows without minding Mother or me. I knew he was mad. Every time I made a remark Mother hushed me irritably. I was mortified. I felt it wasn't fair; there was even something sinister in it. Every time I had pointed out to her the waste of making two beds when we could both sleep in one, she had told me it was healthier like that, and now here was this man, this stranger sleeping with her without the least regard for her health!

He got up early and made tea but though he brought Mother a cup he brought none for me.

"Mummy," I shouted, "I want a cup of tea, too."

"Yes, dear," she said patiently. "You can drink from Mummy's saucer."

That settled it. Either Father or I would have to leave the house. I didn't want to drink from Mother's saucer; I wanted to be treated as an equal in my own home, so, just to spite her, I drank it all and left none for her. She took that quietly, too.

But that night when she was putting me to bed she said gently:

"Larry, I want you to promise me something."

"What is it?" I asked.

"Not to come in and disturb poor Daddy in the morning. Promise?"

"Poor Daddy" again! I was becoming suspicious of everything involving that quite impossible man.

"Why?" I asked.

"Because poor Daddy is worried and tired and he doesn't sleep well."

"Why doesn't he, Mummy?"

"Well, you know, don't you, that while he was at the war Mummy got the pennies from the Post Office?"

"From Miss MacCarthy?"

"That's right. But now, you see, Miss MacCarthy hasn't any more pennies, so Daddy must go out and find us some. You know what would happen if he couldn't?"

"No," I said, "tell us."

"Well, I think we might have to go out and beg for them like the poor old woman on Fridays. We wouldn't like that, would we?"

"No," I agreed. "We wouldn't."

"So you'll promise not to come in and wake him?"

"Promise."

Mind you, I meant that. I knew pennies were a serious matter, and I was all against having to go out and beg like the old woman on Fridays. Mother laid out all my toys in a complete ring round the bed so that, whatever way I got out, I was bound to fall over one of them.

When I woke I remembered my promise all right. I got up and sat on the floor and played— for hours, it seemed to me. Then I got my chair and looked out the attic window for more hours. I wished it was time for Father to wake; I wished someone would make me a cup of tea. I didn't feel in the least like the sun; instead, I was bored and so very, very cold! I simply longed for the warmth and depth of the big featherbed.

At last I could stand it no longer. I went into the next room. As there was still no room at Mother's side I climbed over her and she woke with a start.

"Larry," she whispered, gripping my arm very tightly, "what did you promise?"

"But I did, Mummy," I wailed, caught in the very act. "I was quiet for ever so long."

"Oh, dear, and you're perished!" she said sadly, feeling me all over. "Now, if I let you stay will you promise not to talk?"

13

"But I want to talk, Mummy," I wailed.

"That has nothing to do with it," she said with a firmness that was new to me. "Daddy wants to sleep. Now, do you understand that?"

I understood it only too well. I wanted to talk, he wanted to sleep—whose house was it, anyway?

"Mummy," I said with equal firmness, "I think it would be healthier for Daddy to sleep in his own bed."

That seemed to stagger her, because she said nothing for a while.

"Now, once for all," she went on, "you're to be perfectly quiet or go back to your own bed. Which is it to be?"

The injustice of it got me down. I had convicted her out of her own mouth of inconsistency and unreasonableness, and she hadn't even attempted to reply. Full of spite, I gave Father a kick, which she didn't notice but which made him grunt and open his eyes in alarm.

"What time is it?" he asked in a panic-stricken voice, not looking at Mother but at the door, as if he saw someone there.

"It's early yet," she replied soothingly. "It's only the child. Go to sleep again. . . . Now, Larry," she added, getting out of bed, "you've wakened Daddy and you must go back."

This time, for all her quiet air, I knew she meant it, and knew that my principal rights and privileges were as good as lost unless I asserted them at once. As she lifted me, I gave a screech, enough to wake the dead, not to mind Father. He groaned.

"That damn child! Doesn't he ever sleep?"

"It's only a habit, dear," she said quietly, though I could see she was vexed.

"Well, it's time he got out of it," shouted Father, beginning to heave in the bed. He suddenly gathered all the bedclothes about him, turned to the wall, and then looked back over his shoulder with nothing showing only two small, spiteful, dark eyes. The man looked very wicked.

To open the bedroom door, Mother had to let me down, and I broke free and dashed for the farthest corner, screeching. Father sat bolt upright in bed.

"Shut up, you little puppy!" he said in a choking voice.

I was so astonished that I stopped screeching. Never, never had anyone spoken to me in that tone before. I looked at him incredulously and saw his face convulsed with rage. It was only then that I fully realized how God had codded me, listening to my prayers for the safe return of this monster.

"Shut up, you!" I bawled, beside myself.

"What's that you said?" shouted Father, making a wild leap out of the bed.

"Mick, Mick!" cried Mother. "Don't you see the child isn't used to you?"

"I see he's better fed than taught," snarled Father, waving his arms wildly. "He wants his bottom smacked."

All his previous shouting was as nothing to these obscene words referring to my person. They really made my blood boil.

"Smack your own!" I screamed hysterically. "Smack your own! Shut up! Shut up!"

At this he lost his patience and let fly at me. He did it with the lack of conviction you'd expect of a man under Mother's horrified eyes, and it ended up as a mere tap, but the sheer indignity of being struck at all by a stranger, a total stranger who had cajoled his way back from the war into our big bed as a result of my innocent intercession, made me completely dotty. I shrieked and shrieked, and danced in my bare feet, and Father, looking awkward and hairy in nothing but a short grey army shirt, glared down at me like a mountain out for murder. I think it must have been then that I realized he was jealous too. And there stood Mother in her nightdress, looking as if her heart was broken between us. I hoped she felt as she looked. It seemed to me that she deserved it all.

From that morning out my life was a hell. Father and I were enemies, open and avowed. We conducted a series of skirmishes against one another, he trying to steal my time with Mother and I his. When she was sitting on my bed, telling me a story, he took to looking for some pair of old boots which he alleged he had left behind him at the beginning of the war. While he talked to

 14

Mother I played loudly with my toys to show my total lack of concern. He created a terrible scene one evening when he came in from work and found me at his box, playing with his regimental badges, Gurkha knives and button-sticks. Mother got up and took the box from me.

"You mustn't play with Daddy's toys unless he lets you, Larry," she said severely. "Daddy doesn't play with yours."

For some reason Father looked at her as if she had struck him and then turned away with a scowl.

"Those are not toys," he growled, taking down the box again to see had I lifted anything. "Some of those curios are very rare and valuable."

But as time went on I saw more and more how he managed to alienate Mother and me. What made it worse was that I couldn't grasp his method or see what attraction he had for Mother. In every possible way he was less winning than I. He had a common accent and made noises at his tea. I thought for a while that it might be the newspapers she was interested in, so I made up bits of news of my own to read to her. Then I thought it might be the smoking, which I personally thought attractive, and took his pipes and went round the house dribbling into them till he caught me. I even made noises at my tea, but Mother only told me I was disgusting. It all seemed to hinge round that unhealthy habit of sleeping together, so I made a point of dropping into their bedroom and nosing round, talking to myself, so that they wouldn't know I was watching them, but they were never up to anything that I could see. In the end it beat me. It seemed to depend on being grown-up and giving people rings, and I realized I'd have to wait.

But at the same time I wanted him to see that I was only waiting, not giving up the fight. One evening when he was being particularly obnoxious, chattering away well above my head, I let him have it.

"Mummy," I said, "do you know what I'm going to do when I grow up?"

"No, dear," she replied. "What?"

"I'm going to marry you," I said quietly. Father gave a great guffaw out of him, but he didn't take me in. I knew it must only be pretence. And Mother, in spite of everything, was pleased. I felt she was probably relieved to know that one day Father's hold on her would be broken.

"Won't that be nice?" she said with a smile.

"It'll be very nice," I said confidently. "Because we're going to have lots and lots of babies."

"That's right, dear," she said placidly. "I think we'll have one soon, and then you'll have plenty of company."

I was no end pleased about that because it showed that in spite of the way she gave in to Father she still considered my wishes. Besides, it would put the Geneys in their place.

It didn't turn out like that, though. To begin with, she was very preoccupied—I suppose about where she would get the seventeen and six—and though Father took to staying out late in the evenings it did me no particular good. She stopped taking me for walks, became as touchy as blazes, and smacked me for nothing at all. Sometimes I wished I'd never mentioned the confounded baby—I seemed to have a genius for bringing calamity on myself.

And calamity it was! Sonny arrived in the most appalling hullabaloo—even that much he couldn't do without a fuss—and from the first moment I disliked him. He was a difficult child—so far as I was concerned he was always difficult—and demanded far too much attention. Mother was simply silly about him, and couldn't see when he was only showing off. As company he was worse than useless. He slept all day, and I had to go round the house on tiptoe to avoid waking him. It wasn't any longer a question of not waking Father. The slogan now was "Don't-wake-Sonny!" I couldn't understand why the child wouldn't sleep at the proper time, so whenever Mother's back was turned I woke him. Sometimes to keep him awake I pinched him as well. Mother caught me at it one day and gave me a most unmerciful flaking.

One evening, when Father was coming in from work, I was playing trains in the front garden. I let on not to notice him; instead, I pretended to be talking to myself, and said in a loud voice: "If another bloody baby comes into this house, I'm going out."

Father stopped dead and looked at me over his shoulder.

"What's that you said?" he asked sternly.

"I was only talking to myself," I replied, trying to conceal my panic. "It's private."

He turned and went in without a word. Mind you, I intended it as a solemn warning, but its effect was quite different. Father started being quite nice to me. I could understand that, of course. Mother was quite sickening about Sonny. Even at mealtimes she'd get up and gawk at him in the cradle with an idiotic smile, and tell Father to do the same. He was always polite about it, but he looked so puzzled you could see he didn't know what she was talking about. He complained of the way Sonny cried at night but she only got cross and said that Sonny never cried except when there was something up with him—which was a flaming lie, because Sonny never had anything up with him, and only cried for attention. It was really painful to see how simple-minded she was. Father wasn't attractive, but he had a fine intelligence. He saw through Sonny, and now he knew that I saw through him as well.

One night I woke with a start. There was someone beside me in the bed. For one wild moment I felt sure it must be Mother, having come to her senses and left Father for good, but then I heard Sonny in convulsions in the next room, and Mother saying: "There! There! There!" and I knew it wasn't she. It was Father. He was lying beside me, wide awake, breathing hard and apparently as mad as hell.

After a while it came to me what he was mad about. It was his turn now. After turning me out of the big bed, he had been turned out himself. Mother had no consideration now for anyone but that poisonous pup, Sonny. I couldn't help feeling sorry for Father. I had been through it all myself, and even at that age I was magnanimous. I began to stroke him down and say: "There! There!" He wasn't exactly responsive.

"Aren't you asleep either?" he snarled.

"Ah, come on and put your arm around us, can't you?" I said, and he did, in a sort of way. Gingerly, I suppose, is how you'd describe it. He was very bony but better than nothing.

At Christmas he went out of his way to buy me a really nice model railway.

Daddy was a big man
Very big and fat.
Daddy had a double chin.
Daddy wore a hat.
Daddy always bellowed
"Bessie, where you at?"
Daddy wore his glasses.
Daddy had a frown.
And when you didn't mind him,
Daddy knocked you down.
Daddy had a temper.
Daddy had a mad.
Daddy wouldn't talk to you
Whenever you was bad.
Daddy's lying in the ground
Turning into rot.
Daddy might be living,
But I'm glad he's not.
Daddy had a belly.
Daddy had a smile.
Daddy was a big man
Who could run a mile.
Daddy had a bullet hole
Sticking in his arm.
Daddy drove a team of horses
On a western farm.
Daddy used to hit you.
Daddy used to yell.
In the middle of the summer
Daddy went to hell.
Daddy spit out all his blood.
Daddy closed his eyes.
All your insides turn to ice
When your daddy dies.
Mamma heard him calling
Calling from above.
Daddy is the only one
I will ever love.

Written by a 14-year-old DuSable High School student, 1953.

THE BLOOD JET IS POETRY

ARIEL *by Sylvia Plath.* 85 pages. *Harper & Row.* $4.95.

On a dank day in February 1963, a pretty young mother of two children was found in a London flat with her head in the oven and the gas jets wide open. The dead woman was Sylvia Plath, 30, an American poet whose marriage to Ted Hughes, a British poet, had gone on the rocks not long before. Her published verses, appearing occasionally in American magazines and gathered in a single volume, *The Colossus,* had displayed accents of refinement, but had not yet achieved authority of tone.

But within a week of her death, intellectual London was hunched over copies of a strange and terrible poem she had written during her last sick slide toward suicide. *Daddy* was its title; its subject was her morbid love-hatred of her father; its style was as brutal as a truncheon. What is more, *Daddy* was merely the first jet of flame from a literary dragon who in the last months of her life breathed a burning river of bale across the literary landscape.

Published last year in Britain, the last poems of Sylvia Plath sold 15,000 copies in ten months, almost as many as a best-selling novel, and inspired a vigorous new group of confessional poets. Published last week in the U.S., *Ariel* adds a powerful voice to the rising chorus of American bards (Robert Lowell, Ann Sexton, Frederick Seidel) who practice poetry as abreaction.

Worms like Sticky Pearls. Outwardly, Sylvia's psychosis has standard Freudian trimmings. Her father, born in the Polish town of Grabow in East Prussia, became a professor of entomology at Boston University and is presented in her poetry as an intellectual tyrant with "a love of the rack and the screw." The mother of the heroine in *The Bell Jar,* an autobiographical novel published in England just before Sylvia's death, is described as a metallic New England schoolmarm. Little Sylvia tried to be Daddy's darling. At three she knew the Latin names of hundreds of insects—whenever a bumblebee bumbled by, the pretty little poppet would squeak: *"Bombus bimaculatus!"*

But when she was ten, Daddy died. It was the trauma of her life, or so she came to think in later years. At any rate, she became a compulsive talker, a compulsive learner, a compulsive writer. All through her teens she scribbled stories, plays, poems—many of them sufficiently professional to be published in *Seventeen* and *Mademoiselle.* She won a scholarship to Smith, where she made straight A's. But her feelings took their revenge. At 19, after an unhappy month in New York City, she ran home to Wellesley, Mass., crawled under the front porch, hid behind a stack of kindling and swallowed 50 sleeping pills. Three days later she was found alive but in ghastly condition. "They had to call and call," she wrote later, "and pick the worms off me like sticky pearls."

Words like Missiles. A series of shock treatments put her back on her feet, but she needed "to be bolstered by someone," and a few years later she found that someone

Time, June 10, 1966

 18

in Poet Hughes, whom she met during her Fulbright year at Cambridge. As a poet, Sylvia matured rapidly during her marriage; after the birth of her daughter Frieda, she found in the woman's world the subject she could call her own.

Love set you going like a fat gold watch.
The midwife slapped your footsoles, and
*   your bald cry*
Took its place among the elements.

All night your moth-breath
Flickers among the flat pink roses. I
*   wake to listen:*
A far sea moves in my ear.

One cry, and I stumble from bed, cow-
*   heavy and floral*
In my Victorian nightgown.
Your mouth opens clean as a cat's.

But life was more difficult than poetry. In the fall of 1962, just after the birth of her son Nicholas, she and Hughes separated permanently. Alone with the children in Devon, Sylvia hurled herself into a heroic but foolhardy attempt to probe her deepest problems with the point of a pen.

All day she kept house and cared for the children. Most of the night she wrote "like a woman on fire"—two, three, six complete poems night after night. Her fire was black and its name was hatred. Her words were hard and small like missiles, and they were flung with flat force.

Now I break up in pieces that fly about
*   like clubs.*
A wind of such violence
Will tolerate no bystanding: I must
*   shriek.*

But beneath the hatred she found fear.

I am terrified by this dark thing
That sleeps in me;
All day I feel its soft, feathery turnings,
*   its malignity . . .*
What is this, this face
So murderous in its strangle of branches?

And beneath the fear, she found a sinister love of death. She longed to feel

the knife not carve, but enter
Pure and clean as the cry of a baby,
And the universe slide from my side.

Death like a Poem. In her most ferocious poems, *Daddy* and *Lady Lazarus,* fear, hate, love, death and the poet's own identity become fused at black heat with the figure of her father, and through him, with the guilt of the German exterminators and the suffering of their Jewish victims. They are poems, as Robert Lowell says in his preface to *Ariel,* that "play Russian roulette with six cartridges in the cylinder."

For six months, first in Devon and later in London, Sylvia wrote without letup. By the end of January 1963, her nerves were a shirt of nettles. On Feb. 4 she arrived at a friend's house, lugging the children. "She was in an inferno," the friend remembers. "Depression is not the word." For six days she let herself be looked after, but on Feb. 10 she went back to her flat to spend the night. The next morning, in an Auschwitz all her own, she executed what one critic calls her "last unwritten poem." The epithet is appropriate. In the last week of her life she laid bare the heart of her art in a clouting couplet:

The blood jet is poetry;
There is no stopping it.

19

DADDY

You do not do, you do not do
Any more, black shoe
In which I have lived like a foot
For thirty years, poor and white,
Barely daring to breathe or Achoo.

Daddy, I have had to kill you.
You died before I had time—
Marble-heavy, a bag full of God,
Ghastly statue with one grey toe
Big as a Frisco seal

And a head in the freakish Atlantic
Where it pours bean green over blue
In the waters off beautiful Nauset.
I used to pray to recover you.
Ach, du.

In the German tongue, in the Polish town
Scraped flat by the roller
Of wars, wars, wars.
But the name of the town is common.
My Polack friend

Says there are a dozen or two.
So I never could tell where you
Put your foot, your root,
I never could talk to you.
The tongue stuck in my jaw.

It stuck in a barb wire snare.
Ich, ich, ich, ich,
I could hardly speak.
I thought every German was you.
And the language obscene

An engine, an engine
Chuffing me off like a Jew.
A Jew to Dachau, Auschwitz, Belsen.
I began to talk like a Jew.
I think I may well be a Jew.

The snows of the Tyrol, the clear beer of Vienna
Are not very pure or true.
With my gypsy ancestress and my weird luck
And my Taroc pack and my Taroc pack
I may be a bit of a Jew.

I have always been scared of *you*,
With your Luftwaffe, your gobbledygoo.
And your neat moustache
And your Aryan eye, bright blue.
Panzer-man, panzer-man, O You—

Not God but a swastika
So black no sky could squeak through.
Every woman adores a Fascist,
The boot in the face, the brute
Brute heart of a brute like you.

You stand at the blackboard, daddy,
In the picture I have of you,
A cleft in your chin instead of your foot
But no less a devil for that, no not
Any less the black man who

Bit my pretty red heart in two.
I was ten when they buried you.
At twenty I tried to die
And get back, back, back to you.
I thought even the bones would do.

But they pulled me out of the sack,
And they stuck me together with glue.
And then I knew what to do.
I made a model of you,
A man in black with a Meinkampf look

And a love of the rack and the screw.
And I said I do, I do.
So daddy, I'm finally through.
The black telephone's off at the root,
The voices just can't worm through.

If I've killed one man, I've killed two—
The vampire who said he was you
And drank my blood for a year,
Seven years, if you want to know.
Daddy, you can lie back now.

There's a stake in your fat black heart
And the villagers never liked you.
They are dancing and stamping on you.
They always *knew* it was you.
Daddy, daddy, you bastard, I'm through.

Sylvia Plath

20

DADDY

You do not do, you do not do
Any more, black shoe
In which I have lived like a foot
For thirty years, poor and white,
Barely daring to breathe or Achoo.

Daddy, I have had to kill you.
You died before I had time—
Marble-heavy, a bag full of God,
Ghastly statue with one grey toe
Big as a Frisco seal

And a head in the freakish Atlantic
Where it pours bean green over blue
In the waters off beautiful Nauset.
I used to pray to recover you.
Ach, du.

In the German tongue, in the Polish town
Scraped flat by the roller
Of wars, wars, wars.
But the name of the town is common.
My Polack friend

Says there are a dozen or two.
So I never could tell where you
Put your foot, your root,
I never could talk to you.
The tongue stuck in my jaw.

It stuck in a barb wire snare.
Ich, ich, ich, ich,
I could hardly speak.
I thought every German was you.
And the language obscene

An engine, an engine
Chuffing me off like a Jew.
A Jew to Dachau, Auschwitz, Belsen.
I began to talk like a Jew.
I think I may well be a Jew.

The snows of the Tyrol, the clear beer of Vienna
Are not very pure or true.
With my gypsy ancestress and my weird luck
And my Taroc pack and my Taroc pack
I may be a bit of a Jew.

I have always been scared of you,
With your Luftwaffe, your gobbledygoo.
And your neat moustache
And your Aryan eye, bright blue.
Panzer-man, panzer-man, O You—

Not God but a swastika
So black no sky could squeak through.
Every woman adores a Fascist,
The boot in the face, the brute
Brute heart of a brute like you.

You stand at the blackboard, daddy,
In the picture I have of you,
A cleft in your chin instead of your foot
But no less a devil for that, no not
Any less the black man who

Bit my pretty red heart in two.
I was ten when they buried you.
At twenty I tried to die
And get back, back, back to you.
I thought even the bones would do.

But they pulled me out of the sack,
And they stuck me together with glue.
And then I knew what to do.
I made a model of you,
A man in black with a Meinkampf look

And a love of the rack and the screw.
And I said I do, I do.
So daddy, I'm finally through.
The black telephone's off at the root,
The voices just can't worm through.

If I've killed one man, I've killed two—
The vampire who said he was you
And drank my blood for a year,
Seven years, if you want to know.
Daddy, you can lie back now.

There's a stake in your fat black heart
And the villagers never liked you.
They are dancing and stamping on you.
They always knew it was you.
Daddy, daddy, you bastard, I'm through.

Sylvia Plath

"Woman With Flowered Hat"

Her doctor had told Julian's mother that she must lose twenty pounds on account of her blood pressure, so on Wednesday nights Julian had to take her downtown on the bus for a reducing class at the Y. The reducing class was designed for working girls over fifty, who weighed from 165 to 200 pounds. His mother was one of the slimmer ones, but she said ladies did not tell their age or weight. She would not ride the buses by herself at night since they had been integrated, and because the reducing class was one of her few pleasures, necessary for her health, and *free,* she said Julian could at least put himself out to take her, considering all she did for him. Julian did not like to consider all she did for him, but every Wednesday night he braced himself and took her.

She was almost ready to go, standing before the hall mirror, putting on her hat, while he, his hands behind him, appeared pinned to the door frame, waiting like Saint Sebastian for the arrows to begin piercing him. The hat was new and had cost her seven dollars and a half. She kept saying, "Maybe I shouldn't have paid that for it. No, I shouldn't have. I'll take it off and return it tomorrow. I shouldn't have bought it."

Everything That Rises Must Converge

Flannery O'Connor

Julian raised his eyes to heaven. "Yes, you should have bought it," he said. "Put it on and let's go." It was a hideous hat. A purple velvet flap came down on one side of it and stood up on the other; the rest of it was green and looked like a cushion with the stuffing out. He decided it was less comical than jaunty and pathetic. Everything that gave her pleasure was small and depressed him.

She lifted the hat one more time and set it down slowly on top of her head. Two wings of gray hair protruded on either side of her florid face, but her eyes, sky-blue, were as innocent and untouched by experience as they must have been when she was ten. Were it not that she was a widow who had struggled fiercely to feed and clothe and put him through school and who was supporting him still, "until he got on his feet," she might have been a little girl that he had to take to town.

"It's all right, it's all right," he said. "Let's go." He opened the door himself and started down the walk to get her going. The sky was a dying violet and the houses stood out darkly against it, bulbous liver-colored monstrosities of a uniform ugliness though no two were alike. Since this had been a fashionable neighborhood forty years ago, his mother persisted in thinking they did well to have an apartment in it. Each house had a narrow collar of dirt around it in which sat, usually, a grubby child. Julian walked with his hands in his pockets, his head down and thrust forward and his eyes glazed with the determination to make himself completely numb during the time he would be sacrificed to her pleasure.

The door closed and he turned to find the dumpy figure, surmounted by the atrocious hat, coming toward him. "Well," she said, "you only live once and paying a little more for it, I at least won't meet myself coming and going."

"Some day I'll start making money," Julian said gloomily—he knew he never would—"and you can have one of those jokes whenever you take the fit." But first they would move. He visualized a place where the nearest neighbors would be three miles away on either side.

"I think you're doing fine," she said, drawing on her gloves. "You've only been out of school a year. Rome wasn't built in a day."

She was one of the few members of the Y reducing class who arrived in hat and gloves and who had a son who had been to college. "It takes time," she said, "and the world is in such a mess. This hat looked better on me than any of the others, though when she brought it out I said, 'Take that thing back. I wouldn't have it on my head,' and she said, 'Now wait till you see it on,' and when she put it on me, I said, 'We-ull,' and she said, 'If you ask me, that hat does something for you and you do something for the hat, and besides,' she said, 'with that hat, you won't meet yourself coming and going.'"

Julian thought he could have stood his lot better if she had been selfish, if she had been an old hag who drank and screamed at him. He walked along, saturated in depression, as if in the midst of his martyrdom he had lost his faith. Catching sight of his long, hopeless, irritated face, she stopped suddenly with a grief-stricken look, and pulled back on his arm. "Wait on me," she said. "I'm going back to the house and take this thing off and tomorrow I'm going to return it. I was out of my head. I can pay the gas bill with that seven-fifty."

He caught her arm in a vicious grip. "You are not going to take it back," he said. "I like it."

"Well," she said, "I don't think I ought . . ."

"Shut up and enjoy it," he muttered, more depressed than ever.

"With the world in the mess it's in," she said, "it's a wonder we can enjoy anything. I tell you, the bottom rail is on the top."

Julian sighed.

"Of course," she said, "if you know who you are, you can go anywhere." She said this every time he took her to the reducing class. "Most of them in it are not our kind of people," she said, "but I can be gracious to anybody. I know who I am."

"They don't give a damn for your graciousness," Julian said savagely. "Knowing who you are is good for one generation only. You haven't the foggiest idea where you stand now or who you are."

She stopped and allowed her eyes to flash at him. "I most certainly do know who I am," she said, "and if you don't know who you are, I'm ashamed of you."

"Oh hell," Julian said.

"Your great-grandfather was a former governor of this state," she said. "Your grand-father was a prosperous landowner. Your grandmother was a Godhigh."

"Will you look around you," he said tensely, "and see where you are now?" and he swept his arm jerkily out to indicate the neighborhood, which the growing darkness at least made less dingy.

"You remain what you are," she said. "Your great-grandfather had a plantation and two hundred slaves."

"There are no more slaves," he said irritably.

"They were better off when they were," she said. He groaned to see that she was off on that topic. She rolled onto it every few days like a train on an open track. He knew every stop, every junction, every swamp along the way, and knew the exact point at which her conclusion would roll majestically into the station: "It's ridiculous. It's simply not realistic. They should rise, yes, but on their own side of the fence."

"Let's skip it," Julian said.

"The ones I feel sorry for," she said, "are the ones that are half white. They're tragic."

"Will you skip it?"

"Suppose we were half white. We would certainly have mixed feelings."

"I have mixed feelings now," he groaned.

"Well let's talk about something pleasant," she said. "I remember going to Grandpa's when I was a little girl. Then the house had double stairways that went up to what was really the second floor—all the cooking was done on the first. I used to like to stay down in the kitchen on account of the way the walls smelled. I would sit with my nose pressed against the plaster and take deep breaths. Actually the place belonged to the Godhighs but your grandfather Chestny paid the mortgage and saved it for them. They were in reduced circumstances," she said, "but reduced or not, they never forgot who they were."

"Doubtless that decayed mansion reminded them," Julian muttered. He never spoke of it without contempt or thought of it without longing. He had seen it once when he was a child before it had been sold. The double stairways had rotted and been torn down. Negroes were living in it. But it remained in his mind as his mother had known it. It appeared in his dreams regularly. He would stand on the wide porch, listening to the rustle of oak leaves, then wander through the high-ceilinged hall into the parlor that opened onto it and gaze at the worn rugs and faded draperies. It occurred to him that it was he, not she, who could have appreciated it. He preferred its threadbare elegance to anything he could name and it was because of it that all the neighborhoods they had lived in had been a torment to him—whereas she had hardly known the difference. She called her insensitivity "being adjustable."

"And I remember the old darky who was my nurse, Caroline. There was no better person in the world. I've always had a great respect for my colored friends," she said. "I'd do anything in the world for them and they'd . . ."

"Will you for God's sake get off that subject?" Julian said. When he got on a bus by himself, he made it a point to sit down beside a Negro, in reparation as it were for his mother's sins.

"You're mighty touchy tonight," she said. "Do you feel all right?"

"Yes I feel all right," he said. "Now lay off."

She pursed her lips. "Well, you certainly are in a vile humor," she observed. "I just won't speak to you at all."

They had reached the bus stop. There was no bus in sight and Julian, his hands still jammed in his pockets and his head thrust forward, scowled down the empty street. The frustration of having to wait on the bus as well as ride on it began to creep up his neck like a hot hand. The presence of his mother was borne in upon him as she gave a pained sigh. He looked at her bleakly. She was holding herself very erect under the preposterous hat, wearing it like a banner of her imaginary dignity. There was in him an evil urge to break her spirit. He suddenly unloosened his tie and pulled it off and put it in his pocket.

She stiffened. "Why must you look like *that* when you take me to town?" she said. "Why must you deliberately embarrass me?"

"If you'll never learn where you are," he said, "you can at least learn where I am."

"You look like a—thug," she said.

"Then I must be one," he murmured.

"I'll just go home," she said. "I will not bother you. If you can't do a little thing like that for me . . ."

Rolling his eyes upward, he put his tie back on. "Restored to my class," he muttered. He thrust his face toward her and hissed, "True culture is in the mind, the *mind*," he said, and tapped his head, "the mind."

"It's in the heart," she said, "and in how you do things and how you do things is because of who you *are*."

"Nobody in the damn bus cares who you are."

"I care who I am," she said icily.

The lighted bus appeared on top of the next hill and as it approached, they moved out into the street to meet it. He put his hand under her elbow and hoisted her up on the creaking step. She entered with a little smile, as if she were going into a drawing room where everyone had been waiting for her. While he put in the tokens, she sat down on one of the broad front seats for three which faced the aisle. A thin woman with protruding teeth and long yellow hair was sitting on the end of it. His mother moved up beside her and left room for Julian beside herself. He sat down and looked at the floor across the aisle where a pair of thin feet in red and white canvas sandals were planted.

His mother immediately began a general conversation meant to attract anyone who felt like talking. "Can it get any hotter?" she said and removed from her purse a folding fan, black with a Japanese scene on it, which she began to flutter before her.

"I reckon it might could," the woman with the protruding teeth said, "but I know for a fact my apartment couldn't get no hotter."

"It must get the afternoon sun," his mother said. She sat forward and looked up and down the bus. It was half filled. Everybody was white. "I see we have the bus to ourselves," she said. Julian cringed.

"For a change," said the woman across the aisle, the owner of the red and white canvas sandals. "I come on one the other day and they were thick as fleas—up front and all through."

"The world is in a mess everywhere," his mother said. "I don't know how we've let it get in this fix."

"What gets my goat is all those boys from good families stealing automobile tires," the woman with the protruding teeth said. "I told my boy, I said you may not be rich but you been raised right and if I ever catch you in any such mess, they can send you on to the reformatory. Be exactly where you belong."

"Training tells," his mother said. "Is your boy in high school?"

"Ninth grade," the woman said.

"My son just finished college last year. He wants to write but he's selling typewriters until he gets started," his mother said.

The woman leaned forward and peered at Julian. He threw her such a malevolent look that she subsided against the seat. On the floor across the aisle there was an abandoned newspaper. He got up and got it and opened it out in front of him. His mother discreetly continued the conversation in a lower tone but the woman across the aisle said in a loud voice, "Well that's nice. Selling typewriters is close to writing. He can go right from one to the other."

"I tell him," his mother said, "that Rome wasn't built in a day."

Behind the newspaper Julian was withdrawing into the inner compartment of his mind where he spent most of his time. This was a kind of mental bubble in which he established himself when he could not bear to be a part of what was going on around him. From it he could see out and judge but in it he was safe from any kind of penetration from without. It was the only place where he felt free of the general idiocy of his fellows. His mother had never entered it but from it he could see her with absolute clarity.

The old lady was clever enough and he thought that if she had started from any of the right premises, more might have been expected of her. She lived according to the laws of her own fantasy world, outside of which he had never seen her set foot. The law of it was to sacrifice herself for him after she had first created the necessity to do so by making a mess of things. If he had permitted her sacrifices, it was only because her lack of foresight had made them necessary. All of her life had been a struggle to act like a Chestny without the Chestny goods, and to give him everything she thought a Chestny ought to have; but since, said she, it was fun to struggle, why complain? And when you had won, as she had won, what fun to look back on the hard times! He could not forgive her that she had enjoyed the struggle and that she thought *she* had won.

What she meant when she said she had won was that she had brought him up successfully and had sent him to college and that he had turned out so well—good looking (her teeth had gone unfilled so that his could be straightened), intelligent (he realized he was too intelligent to be a success), and with a future ahead of him (there was of course no future ahead of him). She excused his gloominess on the grounds that he was still growing up and his radical ideas on his lack of practical experience. She said he didn't yet know a thing about "life," that he hadn't even entered the real world—when already he was as disenchanted with it as a man of fifty.

The further irony of all this was that in spite of her, he had turned out so well. In spite of going to only a third-rate college, he had, on his own initiative, come out with a first-rate education; in spite of growing up dominated by a small mind, he had ended up with a large one; in spite of all her foolish views, he was free of prejudice and unafraid to face facts. Most miraculous of all, instead of being blinded by love for her as she was for him, he had cut himself emotionally free of her and could see her with complete objectivity. He was not dominated by his mother.

The bus stopped with a sudden jerk and shook him from his meditation. A woman from the back lurched forward with little steps and barely escaped falling in his newspaper as she righted herself. She got off and a large Negro got on. Julian kept his paper lowered to watch. It gave him a certain satisfaction to see injustice in daily operation. It confirmed his view that with a few exceptions there was no one worth knowing within a radius of three hundred miles. The Negro was well dressed and carried a briefcase. He looked around and then sat down on the other end of the seat where the woman with the red and white canvas sandals was sitting. He immediately unfolded a newspaper and obscured himself behind it. Julian's mother's elbow at once prodded insistently into his ribs. "Now you see why I won't ride on these buses by myself," she whispered.

The woman with the red and white canvas sandals had risen at the same time the Negro sat down and had gone further back in the bus and taken the seat of the woman who had got off. His mother leaned forward and cast her an approving look.

Julian rose, crossed the aisle, and sat down in the place of the woman with the canvas sandals. From this position, he looked serenely across at his mother. Her face had turned an angry red. He stared at her, making his eyes the eyes of a stranger. He felt his tension suddenly lift as if he had openly declared war on her.

He would have liked to get in conversation with the Negro and to talk with him about art or politics or any subject that would be above the comprehension of those around them, but the man remained entrenched behind his paper. He was either ignoring the change of seating or had never noticed it. There was no way for Julian to convey his sympathy.

His mother kept her eyes fixed reproachfully on his face. The woman with the protruding teeth was looking at him avidly as if he were a type of monster new to her.

"Do you have a light?" he asked the Negro.

Without looking away from his paper, the man reached in his pocket and handed him a packet of matches.

"Thanks," Julian said. For a moment he held the matches foolishly. A NO SMOKING sign looked down upon him from over the door. This alone would not have deterred him; he had no cigarettes. He had quit smoking some months before because he could not afford it. "Sorry," he muttered and handed back the matches. The Negro lowered the paper and gave him an annoyed look. He took the matches and raised the paper again.

His mother continued to gaze at him but she did not take advantage of his momentary discomfort. Her eyes retained their battered look. Her face seemed to be unnaturally red, as if her blood pressure had risen. Julian allowed no glimmer of sympathy to show on his face. Having got the advantage, he wanted desperately to keep it and carry it through. He would have liked to teach her a lesson that would last her a while, but there seemed no way to continue the point. The Negro refused to come out from behind his paper.

Julian folded his arms and looked stolidly before him, facing her but as if he did not see her, as if he had ceased to recognize her existence. He visualized a scene in which, the bus having reached their stop, he would remain in his seat and when she said, "Aren't you going to get off?" he would look at her as at a stranger who had rashly addressed him. The corner they got off on was usually deserted, but it was well lighted and it would not hurt her to walk by herself the four blocks to the Y. He decided to wait until the time came and then decide whether or not he would let her get off by herself. He would have to be at the Y at ten to bring her back, but he could leave her wondering if he was going to show up. There was no reason for her to think she could always depend on him.

He retired again into the high-ceilinged room sparsely settled with large pieces of antique furniture. His soul expanded momentarily but then he became aware of his mother across from him and the vision shriveled. He studied her coldly. Her feet in little pumps dangled like a child's and did not quite reach the floor. She was training on him an exaggerated look of reproach. He felt completely detached from her. At that moment he could with pleasure have slapped her as he would have slapped a particularly obnoxious child in his charge.

He began to imagine various unlikely ways by which he could teach her a lesson. He might make friends with some distinguished Negro professor or lawyer and bring him home to spend the evening. He would be entirely justified but her blood pressure would rise to 300. He could not push her to the extent of making her have a stroke, and moreover, he had never been successful at making any Negro friends. He had tried to strike up an acquaintance on the bus with some of the better types, with ones that looked like professors or ministers or lawyers. One morning he had sat down next to a distinguished-looking dark brown man who had answered his questions with a sonorous solemnity but who had turned out to be an undertaker. Another day he had sat down beside a cigar-smoking Negro with a diamond ring on his finger, but after a few stilted pleasantries, the Negro had rung the buzzer and risen, slipping two lottery tickets into Julian's hand as he climbed over him to leave.

He imagined his mother lying desperately ill and his being able to secure only a Negro doctor for her. He toyed with that idea for a few minutes and then dropped it for a momentary vision of himself participating as a sympathizer in a sit-in demonstration. This was possible but he did not linger with it. Instead, he approached the ultimate horror. He brought home a beautiful suspiciously Negroid woman. Prepare yourself, he said. There is nothing you can do about it. This is the woman I've chosen. She's intelligent, dignified, even good, and she's suffered and she hasn't thought it *fun*. Now persecute us, go ahead and persecute us. Drive her out of here, but remember, you're driving me too. His eyes were narrowed and through the indignation he had generated, he saw his mother across the aisle, purple-faced, shrunken to the dwarf-like proportions of her moral nature, sitting like a mummy beneath the ridiculous banner of her hat.

He was tilted out of his fantasy again as the bus stopped. The door opened with a sucking hiss and out of the dark a large, gaily dressed, sullen-looking colored woman got on with a little boy. The child, who might have been four, had on a short plaid suit and a Tyrolean hat with a blue feather in it. Julian hoped that he would sit down beside him and that the woman would push in beside his mother. He could think of no better arrangement.

As she waited for her tokens, the woman was surveying the seating possibilities—he hoped with the idea of sitting where she was least wanted. There was something familiar-looking about her but Julian could not place what it was. She was a giant of a woman. Her face was set not only to meet opposition but to seek it out. The downward tilt of her large lower lip was like a warning sign: DON'T TAMPER WITH ME. Her bulging figure was encased in a green crepe dress and her feet overflowed in red shoes. She had on a hideous hat. A purple velvet flap came down on one side of it and stood up on the other; the rest of it was green and looked like a cushion with the stuffing out. She carried a mammoth red pocketbook that bulged throughout as if it were stuffed with rocks.

To Julian's disappointment, the little boy climbed up on the empty seat beside his mother. His mother lumped all children, black and white, into the common category, "cute," and she thought little Negroes were on the whole cuter than little white children. She smiled at the little boy as he climbed on the seat.

Meanwhile the woman was bearing down upon the empty seat beside Julian. To his annoyance, she squeezed herself into it. He saw his mother's face change as the woman settled herself next to him and he realized with satisfaction that this was more objectionable to her than it was to him. Her face seemed almost gray and there was a look of dull recognition in her eyes, as if suddenly she had sickened at some awful confrontation. Julian saw that it was because she and the woman had, in a sense, swapped sons. Though his mother would not realize the symbolic significance of this, she would feel it. His amusement showed plainly on his face.

The woman next to him muttered something unintelligible to herself. He was conscious of a kind of bristling next to him, a muted growling like that of an angry cat. He could not see anything but the red pocketbook upright on the bulging green thighs. He visualized the woman as she had stood waiting for her tokens—the ponderous figure, rising from the red shoes upward over the solid hips, the mammoth bosom, the haughty face, to the green and purple hat.

His eyes widened.

The vision of the two hats, identical, broke upon him with the radiance of a brilliant sunrise. His face was suddenly lit with joy. He could not believe that Fate had thrust upon his mother such a lesson. He gave a loud chuckle so that she would look at him and see that he saw. She turned her eyes on him slowly. The blue in them seemed to have turned a bruised purple. For a moment he had an uncomfortable sense of her innocence, but it lasted only a second before principle rescued him. Justice entitled him to laugh. His grin hardened until it said to her as plainly as if he were saying aloud: Your punishment exactly fits your pettiness. This should teach you a permanent lesson.

Her eyes shifted to the woman. She seemed unable to bear looking at him and to find the woman preferable. He became conscious again of the bristling presence at his side. The woman was rumbling like a volcano about to become active. His mother's mouth began to twitch slightly at one corner. With a sinking heart, he saw incipient signs of recovery on her face and realized that this was going to strike her suddenly as funny and was going to be no lesson at all. She kept her eyes on the woman and an amused smile came over her face as if the woman were a monkey that had stolen her hat. The little Negro was looking up at her with large fascinated eyes. He had been trying to attract her attention for some time.

"Carver!" the woman said suddenly. "Come heah!"

When he saw that the spotlight was on him at last, Carver drew his feet up and turned himself toward Julian's mother and giggled.

"Carver!" the woman said. "You heah me? Come heah!"

Carver slid down from the seat but remained squatting with his back against the base of it, his head turned slyly around toward Julian's mother, who was smiling at him. The woman reached a hand across the aisle and snatched him to her. He righted himself and hung backwards on her knees, grinning at Julian's mother. "Isn't he cute?" Julian's mother said to the woman with the protruding teeth.

"I reckon he is," the woman said without conviction.

The Negress yanked him upright but he eased out of her grip and shot across the aisle and scrambled, giggling wildly, onto the seat beside his love.

"I think he likes me," Julian's mother said, and smiled at the woman. It was the smile she used when she was being particularly gracious to an inferior. Julian saw everything lost. The lesson had rolled off her like rain on a roof.

The woman stood up and yanked the little boy off the seat as if she were snatching him from contagion. Julian could feel the rage in her at having no weapon like his mother's smile. She gave the child a sharp slap across his leg. He howled once and then thrust his head into her stomach and kicked his feet against her shins. "Be-have," she said vehemently.

The bus stopped and the Negro who had been reading the newspaper got off. The woman moved over and set the little boy down with a thump between herself and Julian. She held him firmly by the knee. In a moment he put his hands in front of his face and peeped at Julian's mother through his fingers.

"I see yooooooooo!" she said and put her hand in front of her face and peeped at him.

The woman slapped his hand down. "Quit yo' foolishness," she said, "before I knock the living Jesus out of you!"

Julian was thankful that the next stop was theirs. He reached up and pulled the cord. The woman reached up and pulled it at the same time. Oh my God, he thought. He had the terrible intuition that when they got off the bus together, his mother would open her purse and give the little boy a nickel. The gesture would be as natural to her as breathing. The bus stopped and the woman got up and lunged to the front, dragging the child, who wished to stay on, after her. Julian and his mother got up and followed. As they neared the door, Julian tried to relieve her of her pocketbook.

"No," she murmured, "I want to give the little boy a nickel."

"No!" Julian hissed. "No!"

She smiled down at the child and opened her bag. The bus door opened and the woman picked him up by the arm and descended with him, hanging at her hip. Once in the street she set him down and shook him.

Julian's mother had to close her purse while she got down the bus step but as soon as her feet were on the ground, she opened it again and began to rummage inside. "I can't find but a penny," she whispered, "but it looks like a new one."

"Don't do it!" Julian said fiercely between his teeth. There was a streetlight on the corner and she hurried to get under it so that she could better see into her pocketbook. The woman was heading off rapidly down the street with the child still hanging backward on her hand.

"Oh little boy!" Julian's mother called and took a few quick steps and caught up with them just beyond the lamppost. "Here's a bright new penny for you," and she held out the coin, which shone bronze in the dim light.

The huge woman turned and for a moment stood, her shoulders lifted and her face frozen with frustrated rage, and stared at Julian's mother. Then all at once she seemed to explode like a piece of machinery that had been given one ounce of pressure too much. Julian saw the black fist swing out with the red pocketbook. He shut his eyes and cringed as he heard the woman shout, "He don't take nobody's pennies!" When he opened his eyes, the woman was disappearing down the street with the little boy staring wide-eyed over her shoulder. Julian's mother was sitting on the sidewalk.

"I told you not to do that," Julian said angrily. "I told you not to do that!"

He stood over her for a minute, gritting his teeth. Her legs were stretched out in front of her and her hat was on her lap. He squatted down and looked her in the face. It was totally expressionless. "You got exactly what you deserved," he said. "Now get up."

He picked up her pocketbook and put what had fallen out back in it. He picked the hat up off her lap. The penny caught his eye on the sidewalk and he picked that up and let it drop before her eyes into the purse. Then he stood up and leaned over and held his hands out to pull her up. She remained immobile. He sighed. Rising above them on either side were black apartment buildings, marked with irregular rectangles of light. At the end of the block a man came out of a door and walked off in the opposite direction. "All right," he said, "suppose somebody happens by and wants to know why you're sitting on the sidewalk?"

She took the hand and, breathing hard, pulled heavily up on it and then stood for a moment, swaying slightly as if the spots of light in the darkness were circling around her. Her eyes, shadowed and confused, finally settled on his face. He did not try to conceal his irritation. "I hope this teaches you a lesson," he said. She leaned forward and her eyes raked his face. She seemed trying to determine his identity. Then, as if she found nothing familiar about him, she started off with a headlong movement in the wrong direction.

"Aren't you going on to the Y?" he asked.

"Home," she muttered.

"Well, are we walking?"

For answer she kept going. Julian followed along, his hands behind him. He saw no reason to let the lesson she had had go without backing it up with an explanation of its meaning. She might as well be made to understand what had happened to her. "Don't think that was just an uppity Negro woman," he said. "That was the whole colored race which will no longer take your condescending pennies. That was your black double. She can wear the same hat as you, and to be sure," he added gratuitously (because he thought it was funny), "it looked better on her than it did on you. What all this means," he said, "is that the old world is gone. The old manners are obsolete and your graciousness is not worth a damn." He thought bitterly of the house that had been lost for him. "You aren't who you think you are," he said.

She continued to plow ahead, paying no attention to him. Her hair had come undone on one side. She dropped her pocketbook and took no notice. He stooped and picked it up and handed it to her but she did not take it.

"You needn't act as if the world had come to an end," he said, "because it hasn't. From now on you've got to live in a new world and face a few realities for a change. Buck up," he said, "it won't kill you."

She was breathing fast.

"Let's wait on the bus," he said.

"Home," she said thickly.

"I hate to see you behave like this," he said. "Just like a child. I should be able to expect more of you." He decided to stop where he was and make her stop and wait for a bus. "I'm not going any farther," he said, stopping. "We're going on the bus."

 34

She continued to go on as if she had not heard him. He took a few steps and caught her arm and stopped her. He looked into her face and caught his breath. He was looking into a face he had never seen before. "Tell Grandpa to come get me," she said.

He stared, stricken.

"Tell Caroline to come get me," she said.

Stunned, he let her go and she lurched forward again, walking as if one leg were shorter than the other. A tide of darkness seemed to be sweeping her from him. "Mother!" he cried. "Darling, sweetheart, wait!" Crumpling, she fell to the pavement. He dashed forward and fell at her side, crying, "Mamma, Mamma!" He turned her over. Her face was fiercely distorted. One eye, large and staring, moved slightly to the left as if it had become unmoored. The other remained fixed on him, raked his face again, found nothing and closed.

"Wait here, wait here!" he cried and jumped up and began to run for help toward a cluster of lights he saw in the distance ahead of him. "Help, help!" he shouted, but his voice was thin, scarcely a thread of sound. The lights drifted farther away the faster he ran and his feet moved numbly as if they carried him nowhere. The tide of darkness seemed to sweep him back to her, postponing from moment to moment his entry into the world of guilt and sorrow.

The Last Echo

And the curtain's disbelieving edges
    dissolve behind the oakleaf
where the shell on the beach bends
    and the lie disappears around the corner
        drugstore
and our pillow cases and medicine chests
    can't save us
from oyster beds repeating
    their parents' eternal commandment:
        I Told You So.

Walter Lowenfels

36

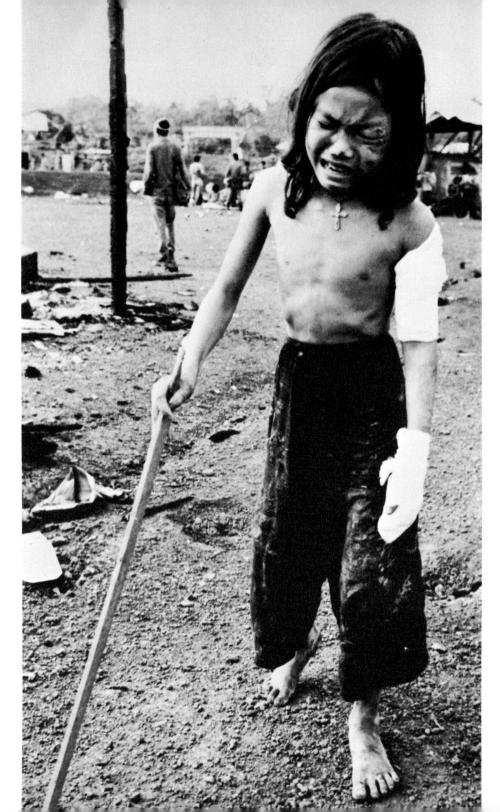

Children's Elegy

From *Eighth Elegy*

. . . This what they say, who were broken off from love:
However long we were loved, it was not long enough.

We were afraid of the broad big policeman,
of lions and tigers, the dark hall and the moon.

After our father went, nothing was ever the same,
when mother did not come back, we made up a war-game.

My cat was sitting in the doorway when the planes
went over, and my cat saw mother cry;
furry tears, fire fell, wall went down;
did my cat see mother die?

Mother is gone away, my cat sits here coughing.
I cough and sit. I am nobody's nothing.

However long they loved us, it was not long enough.
For we have to be strong, to know what they did, and then
our people are saved in time, our houses built again.

You will not know, you have a sister and brother;
My doll is not my child, my doll is my mother.

However strong we are, it is not strong enough.
I want to grow up. To come back to love. . . .

Muriel Rukeyser

Photograph by Fred Eng.

YOUNG WOMAN

Naked before the glass she said,
"I see my body as no man has,
Nor any shall unless I wed
And naked in a stranger's house
Stand timid beside his bed.
There is no pity in the flesh."

"Or else I shall grow old," she said,
"Alone, and change my likeliness
For a vile, slack shape, a head
Shriveled with thinking wickedness
Against the day I must be dead
And eaten by my crabbed wish."

"One or the other way," she said,
"How shall I know the difference,
When wrinkles come, to spinster or bride?
Whether to marry or burn is bless-
ed best, O stranger to my bed,
There is no pity in the flesh."

Howard Nemerov

MARRIAGE

Should I get married? Should I be good?
Astound the girl next door with my velvet suit and faustus hood?
Don't take her to movies but to cemeteries
tell all about werewolf bathtubs and forked clarinets
then desire her and kiss her and all the preliminaries
and she going just so far and I understanding why
not getting angry saying You must feel! It's beautiful to feel!
Instead take her in my arms lean against an old crooked tombstone
and woo her the entire night the constellations in the sky—

 40

When she introduces me to her parents
back straightened, hair finally combed, strangled by a tie,
should I sit knees together on their 3rd degree sofa
and not ask Where's the bathroom?
How else to feel other than I am,
often thinking Flash Gordon soap—
O how terrible it must be for a young man
seated before a family and the family thinking
We never saw him before! He wants our Mary Lou!
After tea and homemade cookies they ask What do you do for a living?

Should I tell them? Would they like me then?
Say All right get married, we're losing a daughter
but we're gaining a son—
And should I then ask Where's the bathroom?

O God, and the wedding! All her family and her friends
and only a handful of mine all scroungy and bearded
just wait to get at the drinks and food—
And the priest! he looking at me as if I masturbated
asking me Do you take this woman for your lawful wedded wife?
And I trembling what to say say Pie Glue!
I kiss the bride all those corny men slapping me on the back
She's all yours, boy! Ha-ha-ha!
And in their eyes you could see some obscene honeymoon going on—
Then all that absurd rice and clanky cans and shoes
Niagara Falls! Hordes of us! Husbands! Wives! Flowers! Chocolates!
All streaming into cozy hotels
All going to do the same thing tonight
The indifferent clerk he knowing what was going to happen
The lobby zombies they knowing what
The whistling elevator man he knowing
The winking bellboy knowing
Everybody knowing! I'd be almost inclined not to do anything!
Stay up all night! Stare that hotel clerk in the eye!
Screaming: I deny honeymoon! I deny honeymoon!
running rampant into those almost climactic suites
yelling Radio belly! Cat shovel!
O I'd live in Niagara forever! in a dark cave beneath the Falls
I'd sit there the Mad Honeymooner
devising ways to break marriages, a scourge of bigamy
a saint of divorce—

But I should get married I should be good
How nice it'd be to come home to her
and sit by the fireplace and she in the kitchen
aproned young and lovely wanting my baby
and so happy about me she burns the roast beef
and comes crying to me and I get up from my big papa chair
saying Christmas teeth! Radiant brains! Apple deaf!
God what a husband I'd make! Yes, I should get married!
So much to do! like sneaking into Mr. Jones' house late at night
and cover his golf clubs with 1920 Norwegian books
Like hanging a picture of Rimbaud on the lawnmower
like pasting Tannu Tuva postage stamps all over the picket fence
like when Mrs. Kindhead comes to collect for the Community Chest
grab her and tell her There are unfavorable omens in the sky.
And when the mayor comes to get my vote tell him
When are you going to stop people killing whales!
And when the milkman comes leave him a note in the bottle
Penguin dust, bring me penguin dust, I want penguin dust—

Yet if I should get married and it's Connecticut and snow
and she gives birth to a child and I am sleepless, worn,
up for nights, head bowed against a quiet window, the past behind me,
finding myself in the most common of situations a trembling man
knowledged with responsibility not twig-smear nor Roman coin soup—
O what would that be like!
Surely I'd give it for a nipple a rubber Tacitus
For a rattle a bag of broken Bach records
Tack Della Francesca all over its crib
Sew the Greek alphabet on its bib
And build for its playpen a roofless Parthenon

No, I doubt I'd be that kind of father
not rural not snow no quiet window
but hot smelly tight New York City
seven flights up, roaches and rats in the walls
a fat Reichian wife screeching over potatoes Get a job!
And five nose running brats in love with Batman
And the neighbors all toothless and dry haired
like those hag masses of the 18th century
all wanting to come in and watch TV
The landlord wants his rent
Grocery store Blue Cross Gas & Electric Knights of Columbus
Impossible to lie back and dream Telephone snow, ghost parking—
No! I should not get married I should never get married!
But—imagine If I were married to a beautiful sophisticated woman
tall and pale wearing an elegant black dress and long black gloves
holding a cigarette holder in one hand and a highball in the other
and we lived high up in a penthouse with a huge window
from which we could see all of New York and ever farther on clearer days
No, can't imagine myself married to that pleasant prison dream—

O but what about love? I forget love
not that I am incapable of love
it's just that I see love as odd as wearing shoes—
I never wanted to marry a girl who was like my mother
And Ingrid Bergman was always impossible
And there's maybe a girl now but she's already married
And I don't like men and—
but there's got to be somebody!
Because what if I'm 60 years old and not married,
all alone in a furnished room with pee stains on my underwear
and everybody else is married! All the universe married but me!

Ah, yet well I know that were a woman possible as I am possible
then marriage would be possible—
Like SHE in her lonely alien gaud waiting her Egyptian lover
so I wait—bereft of 2,000 years and the bath of life.

                    Gregory Corso

How do I love thee? Let me count the ways.
I love thee to the depth and breadth and height
My soul can reach, when feeling out of sight
For the ends of Being and ideal Grace.
I love thee to the level of everyday's
Most quiet need, by sun and candlelight.
I love thee freely, as men strive for Right;
I love thee purely, as they turn from Praise.
I love thee with the passion put to use
In my old griefs, and with my childhood's faith.
I love thee with a love I seemed to lose
With my lost saints,—I love thee with the breath,
Smiles, tears, of all my life!—and, if God choose,
I shall but love thee better after death.

Elizabeth Barrett Browning

43

THREE

You see how easily we fit together,
as if God's own hand had cradled only us
and this beach town's population were but two
and this wide bed but a child's cradle
with room enough left over for presents.

Tomorrow I'll buy you presents.
Pomegranates and breadsticks,
tickets round the room and back
and red red roses like everybody buys everybody.

Everybody's got a diamond ring
and Sunday shoes.
Neckties and petticoats,
pistols and tennis balls.

What pleases you?
I'd hock my watch to buy you Greece
or sell my car to bring you rickshaws from Rangoon.
All they had down at the corner
were poppies with some lemon leaves.
They'll have to do
till I can bring home Union Square.

I found a twenty-dollar bill when I was ten.
I bought a cardboard circus and a fountain pen
and a jackknife because I never had one before.
My mother thought I'd stolen the money.
I brought her perfume from the dime store.
She believed me then.

I was rich in those days,
for a week I had everything.

I wish I'd known you then.

ROD McKUEN

The pain of loving you
Is almost more than I can bear.

I walk in fear of you.
The darkness starts up where
You stand, and the night comes through
Your eyes when you look at me.

Ah, never before did I see
The shadows that live in the sun!

Now every tall glad tree
Turns round its back to the sun
And looks down on the ground, to see
The shadow it used to shun.

At the foot of each glowing thing
A night lies looking up.

Oh, and I want to sing
And dance, but I can't lift up
My eyes from the shadows: dark
They lie spilt round the cup.

What is it?—Hark
The faint fine seethe in the air!

Like the seething sound in a shell!
It is death still seething where
The wild-flower shakes its bell
And the skylark twinkles blue—

The pain of loving you
Is almost more than I can bear.

D. H. Lawrence

45

46

ITEM

this man is o so
Waiter
this;   woman is

please shut that
the pout And Affectionate leer
interminable pyramidal, napkins
(this man is oh so tired of this
a door opens by itself
woman.) they so to speak were in

Love once?
now
     her mouth opens too far
and: she attacks her Lobster without
feet mingle under the
mercy.
          (exit the hors d'oeuvres)

E. E. Cummings

E. E. Cummings

(exit the hors d'oeuvres)
mercy.
feet mingle under the
and: she attacks her Lobster without
her mouth opens too far
now
Love once?

woman.) they so to speak were in
a door opens by itself
(this man is oh so tired of this
interminable pyramidal, napkins
the pout And Affectionate leer
please shut that

this;   woman is
Waiter
this man is o so

ITEM

BY THE TIME
GEORGE TOLD
ME HE WAS
LEAVING ON A
BUSINESS
TRIP FOR A
MONTH I HAD
LOST ALL
FEELING
FOR HIM.

EACH DINNER WHEN
HE'D COME HOME I'D
TRY TO REKINDLE
THE FLAME, BUT
ALL I COULD
THINK OF AS HE
GOBBLED UP MY
CHICKEN WAS:
"ALL I AM IS A
SERVANT TO
YOU, GEORGE."

SO WHEN HE
ANNOUNCED HE
HAD TO GO AWAY
I WAS **DELIGHTED.**
WHILE GEORGE
WAS AWAY I
COULD **FIND** MY-
SELF AGAIN! I
COULD MAKE
PLANS!

THE FIRST WEEK
GEORGE WAS
AWAY I WENT
OUT SEVEN TIMES.
THE TELEPHONE
NEVER STOPPED
RINGING. I HAD
A **MAR**VELOUS
TIME!

12/8

© 1963
JULES
FEIFFER

THE SECOND WEEK GEORGE WAS AWAY I GOT **TIRED** OF THE SAME OLD FACES, SAME OLD LINES. I REMEMBERED WHAT DROVE ME TO MARRY GEORGE IN THE FIRST PLACE.

THE THIRD WEEK GEORGE WAS AWAY I FELT CLOSER TO HIM THAN I HAD IN **YEARS.** I STAYED HOME, READ JANE AUSTEN AND SLEPT ON GEORGE'S SIDE OF THE BED.

THE FOURTH WEEK GEORGE WAS AWAY, I FELL MADLY IN LOVE WITH HIM. I HATED MYSELF FOR MY WITHDRAWAL, FOR MY FAILURE OF HIM.

THE FIFTH WEEK GEORGE CAME HOME. THE MINUTE HE WALKED IN AND SAID, "I'M BACK, DARLING!" I WITHDREW.

I CAN HARDLY WAIT FOR HIS NEXT BUSINESS TRIP SO I CAN LOVE GEORGE AGAIN.

50

Home

published by Harper & Row. Originally printed in *The New Yorker*.

The Crisis of American Masculinity

Arthur Schlesinger, Jr.

What has happened to the American male? For a long time, he seemed utterly confident in his manhood, sure of his masculine role in society, easy and definite in his sense of sexual identity. The frontiersmen of James Fenimore Cooper, for example, never had any concern about masculinity; they were men, and it did not occur to them to think twice about it. Even well into the twentieth century, the heroes of Dreiser, of Fitzgerald, of Hemingway remain men. But one begins to detect a new theme emerging in some of these authors, especially in Hemingway: the theme of the male hero increasingly preoccupied with proving his virility to himself. And by mid-century, the male role had plainly lost its rugged clarity of outline. Today men are more and more conscious of maleness not as a fact but as a problem. The ways by which American men affirm their masculinity are uncertain and obscure. There are multiplying signs, indeed, that something has gone badly wrong with the American male's conception of himself.

On the most superficial level, the roles of male and female are increasingly merged in the American household. The American man is found as never before as a substitute for wife and mother—changing diapers, washing dishes, cooking meals and performing a whole series of what once were considered female duties. The American woman meanwhile takes over more and more of the big decisions, controlling them indirectly when she cannot do so directly. Outside the home, one sees a similar blurring of function. While men design dresses and brew up cosmetics, women become doctors, lawyers, bank cashiers and executives. "Women now fill many 'masculine' roles," writes the psychologist, Dr. Bruno Bettelheim, "and expect their husbands to assume many of the tasks once reserved for their own sex." They seem an expanding, aggressive force, seizing new domains like a conquering army, while men, more and more on the defensive, are hardly able to hold their own and gratefully accept assignments from their new rulers. A recent book bears the stark and melancholy title *The Decline of the American Male.*

Some of this evidence, it should be quickly said, has been pushed too far. The willingness of a man to help his wife around the house may as well be evidence of confidence in masculinity as the opposite; such a man obviously does not have to cling to masculine symbols in order to keep demonstrating his maleness to himself. But there is more impressive evidence than the helpful husband that this is an age of sexual ambiguity. It appears no accident, for example, that the changing of sex—the Christine Jorgensen phenomenon—so fascinates our newspaper editors and readers; or that homosexuality, that incarnation of sexual ambiguity, should be enjoying a cultural boom new in our history. Such developments surely express a deeper tension about the problem of sexual identity.

Consider the theatre, that faithful mirror of a society's preoccupations. There have been, of course, popular overt inquiries into sexual ambiguities, like *Compulsion* or *Tea and Sympathy.* But in a sense these plays prove the case too easily. Let us take rather two uncommonly successful plays by the most discussed young playwrights of the United States and Great Britain—Tennessee Williams's *Cat On A Hot Tin Roof* and John Osborne's *Look Back in Anger.* Both deal with the young male in a singular state of confusion and desperation. In *Cat On A Hot Tin Roof,* Brick Pollitt, the professional football

player, refuses to sleep with his wife because of guilty memories of his relations with a dead team mate. In *Look Back in Anger,* Jimmy Porter, the embittered young intellectual who can sustain a relationship with his wife only by pretending they are furry animals together, explodes with hatred of women and finds his moments of happiness rough-housing around the stage with a male pal.

Brick Pollitt and Jimmy Porter are all too characteristic modern heroes. They are, in a sense, castrated; one is stymied by fear of homosexuality, the other is an unconscious homosexual. Neither is capable of dealing with the woman in his life: Brick surrenders to a strong woman, Jimmy destroys a weak one. Both reject the normal female desire for full and reciprocal love as an unconscionable demand and an intolerable burden. Now not many American males have been reduced to quite the Pollitt-Porter condition. Still the intentness with which audiences have watched these plays suggests that exposed nerves are being plucked—that the Pollitt-Porter dilemma expresses in vivid and heightened form something that many spectators themselves feel or fear.

Or consider the movies. In some ways, the most brilliant and influential American film since the war is *High Noon.* That remarkable movie, which invested the Western with the classic economy of myth, can be viewed in several ways: as an existentialist drama, for example, or as a parable of McCarthyism. It can also be viewed as a mordant comment on the effort of the American woman to emasculate the American man. The sheriff plainly did not suffer from Brick Pollitt's disease. But a large part of the story dealt with the attempt of his girl to persuade him not to use force—to deny him the use of his pistol. The pistol is an obvious masculine symbol, and, in the end, it was the girl herself, in the modern American manner, who used the pistol and killed a villain. (In this connection, one can pause and note why the Gary Coopers, Cary Grants,

Clark Gables and Spencer Tracys continue to play romantic leads opposite girls young enough to be their daughters; it is obviously because so few of the younger male stars can project a convincing sense of masculinity.)

Psychoanalysis backs up the theatre and the movies in emphasizing the obsession of the American male with his manhood. "Every psychoanalyst knows," writes one of them, "how many emotional difficulties are due to those fears and insecurities of neurotic men who are unconsciously doubting their masculinity." "In our civilization," Dr. Theodor Reik says, "men are afraid that they will not be men enough." Reik adds significantly: "And women are afraid that they might be considered only women." Why is it that women worry, not over whether they can fill the feminine role, but whether filling that role is enough, while men worry whether they can fill the masculine role at all? How to account for this rising tide of male anxiety? What has unmanned the American man?

There is currently a fashionable answer to this question. Male anxiety, many observers have declared, is simply the result of female aggression: what has unmanned the American man is the American woman. The present male confusion and desperation, it is contended, are the inevitable consequence of the threatened feminization of American society. The victory of women is the culmination of a long process of masculine retreat, beginning when Puritanism made men feel guilty about sex and the frontier gave women the added value of scarcity. Fleeing from the reality of femininity, the American man, while denying the American woman juridical equality, transformed her into an ideal of remote and transcendent purity with overriding authority over the family, the home, the school and culture. This habit of obeisance left the male psychologically disarmed and vulnerable when the goddess stepped off the pedestal and demanded in addition equal economic, political and legal rights. In the last part of the nineteenth century, women won their battle for equality. They gained the right of entry into one occupation after another previously reserved for males. Today they hold the key positions of personal power in our society and use this power relentlessly to consolidate their mastery. As mothers, they undermine masculinity through the use of love as a technique of reward and punishment. As teachers, they prepare male children for their role of submission in an increasingly feminine world. As wives, they complete the work of subjugation. Their strategy of conquest is deliberately to emasculate men— to turn them into Brick Pollitts and Jimmy Porters.'

Or so a standard indictment runs; and no doubt there is something in it. American women have unquestionably gained through the years a place in our society which American men have not been psychologically prepared to accept. Whether because of Puritanism or the frontier, there has been something immature in the traditional American male attitude toward women—a sense of alarm at times amounting to panic. Almost none of the classic American novels, for example, presents the theme of mature and passionate love. Our nineteenth-century novelists saw women either as unassailable virgins or abandoned temptresses—never simply as women. One looks in vain through *Moby Dick* and *The Adventures of Huckleberry Finn,* through Cooper and Poe and Whitman, for an adult portrayal of relations between men and women. "Where," Leslie Fiedler has asked, "is the American *Madame Bovary, Anna Karenina, Wuthering Heights,* or *Vanity Fair?*"

Yet the implication of the argument that the American man has been unmanned by the emancipation of the American woman is that the American man was incapable of growing up. For the nineteenth-century sense of masculinity was based on the psychological idealization and the legal subjection of women; masculinity so spuriously derived could never—and should never—have endured. The male had to learn to live at some point with the free

54

and equal female. Current attempts to blame "the decline of the American male" on the aggressiveness of the American female amount to a confession that, under conditions of free competition, the female was bound to win. Simple observation refutes this supposition. In a world of equal rights, some women rise; so too do some men; and no pat generalization is possible about the sexual future of society. Women have gained power in certain ways; in others, they have made little progress. It is safe to predict, for example, that we will have a Roman Catholic, perhaps even a Jew, for President before we have a woman. Those amiable prophets of an impending American matriarchy (all men, by the way) are too pessimistic.

Something more fundamental is involved in the unmanning of American men than simply the onward rush of American women. Why is the American man so unsure today about his masculine identity? The basic answer to this is surely because he is so unsure about his identity in general. Nothing is harder in the whole human condition than to achieve a full sense of identity—than to know who you are, where you are going, and what you mean to live and die for. From the most primitive myths to the most contemporary novels—from Oedipus making the horrified discovery that he had married his mother, to Leopold Bloom and Stephen Dedalus searching their souls in Joyce's Dublin and the haunted characters of Kafka trying to make desperate sense out of an incomprehensible universe— the search for identity has been the most compelling human problem. That search has always been ridden with trouble and terror. And it can be plausibly argued that the conditions of modern life make the quest for identity more difficult than it has ever been before.

The pre-democratic world was characteristically a world of status in which people were provided with ready-made identities. But modern western society—free, equalitarian, democratic—has swept away all the old niches in which people for so many centuries found safe refuge. Only a few people at any time in human history have enjoyed the challenge of "making" themselves; most have fled from the unendurable burden of freedom into the womb-like security of the group. The new age of social mobility may be fine for those strong enough to discover and develop their own roles. But for the timid and the frightened, who constitute the majority in any age, the great vacant spaces of equalitarian society can become a nightmare filled with nameless horrors. Thus mass democracy, in the very act of offering the individual new freedom and opportunity, offers new moral authority to the group and thereby sets off a new assault on individual identity. Over a century ago Alexis de Tocqueville, the perceptive Frenchman who ruminated on the contradictions of equality as he toured the United States in the Eighteen Thirties, pointed to the "tyranny of the majority" as a central problem of democracy. John Stuart Mill, lamenting the decline of individualism in Great Britain, wrote: "That so few now dare to be eccentric marks the chief danger of the time." How much greater that danger seems a century later!

For our own time has aggravated the assault on identity by adding economic and technological pressures to the political and social pressures of the nineteenth century. Modern science has brought about the growing centralization of the economy. We work and think and live and even dream in larger and larger units. William H. Whyte, Jr., has described the rise of "the organization man," working by day in immense business concerns, sleeping by night in immense suburban developments, deriving his fantasy life from mass-produced entertainments, spending his existence, not as an individual, but as a member of a group and coming in the end to feel guilty and lost when he deviates from his fellows. Adjustment rather than achievement becomes the social ideal. Men no longer fulfill an inner sense of what they *must* be; indeed, with the cult of the

55

group, that inner sense itself begins to evaporate. Identity consists, not of self-realization, but of smooth absorption into the group. Nor is this just a matter of passive acquiescence. The group is aggressive, imperialistic, even vengeful, forever developing new weapons with which to overwhelm and crush the recalcitrant individual. Nor content with disciplining the conscious mind, the group today is even experimenting with means of violating the subconscious. The subliminal invasion represents the climax of the assault on individual identity.

It may seem a long way from the loss of the sense of self to the question of masculinity. But if people do not know *who* they are, it is hardly surprising that they are no longer sure what sex they are. Nigel Dennis's exuberant novel, *Cards of Identity,* consists of a series of brilliant variations on the quest for identity in contemporary life. It reaches one of its climaxes in the tale of a person who was brought up by enlightened parents to believe that there was no such thing as pure male or female—everyone had elements of both—and who accepted this proposition so rigorously that he (she) could not decide what his (her) own sex was. "In what identity do you intend to face the future?" someone asks. "It seems that nowadays," comes the plaintive reply, "one must choose between being a woman who behaves like a man, and a man who behaves like a woman. In short, I must choose to be one in order to behave like the other." If most of us have not yet quite reached that condition of sexual chaos, yet the loss of a sense of identity is obviously a fundamental step in the decay of masculinity. And the gratification with which some American males contemplate their own decline should not obscure the fact that women, for all their recent legal and economic triumphs, are suffering from a loss of identity too. It is not accidental that the authors of one recent book described modern woman as the "lost sex."

If this is true, then the key to the recovery of masculinity does not lie in any wistful hope of humiliating the aggressive female and restoring the old masculine supremacy. Masculine supremacy, like white supremacy, was the neurosis of an immature society. It is good for men as well as for women that women have been set free. In any case, the process is irreversible; that particular genie can never be put back into the bottle. The key to the recovery of masculinity lies rather in the problem of identity. When a person begins to find out *who* he is, he is likely to find out rather soon what sex he is.

For men to become men again, in short, their first task is to recover a sense of individual spontaneity. And to do this a man must visualize himself as an individual apart from the group, whatever it is, which defines his values and commands his loyalty. There is no reason to suppose that the group is always wrong: to oppose the group automatically is nearly as conformist as to surrender to it automatically. But there is every necessity to recognize that the group is one thing and the individual—oneself—is another. One of the most sinister of present-day doctrines is that of *togetherness.* The recovery of identity means, first of all, a new belief in apartness. It means a determination to resist the overpowering conspiracy of blandness, which seeks to conceal all tension and conflict in American life under a blanket of locker-room affability. And the rebirth of spontaneity depends, at bottom, on changes of attitude *within* people—changes which can perhaps be described, without undue solemnity, as moral changes. These changes will no doubt come about in as many ways as there are individuals involved. But there are some general suggestions that can be made about the techniques of liberation. I should like to mention three such techniques: satire, art, and politics.

Satire means essentially the belief that nothing is sacred—that there is no person or institution or idea which cannot but benefit from the exposure of comedy. Our nation in the past has reveled in satire; it is, after all, the nation of Abraham Lincoln, of

Mark Twain, of Finley Peter Dunne, of H. L. Mencken, of Ring Lardner. Indeed, the whole spirit of democracy is that of satire; as Montaigne succinctly summed up the democratic faith: "Sit he on ever so high a throne, a man still sits on his own bottom." Yet today American society can only be described as a pompous society, at least in its official manifestations. Early in 1958 Mort Sahl, the night-club comedian, made headlines in New York because he dared make a joke about J. Edgar Hoover! It was not an especially good joke, but the fact that he made it at all was an encouraging sign. One begins to feel that the American people can only stand so much reverence—that in the end our native skepticism will break through, sweep aside the stuffed shirts and the stuffed heads and insist that platitudes are platitudinous and the great are made, among other things, to be laughed at. Irony is good for our rulers; and it is even better for ourselves because it is a means of dissolving the pomposity of society and giving the individual a chance to emerge.

If irony is one source of spontaneity, art is another. Very little can so refresh our vision and develop our vision and develop our values as the liberating experience of art. The mass media have cast a spell on us: the popular addiction to prefabricated emotional clichés threatens to erode our capacity for fresh and direct aesthetic experience. Individual identity vanishes in the welter of machine-made reactions. But thoughtful exposure to music, to painting, to poetry, to the beauties of nature, can do much to restore the inwardness, and thereby the identity, of man. There is thus great hope in the immense cultural underground of our age— the paper-bound books, the long-playing records, the drama societies, the art festivals, the new interest in painting and sculpture. All this represents a disdain for existing values and goals, a reaching out for something more exacting and more personal, an intensified questing for identity.

And politics in a true sense can be a means of

57

liberation—not the banal politics of rhetoric and self-congratulation, which aims at burying all real issues under a mass of piety and platitude; but the politics of responsibility, which tries to define the real issues and present them to the people for decision. Our national politics have become boring in recent years because our leaders have offered neither candid and clear-cut formulations of the problems nor the facts necessary for intelligent choice. A virile political life will be definite and hard-hitting, respecting debate and dissent, seeking clarity and decision.

As the American male develops himself by developing his comic sense, his aesthetic sense and his moral and political sense, the lineaments of personality will at last begin to emerge. The achievement of identity, the conquest of a sense of self—these will do infinitely more to restore American masculinity than all the hormones in the test tubes of our scientists. "Whoso would be a *man*," said Emerson, "must be a nonconformist"; and, if it is the present writer who adds the italics, nonetheless one feels that no injustice is done to Emerson's intention. How can masculinity, femininity, or anything else survive in a homogenized society, which seeks steadily and benignly to eradicate all differences between the individuals who compose it? If we want to have *men* again in our theatres and our films and our novels— not to speak of in our classrooms, our business offices and our homes—we must first have a society which encourages each of its members to have a distinct identity.

THE BERRYS by Carl Grubert, courtesy Publishers-Hall Syndicate.

DOTTY by Buford Tune, courtesy Publishers-Hall Syndicate.

THE BERRYS by Carl Grubert, courtesy Publishers-Hall Syndicate.

DOTTY by Buford Tune, courtesy Publishers-Hall Syndicate

THE BERRYS by Carl Grubert, courtesy Publishers-Hall Syndicate

THE BERRYS by Carl Grubert, courtesy Publishers-Hall Syndicate.

The Unicorn in the Garden

Once upon a sunny morning a man who sat in a breakfast nook looked up from his scrambled eggs to see a white unicorn with a gold horn quietly cropping the roses in the garden. The man went up to the bedroom where his wife was still asleep and woke her. "There's a unicorn in the garden," he said. "Eating roses." She opened one unfriendly eye and looked at him. "The unicorn is a mythical beast," she said, and turned her back on him. The man walked slowly downstairs and out into the garden. The unicorn was still there; he was now browsing among the tulips. "Here, unicorn," said the man, and he pulled up a lily and gave it to him. The unicorn ate it gravely. With a high heart, because there was a unicorn in his garden, the man went upstairs and roused his wife again. "The unicorn," he said, "ate a lily." His wife sat up in bed and looked at him, coldly. "You are a booby," she said, "and I am going to have you put in the booby-hatch." The man, who had never liked the words "booby" and "booby-hatch," and who liked them even less on a shining morning when there was a unicorn in the garden, thought for a moment. "We'll see about that," he said. He walked over to the door. "He has a golden horn in the middle of his forehead," he told her. Then he went back to the garden to watch the unicorn; but the unicorn had gone away. The man sat down among the roses and went to sleep.

 62

As soon as the husband had gone out of the house, the wife got up and dressed as fast as she could. She was very excited and there was a gloat in her eye. She telephoned the police and she telephoned a psychiatrist; she told them to hurry to her house and bring a strait-jacket. When the police and the psychiatrist arrived they sat down in chairs and looked at her, with great interest. "My husband," she said, "saw a unicorn this morning." The police looked at the psychiatrist and the psychiatrist looked at the police. "He told me it ate a lily," she said. The psychiatrist looked at the police and the police looked at the psychiatrist. "He told me it had a golden horn in the middle of its forehead," she said. At a solemn signal from the psychiatrist, the police leaped from their chairs and seized the wife. They had a hard time subduing her, for she put up a terrific struggle, but they finally subdued her. Just as they got her into the strait-jacket, the husband came back into the house.

"Did you tell your wife you saw a unicorn?" asked the police. "Of course not," said the husband. "The unicorn is a mythical beast." "That's all I wanted to know," said the psychiatrist. "Take her away. I'm sorry, sir, but your wife is as crazy as a jay bird." So they took her away, cursing and screaming, and shut her up in an institution. The husband lived happily ever after.

Moral: Don't count your boobies until they are hatched.

James Thurber

Gahan Wilson

"... And just what do you think you're going to do with your silly death ray once you've finished it?"

A MARRIAGE

The first retainer
he gave to her
was a golden
wedding ring.

The second—late at night
he woke up,
leaned over on an elbow,
and kissed her.

The third and the last—
he died with
and gave up loving
and lived with her.

Robert Creeley

DIVORCE

 64

A voice from the dark is calling me.
In the close house I nurse a fire.
Out in the dark, cold winds rush free,
To the rock heights of my desire.
I smother in the house in the valley below,
Let me out to the night, let me go, let me go!

Spirits that ride the sweeping blast,
Frozen in rigid tenderness,
Wait! For I leave the fire at last,
My little-love's warm loneliness.
I smother in the house in the valley below,
Let me out in the night, let me go, let me go!

High on the hills are beating drums,
Clear from a line of marching men
To the rock's edge the hero comes.
He calls me, and he calls again.
On the hill there is fighting, victory, or quick death,
In the house is the fire, which I fan with sick breath.
I smother in the house in the valley below,
Let me out in the dark, let me go, let me go!

Anna Wickham

DIVORCE

A voice from the dark is c...
In the close house I nurse ... alling me.
Out in the dark, cold wind ... a fire.
To the rock heights of my ...s rush free,
I smother in the house in t... desire.
Let me out to the night, le... the valley below,
... go, let me go!

Spirits that ride the sweepin...
Frozen in rigid tenderness, ...ng blast,
Wait! For I leave the fire at...
My little-love's warm loneli... last,
I smother in the house in t...ness.
Let me out in the night, le...he valley below,
...me go, let me go!

High on the hills are beatin...
Clear from a line of marching drums,
To the rock's edge the hero...ng men
He calls me, and he calls a...comes.
On the hill there is fighting...gain.
In the house is the fire, wh... victory, or quick death,
I smother in the house in...ich I fan with sick breath.
Let me out in the dark, le...the valley below,
...me go, let me go!

Anna Wickham

A MARRIAGE

The first retainer
he gave to her
was a golden
wedding ring.

The second—late at night
he ... woke up,
lean...ed over on an elbow,
and ... kissed her.

The third and the last—
he died with
and gave up loving
and lived with her.

Robert Creeley

66

Kosti Ruohomaa from Black Star.

"When You Are Old and Gray"

Since I still appreciate you,
Let's find love while we may,
Because I know I'll hate you
When you are old and gray.
So say you love me here and now.
I'll make the most of that.
Say you love and trust me,
For I know you'll disgust me
When you're old and getting fat.
An awful debility, a lessened utility,
A loss of mobility is a strong possibility.
In all probability I'll lose my virility
And you your fertility and desirability.
And this liability of total sterility
Will lead to hostility and a sense of futility.
So let's act with agility while we still have facility
For we'll soon reach senility
And lose the ability.
Your teeth will start to go dear.
Your waist will start to spread.
In twenty years or so dear,
I'll wish that you were dead.
I'll never love you then at all
The way I do today.
So please remember, when I leave in December,
I told you so in May.

Tom Lehrer

67

VIOLENCE

"PISTOL"

Roy Lichtenstein: *Pistol;*
Collection of Donald L. Factor, © TIME, Inc. 1967.

HELLOW TO MY REEDERS

ATOMIC WAR NOW

WHITEY YOU HAVE HAD IT BABY!

Why should the U.S. Govt. fight for fascism in Vietnam?
REPLY:
To fight for the interests of the capitalists.
CONTINUATION:
End the war in Vietnam.
REPLY:
How?
REPLY:
By killing all commies and reactionaries like you.

SCREW YOU

loves HARRY!

loves MARY

WE HATE ALL PEOPLE REGARDLESS OF RACE, CREED OR COLOR

MOM

To THE SHOWERS

SUPPORT MENTAL HEALTH OR I'LL KILL YOU

3146769 After 9 am

BROTHERHOOD

ESCALATE THE WAR.

HI MOM

74

37 Who Saw Murder Didn't Call the Police

For more than half an hour 38 respectable, law-abiding citizens in Queens watched a killer stalk and stab a woman in three separate attacks in Kew Gardens.

Twice the sound of their voices and the sudden glow of their bedroom lights interrupted him and frightened him off. Each time he returned, sought her out and stabbed her again. Not one person telephoned the police during the assault; one witness called after the woman was dead.

—N.Y. Times, March 27.

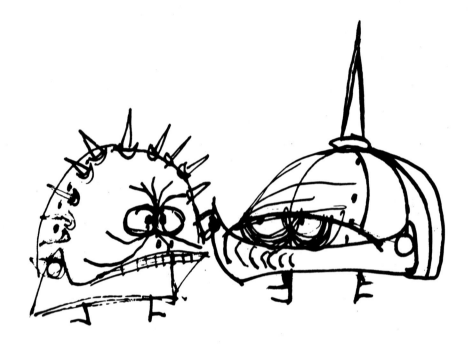

I don't know who you are, but I hate you!

THE LARGE ANT

Howard Fast

There have been all kinds of notions and guesses as to how it would end. One held that sooner or later there would be too many people; another that we would do each other in, and the atom bomb made that a very good likelihood. All sorts of notions, except the simple fact that we were what we were. We could find a way to feed any number of people and perhaps even a way to avoid wiping each other out with the bomb; those things we are very good at, but we have never been any good at changing ourselves or the way we behave.

I know. I am not a bad man or a cruel man; quite to the contrary, I am an ordinary, humane person, and I love my wife and my children and I get along with my neighbours. I am like a great many other men, and I do the things they would do and just as thoughtlessly. There it is in a nutshell.

I am also a writer, and I told Lieberman, the curator, and Fitzgerald, the government man, that I would like to write down the story. They shrugged their shoulders. "Go ahead," they said, "because it won't make one bit of difference."

"You don't think it would alarm people?"

"How can it alarm anyone when nobody will believe it?"

"If I could have a photograph or two."

"Oh, no," they said then. "No photographs."

"What kind of sense does that make?" I asked them. "You are willing to let me write the story—why not the photographs so that people could believe me?"

"They still won't believe you. They will just say you faked the photographs, but no one will believe you. It will make for more confusion, and if we have a chance of getting out of this, confusion won't help."

"What will help?"

They weren't ready to say that, because they didn't know. So here is what happened to me, in a very straightforward and ordinary manner.

Every summer, sometime in August four good friends of mine and I go for a week's fishing on the St. Regis chain of lakes in the Adirondacks. We rent the same shack each summer; we drift around in canoes, and sometimes we catch a few bass. The fishing isn't very good, but we play cards well together, and we cook out and generally relax. This summer past, I had some things to do that couldn't be put off. I arrived three days late, and the weather was so warm and even and beguiling that I decided to stay on by myself for a day or two after the others left. There was a small flat lawn in front of the shack, and I made up my mind to spend at least three or four hours at short putts. That was how I happened to have the putting iron next to my bed.

The first day I was alone, I opened a can of beans and a can of beer for my supper. Then I lay down in my bed with *Life on the Mississippi*, a pack of cigarettes, and an eight-ounce chocolate bar. There was nothing I had to do, no telephone, no demands and no newspapers. At that moment, I was about as contented as any man can be in these nervous times.

It was still light outside, and enough light came in through the window above my head for me to read by. I was just reaching for a fresh cigarette, when I looked up and saw it on the foot of my bed. The edge of my hand was touching the golf club, and with a single motion I swept the club over and down, struck it a savage and accurate blow, and killed it. That was what I referred to before. Whatever kind of a man I am, I react as a man does. I think that any man, black, white or yellow, in China, Africa or Russia, would have done the same thing.

First I found that I was sweating all over, and then I knew I was going to be sick. I went outside to vomit, recalling that this hadn't happened to me since 1943, on my way to Europe on a tub of a Liberty Ship. Then I felt better and was able to go back into the shack and look at it. It was quite dead, but I had already made up my mind that I was not going to sleep alone in this shack.

I couldn't bear to touch it with my bare hands. With a piece of brown paper, I picked it up and dropped it into my fishing creel. That, I put into the trunk case of my car, along with what luggage I carried. Then I closed the door of the shack, got into my car and drove back to New York. I stopped once along the road, just before I reached the Thruway, to nap in the car for a little over an hour. It was almost dawn when I reached the city, and I had shaved, had a hot bath and changed my clothes before my wife awoke.

During breakfast, I explained that I was never much of a hand at the solitary business, and since she knew that, and since driving alone all night was by no means an extraordinary procedure for me, she didn't press me with any questions. I had two eggs, coffee and a cigarette. Then I went into my study, lit another cigarette, and contemplated my fishing creel, which sat upon my desk.

My wife looked in, saw the creel, remarked that it had too ripe a smell, and asked me to remove it to the basement.

"I'm going to dress," she said. The kids were still at camp. "I have a date with Ann for lunch—I had no idea you were coming back. Shall I break it?"

"No, please don't. I can find things to do that have to be done."

Then I sat and smoked some more, and finally I called the Museum, and asked who the curator of insects was. They told me his name was Bertram Lieberman, and I asked to talk to him. He had a pleasant voice. I told him that my name was Morgan, and that I was a writer, and he politely indicated that he had seen my name and read something that I had written. That is normal procedure when a writer introduces himself to a thoughtful person.

I asked Lieberman if I could see him, and he said that he had a busy morning ahead of him. Could it be tomorrow?

"I am afraid it has to be now," I said firmly.

"Oh? Some information you require."

"No. I have a specimen for you."

"Oh?" The "oh" was a cultivated, neutral interval. It asked and answered and said nothing. You have to develop that particular "oh."

"Yes. I think you will be interested."

"An insect?" he asked mildly.

"I think so."

"Oh? Large?"

"Quite large," I told him.

"Eleven o'clock? Can you be here then? On the main floor, to the right, as you enter."

"I'll be there," I said.

"One thing—dead?"

"Yes, it's dead."

"Oh?" again. "I'll be happy to see you at eleven o'clock, Mr. Morgan."

My wife was dressed now. She opened the door to my study and said firmly, "Do get rid of that fishing creel. It smells."

"Yes, darling. I'll get rid of it."

"I should think you'd want to take a nap after driving all night."

"Funny, but I'm not sleepy," I said. "I think I'll drop around to the museum."

My wife said that was what she liked about me, that I never tired of places like museums, police courts and third-rate night clubs.

Anyway, aside from a racetrack, a museum is the most interesting and unexpected place in the world. It was unexpected to have two other men waiting for me, along with Mr. Lieberman, in his office. Lieberman was a skinny, sharp-faced man of about sixty. The government man, Fitzgerald, was small, dark-eyed, and wore gold-rimmed glasses. He was very alert, but he never told me what part of the government he represented. He just said "we," and it meant the government. Hopper, the third man, was comfortable-looking, pudgy, and genial. He was a United States senator with an interest in entomology, although before this morning I would have taken better than even money that such a thing not only wasn't, but could not be.

The room was large and square and plainly furnished, with shelves and cupboards on all walls.

We shook hands, and then Lieberman asked me, nodding at the creel, "Is that it?"

"That's it."

"May I?"

"Go ahead," I told him. "It's nothing that I want to stuff for the parlour. I'm making you a gift of it."

"Thank you, Mr. Morgan," he said, and then he opened the creel and looked inside. Then he straightened up, and the other two men looked at him inquiringly.

He nodded. "Yes."

The senator closed his eyes for a long moment. Fitzgerald took off his glasses and wiped them industriously. Lieberman spread a piece of plastic on his desk, and then lifted the thing out of my creel and laid it on the plastic. The two men didn't move. They just sat where they were and looked at it.

"What do you think it is, Mr. Morgan?" Lieberman asked me.

"I thought that was your department."

"Yes, of course. I only wanted your impression."

"An ant. That's my impression. It's the first time I saw an ant fourteen, fifteen inches long. I hope it's the last."

"An understandable wish," Lieberman nodded.

Fitzgerald said to me, "May I ask how you killed it, Mr. Morgan?"

"With an iron. A golf club, I mean. I was doing a little fishing with some friends up at St. Regis in the Adirondacks, and I brought the iron for my short shots. They're the worst part of my game, and when my friends left, I intended to stay on at our shack and do four or five hours of short putts. You see—"

"There's no need to explain," Hopper smiled, a trace of sadness on his face. "Some of our very best golfers have the same trouble."

"I was lying in bed, reading, and I saw it at the foot of my bed. I had the club—"

"I understand," Fitzgerald nodded.

"You avoid looking at it," Hopper said.

"It turns my stomach."

"Yes—yes, I suppose so."

Lieberman said, "Would you mind telling us why you killed it, Mr. Morgan."

"Why?"

"Yes—why?"

"I don't understand you," I said. "I don't know what you're driving at."

"Sit down, please, Mr. Morgan," Hopper nodded. "Try to relax. I'm sure this has been very trying."

"I still haven't slept. I want a chance to dream before I say how trying."

"We are not trying to upset you, Mr. Morgan," Lieberman said. "We do feel, however, that certain aspects of this are very important. That is why I am asking you why you killed it. You must have had a reason. Did it seem about to attack you?"

"No."

"Or make any sudden motion towards you?"

"No. It was just there."

"Then why?"

"This is to no purpose," Fitzgerald put in. "We know why he killed it."

"Do you?"

"The answer is very simple, Mr. Morgan. You killed it because you are a human being."

"Oh?"

"Yes. Do you understand?"

"No, I don't."

"Then why did you kill it?" Hopper put in.

"I was scared to death. I still am, to tell the truth."

Lieberman said, "You are an intelligent man, Mr. Morgan. Let me show you something." He then opened the doors of one of the wall cupboards, and there eight jars of formaldehyde and in each jar a specimen like mine—and in each case mutilated by the violence of its death. I said nothing. I just stared.

Lieberman closed the cupboard doors. "All in five days," he shrugged.

"A new race of ants," I whispered stupidly.

"No. They're not ants. Come here!" He motioned me to the desk and the other two joined me. Lieberman took a set of dissecting instruments out of his drawer, used one to turn the thing over and then pointed to the underpart of what would be the thorax in an insect.

"That looks like part of him, doesn't it, Mr. Morgan?"

"Yes, it does."

Using two of the tools, he found a fissure and pried the bottom apart. It came open like the belly of a bomber; it was a pocket, a pouch, a receptacle that the thing wore, and in it were four beautiful little tools or instruments or weapons, each about an inch and a half long. They were beautiful the way any object of functional purpose and loving creation is beautiful—the way the creature itself would have been beautiful, had it not been an insect and myself a man. Using tweezers, Lieberman took each instrument off the brackets that held it, offering each to me. And I took each one, felt it, examined it, and then put it down.

I had to look at the ant now, and I realised that I had not truly looked at it before. We don't look carefully at a thing that is horrible or repugnant to us. You can't look at anything through a screen of hatred. But now the hatred and the fear was dilute, and as I looked, I realised it was not an ant although like an ant. It was nothing that I had ever seen or dreamed of.

All three men were watching me, and suddenly I was on the defensive. "I didn't know! What do you expect when you see an insect that size?"

Lieberman nodded.

"What in the name of God is it?"

From his desk Lieberman produced a bottle and four small glasses. He poured and we drank it neat. I would not have expected him to keep good Scotch in his desk.

"We don't know," Hopper said. "We don't know what it is."

Lieberman pointed to the broken skull, from which a white substance oozed. "Brain material—a great deal of it."

"It could be a very intelligent creature," Hopper nodded.

Lieberman said, "It is an insect in developmental structure. We know very little about intelligence in our insects. It's not the same as what we call intelligence. It's a collective phenomenon—as if you were to think of the component parts of our bodies. Each part is alive, but the intelligence is a result of the whole. If that same pattern were to extend to creatures like this one—"

I broke the silence. They were content to stand there and stare at it.

81

"Suppose it were?"

"What?"

"The kind of collective intelligence you were talking about."

"Oh? Well, I couldn't say. It would be something beyond our wildest dreams. To us—well, what we are to an ordinary ant."

"I don't believe that," I said shortly, and Fitzgerald, the government man, told me quietly, "Neither do we. We guess."

"If it's that intelligent, why didn't it use one of those weapons on me?"

"Would that be a mark of intelligence?" Hopper asked mildly.

"Perhaps none of these are weapons," Lieberman said.

"Don't you know? Didn't the others carry instruments?"

"They did," Fitzgerald said shortly.

"Why? What were they?"

"We don't know," Lieberman said.

"But you can find out. We have scientists, engineers—good God, this is an age of fantastic instruments. Have them taken apart!"

"We have."

"Then what have you found out?"

"Nothing."

"Do you mean to tell me," I said, "that you can find out nothing about these instruments—what they are, how they work, what their purpose is?"

"Exactly," Hopper nodded. "Nothing, Mr. Morgan. They are meaningless to the finest engineers and technicians in the United States. You know the old story—suppose you gave a radio to Aristotle? What would he do with it? Where would he find power? And what would he receive with no one to send? It is not that these instruments are complex. They are actually very simple. We simply have no idea of what they can or should do."

"But there must be a weapon of some kind."

"Why?" Lieberman demanded. "Look at yourself, Mr. Morgan—a cultured and intelligent man, yet you cannot conceive of a mentality that does not include weapons as a prime necessity. Yet a weapon is an unusual thing, Mr. Morgan. An instrument of murder. We don't think that way, because the weapon has become the symbol of the world we inhabit. Is that civilised, Mr. Morgan? Or is the weapon and civilisation in the ultimate sense incompatible? Can you imagine a mentality to which the concept of murder is impossible—or let me say absent. We see everything through our own subjectivity. Why shouldn't some other—this creature, for example—see the process of mentation out of his subjectivity? So he approaches a creature of our world—and he is slain. Why? What explanation? Tell me, Mr. Morgan, what conceivable explanation could we offer a wholly rational creature for this—" pointing to the thing on his desk. "I am asking you the question most seriously. What explanation?"

"An accident?" I muttered.

"And the eight jars in my cupboard? Eight accidents?"

"I think, Dr. Lieberman," Fitzgerald said, "that you can go a little too far in that direction."

"Yes, you would think so. It's a part of your own background. Mine is as a scientist. As a scientist, I try to be rational when I can. The creation of a structure of good and evil, or what we call morality and ethics, is a function of intelligence—and unquestionably the ultimate evil may be the destruction of conscious intelligence. That is why, so long ago, we at least recognised the injunction, 'thou shalt not kill!' even if we never gave more than lip service to it. But to a collective intelligence, such as this might be a part of, the concept of murder would be monstrous beyond the power of thought."

I sat down and lit a cigarette. My hands were trembling. Hopper apologised. "We have been rather rough with you, Mr. Morgan. But over the past days, eight other people have done just what you did. We are caught in the trap of being what we are."

"But tell me—where do these things come from?"

"It almost doesn't matter where they come from," Hopper said hopelessly. "Perhaps from another planet—perhaps from inside this one—or the moon or Mars. That doesn't matter. Fitzgerald thinks they come from a smaller planet, because their movements are apparently slow on earth. But Dr. Lieberman thinks that they move slowly because they have not discovered the need to move quickly. Meanwhile, they have the problem of murder and what to do with it. Heaven knows how many of them have died in other places—Africa, Asia, Europe."

"Then why don't you publicise this? Put a stop to it before it's too late!"

"We've thought of that," Fitzgerald nodded. "What then—panic, hysteria, charges that this is the result of the atom bomb? We can't change. We are what we are."

"They may go away," I said.

"Yes, they may," Lieberman nodded. "But if they are without the curse of murder, they may also be without the curse of fear. They may be social in the highest sense. What does society do with a murderer?"

"There are societies that put him to death—and there are other societies that recognise his sickness and lock him away, where he can kill no more," Hopper said. "Of course, when a whole world is on trial, that's another matter. We have atom bombs now and other things, and we are reaching out to the stars—"

"I'm inclined to think that they'll run," Fitzgerald put in. "They may just have that curse of fear, Doctor."

"They may," Lieberman admitted. "I hope so."

But the more I think of it the more it seems to me that fear and hatred are the two sides of the same coin. I keep trying to think back, to recreate the moment when I saw it standing at the foot of my bed in the fishing shack. I keep trying to drag out of my memory a clear picture of what it looked like, whether behind that chitinous face and the two gently waving antennae there was any evidence of fear and anger. But the clearer the memory becomes, the more I seem to recall a certain wonderful dignity and repose. Not fear and not anger.

And more and more, as I go about my work, I get the feeling of what Hopper called "a world on trial." I have no sense of anger myself. Like a criminal who can no longer live with himself, I am content to be judged.

WEATHER FORECAST: Dry and extremely sociable

★ **EXTRA** ★

WEATHER FORECAST: Dry and extremely sociable

SECTION I

CANADA DRY® THE NATION'S LEADING MIXERS

PAGE 1

AMERICA'S GOING DRY!

84

Courtesy Canada Dry Corporation.

Canada Dry makes any drink better. C'mon and mix with us!

©Copyright 1967 Canada Dry Corp.

"Oh, speak up, George! Stop mumbling!"

the snake

It was almost dark when young Dr. Phillips swung his sack to his shoulder and left the tide pool. He climbed up over the rocks and squashed along the street in his rubber boots. The street lights were on by the time he arrived at his little commercial laboratory on the cannery street of Monterey. It was a tight little building, standing partly on piers over the bay water and partly on the land. On both sides the big corrugated-iron sardine canneries crowded in on it.

Dr. Phillips climbed the wooden steps and opened the door. The white rats in their cages scampered up and down the wire, and the captive cats in their pens mewed for milk. Dr. Phillips turned on the glaring light over the dissection table and dumped his clammy sack on the floor. He walked to the glass cages by the window where the rattlesnakes lived, leaned over and looked in.

The snakes were bunched and resting in the corners of the cage, but every head was clear; the dusty eyes seemed to look at nothing, but as the

JOHN STEINBECK

young man leaned over the cage the forked tongues, black on the ends and pink behind, twittered out and waved slowly up and down. Then the snakes recognized the man and pulled in their tongues.

Dr. Phillips threw off his leather coat and built a fire in the tin stove; he set a kettle of water on the stove and dropped a can of beans into the water. Then he stood staring down at the sack on the floor. He was a slight young man with the mild, preoccupied eyes of one who looks through a microscope a great deal. He wore a short blond beard.

The draft ran breathily up the chimney and a glow of warmth came from the stove. The little waves washed quietly about the piles under the building. Arranged on shelves about the room were tier above tier of museum jars containing the mounted marine specimens the laboratory dealt in.

Dr. Phillips opened a side door and went into his bedroom, a book-lined cell containing an army cot, a reading light and an uncomfortable wooden chair. He pulled off his rubber boots and put on a pair of sheep-skin slippers. When he went back to the other room the water in the kettle was already beginning to hum.

He lifted his sack to the table under the white light and emptied out two dozen common starfish. These he laid out side by side on the table. His preoccupied eyes turned to the busy rats in the wire cages. Taking grain from a paper sack, he poured it into the feeding troughs. Instantly the rats scrambled down from the wire and fell upon the food. A bottle of milk stood on a glass shelf between a small mounted octopus and a jellyfish. Dr. Phillips lifted down the milk and walked to the cat cage, but before he filled the containers he reached in the cage and gently picked out a big rangy alley tabby. He stroked her for a moment and then dropped her in a small black painted box, closed the lid and bolted it and then turned on a petcock which admitted gas into the killing chamber. While the short soft struggle went on in the black box he filled the saucers with milk. One of the cats

The tall woman leaned over the table. With the eyedropper the young man gathered fluid from between the rays of the starfish and squirted it into a bowl of water, and then he drew some milky fluid and squirted it in the same bowl and stirred the water gently with the eyedropper. He began his little patter of explanation.

"When starfish are sexually mature they release sperm and ova when they are exposed at low tide. By choosing mature specimens and taking them out of the water, I give them a condition of low tide. Now I've mixed the sperm and eggs. Now I put some of the mixture in each one of these ten watch glasses. In ten minutes I will kill those in the first glass with menthol, twenty minutes later I will kill the second group and then a new group every twenty minutes. Then I will have arrested the process in stages, and I will mount the series on microscope slides for biologic study." He paused. "Would you like to look at this first group under the microscope?"

"No, thank you."

He turned quickly to her. People always wanted to look through the glass. She was not looking at the table at all, but at him. Her black eyes were on him, but they did not seem to see him. He realized why—the irises were as dark as the pupils, there was no color line between the two. Dr. Phillips was piqued at her answer. Although answering questions bored him, a lack of interest in what he was doing irritated him. A desire to arouse her grew in him.

"While I'm waiting the first ten minutes I have something to do. Some people don't like to see it. Maybe you'd better step into that room until I finish."

"No," she said in her soft flat tone. "Do what you wish. I will wait until you can talk to me." Her hands rested side by side on her lap. She was completely at rest. Her eyes were bright but the rest of her was almost in a state of suspended animation. He thought, "Low metabolic rate, almost as low as a frog's, from the looks." The desire to shock her out of her inanition possessed him again.

arched against his hand and he smiled and petted her neck.

The box was quiet now. He turned off the petcock, for the airtight box would be full of gas.

On the stove the pan of water was bubbling furiously about the can of beans. Dr. Phillips lifted out the can with a big pair of forceps, opened it, and emptied the beans into a glass dish. While he ate he watched the starfish on the table. From between the rays little drops of milky fluid were exuding. He bolted his beans and when they were gone he put the dish in the sink and stepped to the equipment cupboard. From this he took a microscope and a pile of little glass dishes. He filled the dishes one by one with sea water from a tap and arranged them in a line beside the starfish. He took out his watch and laid it on the table under the pouring white light. The waves washed with little sighs against the piles under the floor. He took an eyedropper from a drawer and bent over the starfish.

At that moment there were quick soft steps on the wooden stairs and a strong knocking at the door. A slight grimace of annoyance crossed the young man's face as he went to open. A tall, lean woman stood in the doorway. She was dressed in a severe dark suit—her straight black hair, growing low on a flat forehead, was mussed as though the wind had been blowing it. Her black eyes glittered in the strong light.

She spoke in a soft throaty voice, "May I come in? I want to talk to you."

"I'm very busy now," he said half-heartedly. "I have to do things at times." But he stood away from the door. The tall woman slipped in.

"I'll be quiet until you can talk to me."

He closed the door and brought the uncomfortable chair from the bedroom. "You see," he apologized, "the process is started and I must get to it." So many people wandered in and asked questions. He had little routines of explanations for the commoner processes. He could say them without thinking. "Sit here. In a few minutes I'll be able to listen to you."

He brought a little wooden cradle to the table, laid out scalpels and scissors and rigged a big hollow needle to a pressure tube. Then from the killing chamber he brought the limp dead cat and laid it in the cradle and tied its legs to hooks in the sides. He glanced sidewise at the woman. She had not moved. She was still at rest.

The cat grinned up into the light, its pink tongue stuck out between its needle teeth. Dr. Phillips deftly snipped open the skin at the throat; with a scalpel he slit through and found an artery. With flawless technique he put the needle in the vessel and tied it in with gut. "Embalming fluid," he explained. "Later I'll inject yellow mass into the veinous system and red mass into the arterial system—for bloodstream dissection—biology classes."

He looked around at her again. Her dark eyes seemed veiled with dust. She looked without expression at the cat's open throat. Not a drop of blood had escaped. The incision was clean. Dr. Phillips looked at his watch. "Time for the first group." He shook a few crystals of menthol into the first watch-glass.

The woman was making him nervous. The rats climbed about on the wire of their cage again and squeaked softly. The waves under the building beat with little shocks on the piles.

The young man shivered. He put a few lumps of coal in the stove and sat down. "Now," he said. "I haven't anything to do for twenty minutes." He noticed how short her chin was between lower lip and point. She seemed to awaken slowly, to come up out of some deep pool of consciousness. Her head raised and her dark dusty eyes moved about the room and then came back to him.

"I was waiting," she said. Her hands remained side by side on her lap. "You have snakes?"

"Why yes," he said rather loudly. "I have about two dozen rattlesnakes. I milk out the venom and send it to the anti-venom laboratories."

She continued to look at him but her eyes did not center on him, rather they covered him and seemed to see in a big circle all around him. "Have you a male snake, a male rattlesnake?"

"Well, it just happens I know I have. I came in one morning and found a big snake in—in coition with a smaller one. You see, it's very rare in captivity. I do know I have a male snake."

"Where is he?"

"Why, right in the glass cage by the window there."

Her head swung slowly around but her two quiet hands did not move. She turned back toward him. "May I see?"

He got up and walked to the case by the window. On the sand bottom the knot of rattlesnakes lay entwined, but their heads were clear. The tongues came out and flickered a moment and then waved up and down feeling the air for vibrations. Dr. Phillips nervously turned his head. The woman was standing beside him. He had not heard her get up from the chair. He had heard only the splash of water among the piles and the scampering of the rats on the wire screen.

She said softly, "Which is the male you spoke of?"

He pointed to a thick, dusty grey snake lying by itself in one corner of the cage. "That one. He's nearly five feet long. He comes from Texas. Our Pacific coast snakes are usually smaller. He's been taking all the rats, too. When I want the others to eat I have to take him out."

The woman stared down at the blunt dry head. The forked tongue slipped out and hung quivering for a long moment. "And you're sure he's a male."

"Rattlesnakes are funny," he said glibly. "Nearly every generalization proves wrong. I don't like to say anything definite about rattlesnakes, but—yes—I can assure you he's a male."

Her eyes did not move from the flat head. "Will you sell him to me?"

"Sell him?" he cried. "Sell him to you?"

"You do sell specimens, don't you?"

"Oh—yes. Of course I do. Of course I do."

"How much? Five dollars? Ten?"

"Oh! Not more than five. But—do you know anything about rattlesnakes? You might be bitten."

She looked at him for a moment. "I don't

"Maybe he wouldn't kill you, but he'd make you damned sick in spite of what I could do for you."

"You put him in the other cage then," she said quietly.

Dr. Phillips was shaken. He found that he was avoiding the dark eyes that didn't seem to look at anything. He felt that it was profoundly wrong to put a rat into the cage, deeply sinful; and he didn't know why. Often he had put rats in the cage when someone or other had wanted to see it, but this desire tonight sickened him. He tried to explain himself out of it.

"It's a good thing to see," he said. "It shows you how a snake can work. It makes you have a respect for a rattlesnake. Then, too, lots of people have dreams about the terror of snakes making the kill. I think because it is a subjective rat. The person is the rat. Once you see it the whole matter is objective. The rat is only a rat and the terror is removed."

He took a long stick equipped with a leather noose from the wall. Opening the trap he dropped the noose over the big snake's head and tightened the thong. A piercing dry rattle filled the room. The thick body writhed and slashed about the handle of the stick as he lifted the snake out and dropped it in the feeding cage. It stood ready to strike for a time, but the buzzing gradually ceased. The snake crawled into a corner, made a big figure eight with its body and lay still.

"You see," the young man explained, "these snakes are quite tame. I've had them a long time. I suppose I could handle them if I wanted to, but everyone who does handle rattlesnakes gets bitten sooner or later. I just don't want to take the chance." He glanced at the woman. He hated to put in the rat. She had moved over in front of the new cage; her black eyes were on the stony head of the snake again.

She said, "Put in a rat."

Reluctantly he went to the rat cage. For some reason he was sorry for the rat, and such a feeling had never come to him before. His eyes went over the mass of swarming white bodies climbing up intend to take him. I want to leave him here, but—I want him to be mine. I want to come here and look at him and feed him and to know he's mine." She opened a little purse and took out a five dollar bill. "Here! Now he is mine."

Dr. Phillips began to be afraid. "You could come to look at him without owning him."

"I want him to be mine."

"Oh, Lord!" he cried. "I've forgotten the time." He ran to the table. "Three minutes over. It won't matter much." He shook menthol crystals into the second watch-glass. And then he was drawn back to the cage where the woman still stared at the snake.

She asked, "What does he eat?"

"I feed them white rats, rats from the cage over there."

"Will you put him in the other cage? I want to feed him."

"But he doesn't need food. He's had a rat already this week. Sometimes they don't eat for three or four months. I had one that didn't eat for over a year."

In her low monotone she asked, "Will you sell me a rat?"

He shrugged his shoulders. "I see. You want to watch how rattlesnakes eat. All right. I'll show you. The rat will cost twenty-five cents. It's better than a bullfight if you look at it one way, and it's simply a snake eating his dinner if you look at it another." His tone had become acid. He hated people who made sport of natural processes. He was not a sportsman but a biologist. He could kill a thousand animals for knowledge, but not an insect for pleasure. He'd been over this in his mind before.

She turned her head slowly toward him and the beginning of a smile formed on her thin lips. "I want to feed my snake," she said. "I'll put him in the other cage." She had opened the top of the cage and dipped her hand in before he knew what she was doing. He leaped forward and pulled her back. The lid banged shut.

"Haven't you any sense," he asked fiercely.

the screen toward him. "Which one?" he thought. "Which one shall it be?" Suddenly he turned angrily to the woman. "Wouldn't you rather I put in a cat? Then you'd see a real fight. The cat might even win, but if it did it might kill the snake. I'll sell you a cat if you like."

She didn't look at him. "Put in a rat," she said. "I want him to eat."

He opened the rat cage and thrust his hand in. His fingers found a tail and he lifted a plump, red-eyed rat out of the cage. It struggled up to try to bite his fingers and, failing, hung spread out and motionless from its tail. He walked quickly across the room, opened the feeding cage and dropped the rat in on the sand floor. "Now, watch it," he cried.

The woman did not answer him. Her eyes were on the snake where it lay still. Its tongue flicking in and out rapidly, tasted the air of the cage.

The rat landed on its feet, turned around and sniffed at its pink naked tail and then unconcernedly trotted across the sand, smelling as it went. The room was silent. Dr. Phillips did not know whether the water sighed among the piles or whether the woman sighed. Out of the corner of his eye he saw her body crouch and stiffen.

The snake moved out smoothly, slowly. The tongue flicked in and out. The motion was so gradual, so smooth that it didn't seem to be motion at all. In the other end of the cage the rat perked up in a sitting position and began to lick down the fine white hair on its chest. The snake moved on, keeping always a deep S curve in its neck.

The silence beat on the young man. He felt the blood drifting up in his body. He said loudly, "See! He keeps the striking curve ready. Rattlesnakes are cautious, almost cowardly animals. The mechanism is so delicate. The snake's dinner is to be got by an operation as deft as a surgeon's job. He takes no chances with his instruments."

The snake had flowed to the middle of the cage by now. The rat looked up, saw the snake and then unconcernedly went back to licking its chest.

"It's the most beautiful thing in the world,"

Gold bracelet in form of coiled snake, Courtesy of the Oriental Institute, University of Chicago.

the young man said. His veins were throbbing. "It's the most terrible thing in the world."

The snake was close now. Its head lifted a few inches from the sand. The head weaved slowly back and forth, aiming, getting distance, aiming. Dr. Phillips glanced again at the woman. He turned sick. She was weaving too, not much, just a suggestion.

The rat looked up and saw the snake. It dropped to four feet and back up, and then—the stroke. It was impossible to see, simply a flash. The rat jarred as though under an invisible blow. The snake backed hurriedly into the corner from which it had come, and settled down, its tongue working constantly.

"Perfect!" Dr. Phillips cried. "Right between the shoulder blades. The fangs must almost have reached the heart."

The rat stood still, breathing like a little white bellows. Suddenly it leaped in the air and landed on its side. Its legs kicked spasmodically for a second and it was dead.

The woman relaxed, relaxed sleepily.

"Well," the young man demanded, "it was an emotional bath, wasn't it?"

She turned her misty eyes to him. "Will he eat it now?" she asked.

"Of course he'll eat it. He didn't kill it for a thrill. He killed it because he was hungry."

The corners of the woman's mouth turned up a trifle again. She looked back at the snake. "I want to see him eat it."

Now the snake came out of its corner again. There was no striking curve in its neck but it approached the rat gingerly, ready to jump back in case it attacked. It nudged the body gently with its blunt nose, and drew away. Satisfied that it was dead, the snake touched the body all over with its chin, from head to tail. It seemed to measure the body and to kiss it. Finally it opened its mouth and unhinged its jaws at the corners.

Dr. Phillips put his will against his head to keep it from turning toward the woman. He thought, "If she's opening her mouth, I'll be sick.

I'll be afraid." He succeeded in keeping his eyes away.

The snake fitted its jaws over the rat's head and then with a slow peristaltic pulsing, began to engulf the rat. The jaws gripped and the whole throat crawled up, and the jaws gripped again.

Dr. Phillips turned away and went to his work table. "You've made me miss one of the series," he said bitterly. "The set won't be complete." He put one of the watch glasses under a low-power microscope and looked at it, and then angrily he poured the contents of all the dishes into the sink. The waves had fallen so that only a wet whisper came up through the floor. The young man lifted a trapdoor at his feet and dropped the starfish down into the black water. He paused at the cat, crucified in the cradle and grinning comically into the light. Its body was puffed with embalming fluid. He shut off the pressure, withdrew the needle and tied the vein.

"Would you like some coffee?" he asked.

"No, thank you. I shall be going pretty soon."

He walked to her where she stood in front of the snake cage. The rat was swallowed, all except an inch of pink tail that stuck out of the snake's mouth like a sardonic tongue. The throat heaved again and the tail disappeared. The jaws snapped back into their sockets, and the big snake crawled heavily to the corner, made a big eight and dropped its head on the sand.

"He's asleep now," the woman said. "I'm going now. But I'll come back and feed my snake every little while. I'll pay for the rats. I want him to have plenty. And sometime—I'll take him away with me." Her eyes came out of their dusty dream for a moment. "Remember, he's mine. Don't take his poison. I want him to have it. Goodnight." She walked swiftly to the door and went out. He heard her footsteps on the stairs, but he could not hear her walk away on the pavement.

Dr. Phillips turned a chair around and sat down in front of the snake cage. He tried to comb out his thought as he looked at the torpid snake. "I've read so much about psychological sex sym-

bols," he thought. "It doesn't seem to explain. Maybe I'm too much alone. Maybe I should kill the snake. If I knew—no, I can't pray to anything."

For weeks he expected her to return. "I will go out and leave her alone here when she comes," he decided. "I won't see the damned thing again."

She never came again. For months he looked for her when he walked about in the town. Several times he ran after some tall woman thinking it might be she. But he never saw her again—ever.

FROM "STELLA FIGURA"

Her beauty has the serpent's undulant grace,
The rhythm and flow of softly fluctuant line;
And in the stealthy contours of her face,
And in her eyes, the charm is serpentine.

Her face in smiling, wakes strange memories,
Memories of death, and old forgotten woe;
Her eyes are pools where many a drowned hope lies,
They shine above the dead who sleep below.

The very charm of death is in her look,
The fascination of all delicate deaths
Of mortals who in easeful ways forsook
The taking of so many weary breaths.

Arthur Symons

94

Liar, liar, pants on fire,
Nose as long as a telephone wire,

children's

street songs

and cries

Black, black,
Sit on a tack
Blue, blue,
I hate you.
White, white,
Let's fight.
Red, red,
Soak your head.
Green, green,
You're mean.
Soak your head in gasoline.

I see Paris
I see France
I see Linda's underpants
Are they blue?
Are they pink?
I don't know,
But they sure stink.

Johnny's over the ocean
Johnny's over the sea.
Johnny broke a bottle.
And blamed it on me.
I told Ma;
Ma told Pa.
Johnny got a lickin;
So ha, ha, ha.

I'm rubber, your glue
Everything you say
Bounces off me
And sticks to you.

Pete, Pete
Has smelly feet.

Ta, ra, ra, boom de ay!
There is no school today.
The Teacher passed away.
She died of tooth decay.
We threw her in the bay.
She scared all the Fish away.
And when we pulled her out,
She smelled like sauerkraut.

Jean, Jean,
Fell on her beam,
Won't wake up
Till Halloween.

In nineteen forty-four
My father went to war.
He pulled the trigger
And shot a nigger,
And that was the end of the war.

JOE, JOE
FAT AND SLOW
FALL DOWN AND STUB YOUR TOE.

Roses are red,
Violets are blue,
You got a nose like a B-42.

Eenie, Meenie, Miney mo,
Catch a Nigger by the toe.
If he hollers, let him go,
Eenie, Meenie, miney, Mo.

When I was only five
My mother learned to drive
She hit a bump
And skinned her rump
And landed in the city dump.

Sticks and stones may break my bones,
But names will never hurt me.

WHAT A SHAPE!
WHAT A FIGURE!
TWO MORE LEGS
AND YOU'D LOOK LIKE
TRIGGER

I hate Bosco.
It's not the drink for me.
Mommy put it in my milk.
To try and poison me.
But I showed Mommy
And put it in her tea,
And now there's no more Mommy
To try and poison me.

Ooey gooey was a worm
Sitting on a railroad track
The train he did not see.
OOEY GOOEY.

Roses are red
Violets are black
You'd look better
with a knife in your back

PINK, PINK,
YOU STINK.

FATTY, FATTY, TWO BY FOUR,
CAN'T GET THROUGH THE BATHROOM DOOR,
SO SHE MAKES IT
ON THE FLOOR.

Boys are made of greasy, grimy gopher guts,
Marinated monkey meat,
French fried parakeet.
All that vomit rolling down a country street.
Wish I had a spoon.

BAD NEWS AT THE BREAKFAST TABLE . . .

Kennedy Is Killed by Sniper as He Rides in Car in Dallas

DALLAS, Nov. 22—President John Fitzgerald Kennedy was shot and killed by an assassin today.

He died of a wound in the brain caused by a rifle bullet that was fired at him as he was riding through downtown Dallas in a motorcade.
—N.Y. Times

President's Assassin Shot To Death

DALLAS, Nov. 24—President Kennedy's assassin, Lee Harvey Oswald, was fatally shot by a Dallas night-club operator today as the police started to move him from the city jail to the county jail. . . .

Millions of viewers saw the shooting on television.
—N.Y. Times

Criticizes JFK, Is Fatally Stabbed

Cursing "President Kennedy and America" cost a Russian-born Sioux City man his life Sunday afternoon when his stepson plunged a pair of scissors into his body. . . .
—The Sioux City Journal, Nov. 25

Jilted GI Kills 2, Chokes Girl in Catskills Rampage

SMALLWOOD, N. Y. Jan. 1—A rejected suitor broke into his former fiancee's home here, hid in a linen closet until the family had gone to sleep, and then at dawn of New Year's Day used an ax to kill the girl's father and her girl friend who was staying overnight, state police said.

He also choked and left for dead the pretty 20-year-old blonde who had spurned him.
—N.Y. Daily News

Shackup Sadism Costs Life of Beaten Crutch Girl, 7

A chronic sufferer of a debilitating bone disease and an acute victim of "battered child syndrome," 7-year-old Elizabeth Pappolla died yesterday after two weeks of savage beatings by her mother and the woman's lover.

The lover-boy unemployed laborer John Koltosky, 26, allegedly admitted to the police he pummeled the undersized child every night for two weeks because "I enjoy beating her."
—N.Y. Daily News, March 14

3 Policemen Cuffed Together and Killed

LAWRENCEVILLE, Ga., April 17 (UPI)—Three county policemen were manacled together by their own handcuffs and shot to death early today after the surprised a gang of thieves stripping a stolen automobile.

All were shot in the back of the head. Their bodies were found just off a dirt road in a remote wooded area about 20 miles northeast of Atlanta.

Georgia Sniper Kills a Negro Educator

COLBERT, Ga., July 11—A Negro school official from Washington was slain in Georgia today when two shotgun blasts were fired into a car he was driving through early-morning mists. The shotgun was fired from another car.
—N.Y. Times

Experts Identify Mississippi Bodies As Rights Aides'

JACKSON, Miss., Aug. 5—Experts working from dental charts and other evidence identified today the three bodies found buried deep inside a cattle-pond dam as those of three missing civil rights workers.

. . . J. Edgar Hoover, director of the F.B.I., announced this morning that the two white men had been definitely identified as Michael H. Schwerner, a 24-year-old field worker for the Congress of Racial Equality from New York, and Andrew Goodman, 20, a Queens College student from New York, who was a volunteer in the summer civil rights campaign in Mississippi.

Further tests were being made to confirm the tentative identification of the body of James E. Chaney, 21, a Negro plasterer from Meridian, Miss., who also was a CORE field worker.
—N.Y. Times, Aug. 6

Judge's 2 Little Girls Are Slain

JACKSON, Wyo., Aug. 7 (Combined Services)—Two young daughters of a Chicago area judge were raped and murdered early today in a resort motel as their 6-year-old sister slumbered undisturbed a few feet away.

On the floor of the dead girls' room, drunk or pretending drunkenness, was Andrew Pixley, 21, of Dallas, Ore., a transient who apparently had been in the area the past few days.

Teeners Slash New Pupil Because 'She's a Misfit'

TORRANCE, Calif., Sept. 19 (AP)—As she walked home from her third day at Torrance High School, a carload of teen-agers pulled up alongside 15-year-old Margaret Mary Little. One yelled: "We don't want misfits in our school."

Then, said the girl, three boys and two girls jumped out. The others watched as one boy ripped her skirt and her blouse, and, with a rusty razor blade, cut slashes on her cheek and forearm. . . . Margaret is a cerebral palsy victim. She has been handicapped since birth.

97 Stab Wounds Killed L.I. Matron

Mrs. Doris Marcus, 41-year-old housewife found murdered Friday in her $100,000 Great Neck, L.I., home, had been stabbed 97 times 'with the force of a maniac,' an autopsy showed yesterday.
—N.Y. Daily News, October 18

44 Airliner Deaths Laid To Passenger Who Shot 2 Pilots

WASHINGTON, Nov. 2 (AP)—A passenger deeply in debt and insured for $105,000 shot two pilots of an airliner during a flight last May, the Civil Aeronautics Board said today. The plane crashed into a low California hill, killing all 44 persons aboard.

Kills Wife, 4 of 10 Kids & Self

SARTELL, Minn., Nov. 15, 1964 (AP)—A 49-year-old laborer, brooding over a separation from his wife, shot and killed her and four of their 10 children late last night, then took his own life.

Three other children ran screaming in terror to a neighbor's home, telling of the killings.

Dead are John S. Jenderseck; his wife, Catherine, 42; their sons James, 16, Philip, 14, and David, 6, and a daughter, Joan, 10.

The oldest three children—Robert, 20, Judith, 19, and Richard, 18—were out on dates and came home to find sheriff's officers awaiting them.

Violinmaker Murders Ex-Wife in Museum

Climaxing years of bitter disputes over his daughter, a 72-year-old master violinmaker shot and killed his former wife yesterday before scores of horrified onlookers in the main hall of the Museum of Natural History.

Among the shocked and terror-striken witnesses was the girl herself, a pretty, frail 12-year-old.
—N.Y. Daily News, February 8

Malcolm X Slain; 400 Watch

A week after he was firebombed out of his Queens home, Black Nationalist leader Malcolm X was shot to death shortly after 3 P.M. yesterday as he started to address a Washington Heights rally of some 400 of his devoted followers.

Three other men were wounded in the wild burst of firing from at least three weapons—a .38 and a .45 automatic pistol and a sawed-off shotgun—although only the shotgun was recovered.
—N.Y. Daily News, February 22

3 Hold Car in Terror

A 27-year-old man was stabbed to death in a subway train in Brooklyn last night as 11 other passengers sat by, watching in horror.

The man was attacked by three teen-agers who had boarded the car and held it in terror for 10 minutes as it rumbled under the East New York and Bedford-Stuyvesant sections.
—N.Y. Times, March 13

Held for Slaying Husband with Pills, Hammer, Knife

Mrs. Marion G. Adams, 35, a thin blonde, had little to say yesterday as she stood in 1st District Court, Mineola, L.I., at her arraignment on a first degree murder charge.

But there was nothing halting or inarticulate in her speech Saturday night when she told police how she killed her husband, using a combination of sleeping pills, a hammer and a kitchen knife. . . .
—N.Y. Daily News, March 22

Mad Scientist Shoots 3, Kills Self at A-Lab

A "very quiet and friendly" nuclear engineer—naked to the waist, his chest and forehead daubed with lipstick in grotesque, Indian-like designs—strode yesterday into Brookhaven National Laboratory, the hush-hush atomic energy research plant in Suffolk, L.I. He was carrying a sawed-off Mossberg automatic shotgun.

Without a word, 34-year-old Michael Maresca, who had reportedly been under consideration as an astronaut, gunned down three physicists—all friends. He fired at, but missed, a fourth scientist and broke away from fellow researchers who tried to disarm him.

Then Maresca, father of three, ran outside to his car in the parking lot, put the muzzle of the shotgun in his mouth and killed himself.

—N.Y. Daily News, Jan. 19

Rabbi Shot at Temple as Youth Goes Amok

DETROIT, Feb. 12—Rabbi Morris Adler, 59, was felled by two bullets today as he stood in front of his congregation trying to protect a 13-year-old boy from a wild-eyed gunman.

The gunman, Richart Wishnetsky, 24, then turned the pistol on himself and fired a single bullet into his head. The boy, Steven Frank, for whom a bar mitzvah service was being held, was unharmed.

—N.Y. Daily News

2nd Union Officer Is Slain on Coast

HAYWARD, Calif., May 7 (UPI)—A second leader in a bitter fight within the painters union was slain by a charge of buckshot early today as he sat in his office.

Lloyd Green, 45 years old, financial secretary of Local 1178 of the International Brotherhood of Painters, Decorators and Paperhangers of America here, was struck in the face by the shotgun blast.

He was killed a little more than one month after a slayer with a shotgun shot down Dow Wilson, recording secretary of San Francisco Local 4, as he walked along a San Francisco street after a night union meeting.

Mother of 7 Found Guilty in Torture Slaying of Girl

INDIANAPOLIS, May 19 (UPI)—A Criminal Court jury found Mrs. Gertrude Baniszewski, 38, mother of seven, guilty today of first degree murder in the torture-slaying of Sylvia Likens, 16. Four teen-age defendants were convicted on other charges.

... Mrs. Baniszewski ... was accused of leading a pack of youngsters—including her daughter and son—in the "horror chamber" torture of Sylvia ... Sylvia, a boarder in the Baniszewski home, died last October 26.

8 Student Nurses Slain in Chicago Dormitory

CHICAGO, July 14—Eight student nurses were killed here early this morning in one of the most savage multiple murders in the history of crime.

Another nurse, 23-year-old Corazon Amurao, escaped death by rolling under a bed in the row house that served as a dormitory for the South Chicago Community Hospital on the Far South Side.

—N.Y. Times

Mountain Resort Mystery Find Woman & 2 Men Slain

TUXEDO, N. C., July 23 (UPI)—The bodies of two men and a half-nude woman were found near this mountain resort today, victims of a sadistic killer who apparently beat them to death with an auto jack and then left crossed symbols on two of the corpses.

All three bodies were arranged face-up in a semicircle. They were discovered by two men cutting through a wooded area to dispose of some trash.

Mad Sniper Kills 15, Wounds 31 from U of Texas Tower

AUSTIN, Tex., Aug. 1 (Combined Services)—A kill-crazy ex-marine slaughtered his wife and mother today, then hauled an arsenal of guns to a perch high on the University of Texas tower and launched an orgy of sniping in which 13 died and 31 were wounded.

The carnage ended only when police burst into the sniper's 28th story eyrie and shot him dead after a brief gun duel.

The killer was ... identified as ... architecture student Charles Joseph Whitman, 24. ...

Body of Girl, 16, Is Found in Triple Texas Slaying

FORT WORTH, Tex., Aug 8 (AP)—Searchers combing the flatlands south of here recovered a body identified tonight as Edna Louise Sullivan, 16, a rape-strangle victim.

... The blue-eyed high school sophomore was missing early Sunday after fishermen came across the bodies of her two companions, Robert Brand, 17, of nearby Alvarado, and his cousin, Mark Dunnam, 16, of Tarzana, Calif.

A 5th Redhead Slain in Jersey

An attractive redhaired matron—the fifth redhaired woman murdered in a two-county area along the Jersey shore in less than a year—was found shot through the head yesterday in her own car, mired in the sand in Howell Township between Lakewood and Freehold.

The victim was Mrs. Dorothy Louise McKenzie. ...

—N.Y. Daily News, Aug. 11

James Meredith Shot in the Back

HERNANDO, Miss., June 6 (UPI)—Negro James Meredith, 32, was shot in the head by a forest sniper today as he trudged down a lonely highway on the second day of his march through Mississippi.

... Meredith, marching to urge Negro voter registration, was walking past a patch of woods when a shot rang out.

Hint Sex Slayer Beat Jersey Boy in a Rage

Paul Benda, the handsome blond 5-year-old youngster who was found stabbed to death on the shore of Raritan Bay in Union Beach, N.J., had been beaten and tortured, "apparently by someone in a sexual rage," authorities declared yesterday.

... The boy had been stabbed three times—once in the heart—beaten with a stick and tortured with lighted cigarettes ... another source close to the investigation said the tot had been beaten in a sexual rage.

—N.Y. Daily News, June 23

Percy's Daughter Is Slain in Chicago

CHICAGO, Sept. 18—An intruder entered the palatial suburban home of Charles H. Percy early today and killed the Republican Senate candidate's 21-year-old daughter Valerie Jeanne in her second-floor bedroom.

—N.Y. Times

New Haven Man, 26, Guilty of Slaying 6

NEW HAVEN, Nov. 16—Arthur James Davis, accused of slaying six people here in a wild search for his estranged girl friend Aug. 6 was found guilty by a three-judge panel in Superior Court this afternoon of six counts of first-degree murder.

—N.Y. Times

Bomb Kills Civil Rights Aide

NATCHEZ, Miss., Feb. 28 (UPI)—A Negro civil rights leader, recently promoted to a job previously held by a white man, was killed late last night when a bomb shattered his pickup truck.

The victim was Wharlest Jackson, 37, the treasurer of the local branch of the National Association for the Advancement of Colored People.

2 Teen Cousins Forced To Kneel, Shot To Death

ROCKFORD, Ill., March 3 (AP)—Two teen-age cousins were forced to kneel against the stone wall of an isolated park pavilion last night and then were shot to death at point blank range, police said.

Police squads rushed to the area after an anonymous tipster, believed to be a woman, called the Winnebago County sheriff's office and told deputies where to find the bodies.

"To hell with them," the woman shouted over the phone. "Just let them lay there and die."

Top N.Y. Policeman's Neighbors Say Fear Pervades Vicinity

Next door to where Police Commissioner Howard R. Leary lives in Peter Cooper Village, some 100 or more housewives are afflicted with fear.

They fear muggers and rapists. Their dread has been intensified since Feb. 16, when a 13-year-old girl was grabbed by the hair by a youth in the lobby of their apartment building at 441 East 20th Street, forced at knifepoint into an elevator, taken to the sixth floor and raped on the landing of the fire stairwell.

Last night, despairing of ever getting adequate city police protection or enough guards from Metropolitan Life, owners of the project, tenants of No. 441 met and discussed alternative security measures. ...

The building has no doorman. The entrance is never locked. It is the same at No. 511, where Commissioner Leary lives.

But, as the housewives were quick to point out, Commissioner Leary gets a police escort when he goes to work and when he returns at night ...

—Homer Bigart,
N.Y. Times

United Press International Photo.

Arsenal in Action

As the big kill at Tay Ninh demonstrated, the arsenal of American weapons in Viet Nam is the deadliest ever developed for man-to-man combat. The U.S. infantryman in Viet Nam today shoulders six times the firepower of his Korean War counterpart; behind him stand rank upon rank of mobile mortars and howitzers that can be called in by air as quickly as he needs them. Overhead hover helicopters bristling with machine guns, rockets and automatic grenade launchers; above the "gunships" circle jet fighter-bombers armed with searing napalm, white phosphorous and bomblets that can unleash deadly patterns of tiny steel pellets. In no other war has American weaponry so quickly matched the demands of a difficult tactical terrain. From the swamps of the Mekong Delta, where 30-ft. patrol boats packed with unsinkable plastic foam whisk along on water jets, to the shell-pocked "Rockpile" below the Demilitarized Zone, where six-barreled Ontos tracked vehicles rumble, the arsenal last week was in awesome action.

Bloody Mush. Basic element in this lethal complex is what the Viet Cong call "the little black rifle"—the light, fast-firing, plastic-stocked M-16 automatic rifle carried by most of the combat troops in South Viet Nam. At 7.6 lbs., the M-16 is scarcely the size of a farm boy's "varmint" rifle; yet it can spray short bursts at the rate of 750 rounds per minute, though reloading time cuts the effective rate to a far lower figure. Its muzzle velocity is so great that within 100 yds.—the range of most Viet Nam fire fights—an M-16 bullet generates supersonic shock waves that can collapse internal organs into bloody mush, shatter bone or leave arms and legs dangling drunkenly.

Time Magazine, Nov. 18, 1966

THE ENEMY'S TESTAMENT

1

With no other identity than the letters of V.C.
which sound like venereal disease:

I have been softened up,
my backbone as soft as my belly,

I have been gassed,
my eyes as blind as a worm's,

I have been brainwashed,
told of freedom until light
passed out of my brain,

I have been shot,
more bullet holes in my flesh
than holes in a target.

2

They got me out of my lair
for I was infesting my own land,
and they, the foreigners, came to liberate me,
liberate me of my share.

3

So now I have this will to make:

I send my brain to your center of research
so they could see what made me fight,

I send my eyes to your President
so they can look him in the face,

they only knew the darkness of tunnels. . .

I send my teeth to your generals,
they bit more rifle than bread,

for hunger was my companion. . .

I send my tongue to your cardinals,
It will tell them what Jesus said,

about the sword. . .

My body, I leave to the Mekong River.

ETEL ADNAN

Who is the slayer, who the victim? Speak.

Sophocles

"WE BURNED EVERY HUT!"

To The Editor:

   Here are portions of a letter I have just received from my son, who is now stationed in Vietnam.

   My son enlisted in the Army, asked to be sent to Vietnam and backed the government's strong policy toward the war in Vietnam--at least he did when he left this country last November. I believe what he has to say will be of interest to you and to your readers:

DEAR MOM AND DAD:

   Today we went on a mission and I'm not very proud of myself, my friends or my country. We burned every hut in sight!

   It was a small rural network of villages and the people were incredibly poor. My unit burned and plundered their meager possessions. Let me try to explain the situation to you.

   The huts here are thatched palm leaves. Each one has a dried mud bunker inside. These bunkers are to protect the families. Kind of like air raid shelters.

   My unit commanders, however, chose to think that these bunkers are offensive. So every hut we find that has a bunker, we are ordered to burn to the ground!

   WHEN THE 10 helicopters landed this morning, in the midst of these huts, and six men jumped out of each "chopper" we were firing the moment we hit the ground. We fired into all the huts we could. Then we got "on line" and swept the area.

   It is then that we burn these huts and take all men old enough to carry a weapon and the "choppers" come and get them (they take them to a collection point a few miles away for interrogation). The families don't understand this. The Viet Cong fill their minds with tales saying the GIs kill all their men.

   So, everyone is crying, begging and praying that we don't separate them and take their husbands and fathers, sons and grandfathers. The women wail and moan.

   Then they watch in terror as we burn their homes, personal possessions and food. Yes, we burn all rice and shoot all livestock.

   SOME OF the guys are so careless! Today a buddy of mine called "la Dai" ("come here") into a hut and an old man came out of the bomb shelter. My buddy told the old man to get away from the hut and since we have to move quickly on a sweep, just threw a hand grenade into the shelter.

   As he pulled the pin the old man got excited and started jabbering and running toward my buddy and the hut. A GI, not understanding, stopped the old man with a football tackle just as my buddy threw the grenade into the shelter. (There is a four-second delay on a hand grenade.)

   After he threw it, and was running for cover, (during this four-second delay) we all heard a baby crying from inside the shelter!

   THERE WAS nothing we could do...

   After the explosion we found the mother, two children (ages about 6 and 12, boy and girl) and an almost newborn baby. That is what the old man was trying to tell us!

   The shelter was small and narrow. They were all huddled together. The three of us dragged out the bodies onto the floor of the hut.

   IT WAS HORRIBLE!!

   The children's fragile bodies were torn apart, literally mutilated. We looked at each other and burned the hut.

The old man was just whimpering in disbelief outside the burning hut. We walked away and left him there.

My last look was: an old, old man in ragged, torn, dirty clothes on his knees outside the burning hut, praying to Buddha. His white hair was blowing in the wind and tears were rolling down...

WE KEPT on walking then the three of us separated. There was a hut at a distance and my squad leader told me to go over and destroy it. An oldish man came out of the hut.

I checked and made sure no one was in it, then got out my matches. The man came up to me then, and bowed with hands in a praying motion over and over. He looked so sad! He didn't say anything, just kept bowing, begging me not to burn his home.

We were both there, alone, and he was about your age, Dad. With a heavy heart I hesitatingly put the match to the straw and started to walk away.

Dad, it was so hard for me to turn and look at him in the eyes but I did.

I WISH I could have cried but I just can't anymore.

I threw down my rifle and ran into the now blazing hut and took out everything I could save--food, clothes, etc.

Afterward, he took my hand, still saying nothing and bowed down touching the back of my hand to his forehead.

MACHINE GUN fire is coming into our village (base camp). We are being attacked, NOW as I am writing. I must go.

NEXT DAY: Everything's OK. It was just harassing fire. I was up for the better part of the night, though.

Well, Dad, you wanted to know what it's like here. Does this give you an idea? Excuse the poor writing but I was pretty emotional, I guess, even a little shook.

YOUR SON

THE REST of my son's letter goes on to describe what the routines of his life in Vietnam are like. He described an uneventful ambush he participated in, and he got excited about a new type rifle he had been issued. Beyond that, there are personal matters which he discussed.

Needless to say, I was very much disturbed to read this letter. My 16-year-old daughter had read it before I did and when I went to her room to ask her if I could read the letter, I found her crying. I asked her the reason, and she replied by handing me the letter.

I HAVE NOT been a dove as far as the Vietnamese war is concerned, though I have not been a strong hawk either. But I think that the American people should understand what they mean when they advocate a continuation and even an escalation of our war effort in Vietnam.

They should understand that war doesn't consist only of two armies made up of young men in uniform, armed and firing at each other across open fields, with bugles blowing and flags waving. The American people should understand what a war such as this does to our young men whom we send overseas to carry out our government's foreign policy.

I guess what I am saying is that whatever course American public opinion backs should be supported by knowledge and understanding of the concrete results of that course and not by illusions.

A GI'S DAD

FROM CONFESSION

How do I say
that I'm a murderer?

I drag my shadow
as if it were a sack
full of discarded bodies.

My count is indefinite
but probably includes
the 8 mothers
who run through the caves
of my colon
with burning hair;

the baby
shaped like a scream;
the two girls
with hands and wombs
of flaming water;
and, on my spinal road,
the boy who crawls
farther and farther
from his legs.

Morton Marcus

"BALLAD OF THE GREEN BERETS"

Fighting soldiers from the sky,
Fearless men who jump and die
Men who mean just what they say
The Brave Men of the Green Beret.
Silver wings upon their chests
These are men America's best
One hundred men we'll test today
But only three win the Green Beret.

Trained to live off nature's land,
Trained to combat, hand to hand,
Men who fight by night and day
Courage take the Green Beret.
Silver wings upon their chests
These are men America's best.
One hundred men we'll test today
But only three win the Green Beret.

Back at home a young wife waits
Her Green Beret has met his fate
He has died for those oppressed
Leaving her this last request
Put silver wings on my son's chest
Make him one of America's best
He'll be a man they'll test one day.
Have him win the Green Beret.

Staff Sgt. Barry Sadler

107

108

THE DEATH OF THE BALL TURRET GUNNER

From my mother's sleep I fell into the State,
And I hunched in its belly till my wet fur froze.
Six miles from earth, loosed from its dream of life,
I woke to black flak and the nightmare fighters.
When I died they washed me out of the turret with a hose.

Randall Jarrell

Mother, the wardrobe is full of infantrymen

Mother, the wardrobe is full of infantrymen
i did, i asked them
but they snarled saying it was a man's life

Mother, there is a centurion tank in the parlour
i did, i asked the officer
but he laughed saying queen's regulations,
piano was out of tune anyway

Mother, polish your identity bracelet
there is a mushroom cloud in the back garden
i did, i tried to bring in the cat
but it simply came to pieces in my hand
i did, i tried to whitewash the windows
but there weren't any
i did, i tried to hide under the stairs
but i couldn't get in for civil defence leaders
i did, i tried ringing Candid Camera
but they crossed their hearts

I went for a policeman but they were looting the town
i went out for a fire engine but they were all upside down
i went for a priest but they were all on their knees
mother don't just lie there say something please
mother don't just lie there say something please

Roger McGough

109

110

THREE PEOPLE ARE ENJOYING THIS SITUATION: THE MURDERER, THE VICTIM, AND YOU.

The murderer because he is about to take the ultimate risk; the victim because he is about to experience the ultimate sensation; and you because the vicarious thrill is more potent than pornography. Violence has become an obsession. Our heroes and our leaders arrive and depart in violence; our films and plays and books sing its song; our newspapers report its progress; our artists glorify its style. What seemed to be an isolated example of madness—The Unmaking of a President, 1963—proved to be only the first in a series of shock waves which have now lost their shock value. And so we present a dossier of evidence seeking a conclusion: Why are we so obsessed? If, somewhere in your reading, the blood quickens, then you must realize that it is only one more step until that essential moment when the blood flows.

PAUSE, NOW, AND CONSIDER
SOME TENTATIVE CONCLUSIONS
ABOUT THE MEANING OF THIS MASS PERVERSION
CALLED PORNO-VIOLENCE:
WHAT IT IS
AND WHERE IT COMES FROM
AND WHO PUT THE HAIR ON THE WALLS

Tom Wolfe

Keeps His Mom-in-law in Chains, meet *Kills Son and Feeds Corpse to Pigs.* Pleased to meet you. *Teenager Twists Off Corpse's Head . . . To Get Gold Teeth,* meet *Strangles Girl Friend, then Chops Her to Pieces.* Likewise, I'm sure. *Nurse's Aide Sees Fingers Chopped Off in Meat Grinder,* meet. . . .

In ten years of journalism I have covered more conventions than I care to remember. Podiatrists, theosophists, Professional Budget Finance dentists, oyster farmers, mathematicians, truckers, dry cleaners, stamp collectors, Esperantists, nudists and newspaper editors—I have seen them all, together, in vast assemblies, sloughing through the wall-to-wall of a thousand hotel lobbies (the nudists excepted) in their shimmering grey-metal suits and Nicey Short Collar white shirts with white Plasti-Coat name cards on their chests, and I have sat through their speeches and seminars (the nudists included) and attentively endured ear baths such as you wouldn't believe. And yet some of the truly instructive conventions of our times I seem to have missed altogether. One, for example, I only heard about from one of the many anonymous men who have labored in . . . a curious field. This was a convention of the stringers for *The National Enquirer.*

The Enquirer is a weekly newspaper that is probably known by sight to millions more than know it by name. In fact, no one who ever came face-to-face with *The Enquirer* on a newsstand in its wildest days is likely to have forgotten the sight: a tabloid with great inky shocks of type all over the front page saying something on the order of *Gouges Out Wife's Eyes to Make Her Ugly, Dad Hurls Hot Grease in Daughter's Face, Wife Commits Suicide After 2 Years of Poisoning Fails to Kill Husband. . . .*

The stories themselves were supplied largely by stringers, i.e., correspondents, from all over the country, the world, for that matter, mostly copy editors and reporters on local newspapers. Every so often they would come upon a story, usually via the police beat, that was so grotesque the local sheet would discard it or run it in a highly glossed form rather than offend or perplex its readers. The stringers would preserve them for *The Enquirer,* which always rewarded them well and respectfully.

In fact, one year *The Enquirer* convened and feted them at a hotel in Manhattan. It was a success in every way. The only awkward moment was at the outset when the stringers all pulled in. None of them knew each other. Their hosts got around the problem by introducing them by the stories they had supplied. The introductions, I am told, went like this:

"Harry, I want you to meet Frank here. Frank did that story, you remember that story, *Midget Murderer Throws Girl Off Cliff After She Refuses To Dance With Him.*"

"Pleased to meet you. That was some story."

"And Harry did the one about *I Spent Three Days Trapped at Bottom of Forty-foot-deep Mine Shaft and Was Saved by a Swarm of Flies.*"

"Likewise, I'm sure."

And *Midget Murderer Throws Girl Off Cliff* shakes hands with *I Spent Three Days Trapped at Bottom of Forty-foot-deep Mine Shaft,* and *Buries Her Baby Alive* shakes hands with *Boy, Twelve, Strangles Two-year-old Girl,* and *Kills Son and Feeds Corpse to Pigs* shakes hands with *He Strangles Old Woman and Smears Corpse with Syrup, Ketchup and Oatmeal . . .* and. . . .

. . . There was a great deal of esprit about the whole thing. These men were, in fact, the avant-garde of a new genre that since then has become institutionalized throughout the nation without anyone knowing its proper name. I speak of the new pornography, the pornography of violence.

Pornography comes from the Greek word *porne,* meaning harlot, and pornography is literally the depiction of the acts of harlots. In the new pornography, the theme is not sex. The new pornography depicts practitioners acting out another, murkier drive: people staving teeth in, ripping guts open, blowing brains out and getting even with all those bastards. . . .

The success of *The Enquirer* prompted many imitators to enter the field, *Midnight, The Star Chronicle, The National Insider, Inside News, The National Close-up, The National Tattler, The National Examiner.* A truly competitive free press evolved, and soon a reader could go to the newspaper of his choice for *Kill the Retarded!* (*Won't You Join My Movement?*) and *Unfaithful Wife? Burn Her Bed!, Harem Master's Mistress Chops Him with Machete, Babe Bites Off Boy's Tongue,* and *Cuts Buddy's Face to Pieces for Stealing His Business and Fiancée.*

And yet the last time I surveyed the Violence press, I noticed a curious thing. These pioneering journals seem to have pulled back. They seem to be regressing to what is by now the Redi-Mix staple of literate Americans, plain old lust-o-lech sex. *Ecstasy and Me* (*By Hedy Lamarr*), says *The National Enquirer. I Run A Sex Art Gallery,* says *The National Insider.* What has happened, I think, is something that has happened to avant-gardes in many fields, from William Morris and the Craftsmen to the Bauhaus group. Namely, their discoveries have been preempted by the Establishment and so thoroughly dissolved into the mainstream they no longer look original.

Robert Harrison, the former publisher of *Confidential,* and later publisher of the aforementioned *Inside News,* was perhaps the first person to see it coming. I was interviewing Harrison early in January of 1964 for a story in Esquire about six weeks after the assassination of President Kennedy, and we were in a cab in the West Fifties in Manhattan, at a stoplight, by a newsstand, and Harrison suddenly pointed at the newsstand and said, "Look at that. They're doing the same thing *The Enquirer* does."

There on the stand was a row of slick-paper, magazine-size publications, known in the trade as one-shots, with titles like *Four Days That Shook the World, Death of a President, An American Tragedy* or just *John Fitzgerald Kennedy* (*1921–1963*). "You want to know why people buy those things?" said Harrison. "People buy those things to see a man get his head blown off."

And, of course, he was right. Only now the publishers were in many cases the pillars of the American press. Invariably, these "special coverages" of the assassination bore introductions piously commemorating the fallen President, exhorting the American people to strength and unity in a time of crisis, urging greater vigilance and safeguards for the new President, and even raising the nice metaphysical question of collective guilt in "an age of violence."

In the three and a half years since then, of course, there has been an incessant replay, with every recoverable clinical detail, of those less than five seconds in which a man got his head blown off. And throughout this deluge of words, pictures and film frames, I have been intrigued with one thing. The point of view, the vantage point, is almost never that of the victim, riding in the Presidential Lincoln Continental. What you get is . . . the view from Oswald's rifle. You can step right up here and look point-blank right through the very hairline cross in Lee Harvey Oswald's Optics Ordinance four-power Japanese telescopic sight and watch, frame by frame by frame by frame by frame, as that man there's head comes apart. Just a little History there before your very eyes.

The television networks have schooled us in the view from Oswald's rifle and made it seem a normal pastime. The TV viewpoint is nearly always that of the man who is going to strike. The last time I watched *Gunsmoke,* which was not known as a very violent Western in TV terms, the action went like this: The Wellington agents and the stagecoach driver pull guns on the badlands gang leader's daughter and Kitty, the heart-of-gold saloonkeeper, and kidnap them. Then the badlands gang shoots two Wellington agents. Then they tie up five more and talk about shooting them. Then they desist because they might not be able to get a hotel room in the next town if the word got around. Then one badlands gang gunslinger attempts to rape Kitty while the gang leader's younger daughter looks on. Then Kitty resists, so he slugs her one in the jaw. Then the gang leader slugs him. Then the gang leader slugs Kitty. Then Kitty throws hot stew in a gang member's face and hits him over the back of the head with a revolver. Then he knocks her down with a rock. Then the gang sticks up a bank. Here comes the sheriff, Matt Dillon. He shoots a gang member and breaks it up. Then the gang leader shoots the guy who was guarding his daughter and the woman. Then the sheriff shoots the gang leader. The final exploding bullet signals The End.

It is not the accumulated slayings and bone-crushings that make this porno-violence, however. What makes it porno-violence is that in almost every case the camera angle, therefore the viewer, is with the gun, the fist, the rock. The pornography of violence has no point of view in the old sense that novels do. You do not live the action through the hero's eyes. You live with the aggressor, whoever he may be. One moment you are the hero. The next, you are the villain. No matter whose side you may be on consciously, you are in fact with the muscle, and it is you who disintegrate all comers, villains, lawmen, women, anybody. On the rare occasions in which the gun is emptied into the camera—i.e., into your face—the effect is so startling that the pornography of violence all but loses its fantasy charm. There are not nearly so many masochists as sadists among those little devils whispering into your ears.

In fact, sex—"sadomasochism"—is only a part of the pornography of violence. Violence is much more wrapped up, simply, with status. Violence is the simple, ultimate solution for problems of status competition, just as gambling is the simple, ultimate solution for economic competition. The old pornography was the fantasy of easy sexual delights in a world where sex was kept unavailable. The new pornography is the fantasy of easy triumph in a world where status competition has become so complicated and frustrating.

Already the old pornography is losing its kick because of overexposure. In the late Thirties, Nathanael West published his last and best-regarded novel, *The Day of the Locust,* and it was a terrible flop commercially, and his publisher said if he ever published another book about Hollywood it would "have to be *My Thirty-nine Ways of Making Love by Hedy Lamarr." Ecstasy and Me* is not quite that . . . but maybe it is. I stopped counting. I know her account begins: "The men in my life have ranged from a classic case history of impotence, to a whip-brandishing sadist who enjoyed sex only after he tied my arms behind me with the sash of his robe. There was another man who took his pleasure with a girl in my own bed, while he thought I was asleep in it."

Yawns all around. The sin itself is wearing out. Pornography cannot exist without certified taboo to violate. And today Lust, like the rest of the Seven Deadly Sins—Pride, Sloth, Envy, Greed, Anger and Gluttony—is becoming a rather minor vice. The Seven Deadly Sins, after all, are only sins against the self. Theologically, the idea of Lust—well, the idea is that if you seduce some poor girl from Akron, it is not a sin because you are ruining her, but because you are wasting your time and your energies and damaging your own spirit. This goes back to the old work ethic, when the idea was to keep every able-bodied man's shoulder to the wheel. In an age of riches for all, the ethic becomes more nearly: Let him do anything he pleases, as long as he doesn't get in my way. And if he does get in my way, or even if he doesn't . . . well . . . we have *new* fantasies for that. *Put hair on the walls.*

Hair on the walls is the invisible subtitle of Truman Capote's book, *In Cold Blood.* The book is neither a who-done-it nor a will-they-be-caught, since the answers to both questions are known from the outset. It does ask why-did-they-do-it, but the answer is soon as clear as it is going to be. Instead, the book's suspense is based largely on a totally new idea in detective stories: the promise of gory details, and the withholding of them until the end. Early in the game one of the two murderers, Dick, starts promising to put "plenty of hair on them-those walls" with a shotgun. So read on, gentle readers, and on and on; you are led up to the moment before the crime on page 60—yet the specifics, what happened, the gory details, are kept out of sight, in grisly dangle, until page 244.

But Dick and Perry, Capote's killers, are only a couple of lower-class bums. With James Bond the new pornography has already reached dead center, the bureaucratic middle class. The appeal of Bond has been explained as the appeal of the lone man who can solve enormously complicated, even world problems through his own bravery and initiative. But Bond is not a lone man at all, of course. He is not the Lone Ranger. He is much easier to identify than that. He is a salaried functionary in a bureaucracy. He is a sport, but a believable one; not a millionaire, but a bureaucrat on expense account. He is not even a high-level bureaucrat. He is an operative. This point is carefully and repeatedly made by having his superiors dress him down for violations of standard operating procedure. Bond, like the Lone Ranger, solves problems with guns and fists. When it is over, however, the Lone Ranger leaves a silver bullet. Bond, like the rest of us, fills out a report in triplicate.

Marshall McLuhan says we are in a period in which it will become harder and harder to stimulate lust through words and pictures—i.e., the old pornography. In an age of electronic circuitry, he says, people crave tactile, all-involving experiences. The same thing may very well happen to the new pornography of violence. Even such able craftsmen as Truman Capote, Ian Fleming, NBC and CBS may not suffice. Fortunately, there are historical models to rescue us from this frustration. In the latter days of the Roman Empire, the Emperor Commodus became jealous of the celebrity of the great gladiators. He took to the arena himself, with his sword, and began dispatching suitably screened cripples and hobbled fighters. Audience participation became so popular that soon various *illuminati* of the Commodus set, various boys and girls of the year, were out there, suited up, gaily cutting a sequence of dwarves and feebles down to short ribs. Ah, swinging generations, what new delights await?

"Varoom!"

Roy Lichtenstein: *Varoom*
Collection: Kimiko and John Powers, Aspen, Colorado.

The Revolt of Leo Held

There was almost nothing in Leo Held's life that could have presaged the end of it. Held, 40, a burly (6 ft., 200 lbs.), balding lab technician at a Lock Haven, Pa., paper mill, had been a school-board member, Boy Scout leader, secretary of a fire brigade, churchgoer and affectionate father. Certainly he bickered occasionally with his neighbors, drove too aggressively over the hilly highways between his Loganton home and the mill, and sometimes fretted about the job that he held for 19 years. But to most of his neighbors and co-workers, he was a paragon of the responsible, respectable citizen.

That image was shattered in a well-planned hour of bloodshed last week when Held decided to mount a one-man revolt against the world he feared and resented. After seeing his wife off to work and their children to school, Held, a proficient marksman, pocketed two pistols—a .45 automatic and a Smith & Wesson .38—and drove his station wagon to the mill. Parking carefully, he gripped a gun in each fist and stalked into the plant. Then he started shooting with a calculated frenzy that filled his fellow-worker victims with two and three bullets apiece, at least 30 shots in all. One bullet shattered a transformer, adding darkness to the sudden panic; yet throughout his ten-minute rampage, Held displayed the calm proficiency of a man who has mapped his assault in advance. Shot dead were Supervisors Carmen H. Edwards and Richard Davenport, Lab Technicians Allen R. Barrett and Elmer E. Weaver, and Superintendent Donald V. Walden. Picking his targets with care as he strode through the mill, Held also wounded James Allen, a superintendent; Richard Carter, a lab technician; David Overdorf, a machine operator, and a manager, Woodrow Stultz.

No More Bull. Stopping for a few casual words with incoming workers as he left the mill, Held next drove to the Lock Haven airport, where he shot at Switchboard Operator Gerry Ramm four times, wounding her twice. Thinking it was a prank, the airport manager hustled Held outside without a protest. Then Held's obsession sent him to the Sugar Valley School, where three of his own children and some 500 others had been locked inside after police had notified the principal of Held's rampage. After circling the school, Held drove home and invaded the house of Mr. and Mrs. Floyd Quiggle across the street. The Quiggles were still asleep in bed. Held's shots killed Quiggle instantly and critically wounded Mrs. Quiggle while their four-year-old daughter cowered under her own bed in fright. Helping himself to more ammunition and a rifle, Held went home.

A hastily formed posse found him in his doorway, armed and snarling defiance: "Come and get me. I'm not taking any more of their bull." Although Held's brother-in-law pleaded with him to surrender and bullets shattered his shoulder, leg and right wrist, Held switched the .38 to his left hand, firing until it, too, was smashed. Taken to a guarded hospital bed, he never regained full consciousness, dying later from the complications of his many wounds. He left behind a trail of six people wounded, six others dead.

One to Go. As news of Held's bloody rampage reverberated across central Pennsylvania, puzzled officials discovered a tenuous chain of logic behind his actions. Mrs. Ramm had quit a car pool, complaining of Held's driving. Many victims at the paper plant either were in authority over him or had been promoted while he had not. Held and Quiggle had feuded over smoke from burning leaves, and probers soon found that Held's stolid surface had masked truculence, resentment and rage. His doctor, noting that Held had shown paranoid tendencies a year ago, said: "He felt the people at the plant were talking about him." Another neighbor, Mrs. Ella Knisely, told of a spat over a fallen tree limb that so enraged Held he beat the 71-year-old widow with the branch. She took him to court on assault and battery charges, but the magistrate threw out her case and Held's cross complaint. If the jurist "had thought a little more carefully," said Mrs. Knisely, and seen that "here was a man who was sick and sent him to a psychiatrist, this thing could have been prevented."

Mrs. Knisely added that she wished Held had slain her instead of young Quiggle. Indeed, he may well have intended to include her with the rest. As he lay dying, doctors said, Held thanked a nurse for a glass of water, asked about his oldest son, and murmured, "I had one more to go."

119

Time, Nov. 3, 1967

from
"VIOLENCE:
A
NEGLECTED
MODE
OF
BEHAVIOR" Bruno Bettelheim

Nowadays, parents receive a great deal of help in accepting their children's instinctual desires, as far as intake and elimination are concerned. Even about sexual behavior we tend to be more understanding, more accepting in our emotional attitudes. But as far as violence is concerned, Freud might never have written *Civilization and its Discontents*, or have concluded it by saying:

> The fateful question for the human species seems to me to be whether and to what extent their cultural development will succeed in mastering the disturbance of their communal life by the human instinct of aggression and self-destruction.

If this is the fateful question, and I certainly agree that it is, what measures are we taking to help our children do a better job of mastering the disturbance of their communal life that comes from the instinct of aggression? Freud certainly did not mean denial or suppression to be the answer, any more than he meant it for our sexual instincts. About these drives we have followed his teaching and try to be reasonable. We try to satisfy them within acceptable limits, so that they do not generate so much pressure as to cause explosive outbreaks or a crippling of the total personality. In regard to violence I find no such reasonable efforts.

Children are supposed neither to hit, nor to swear at their playmates. They are supposed to refrain from destroying their toys or other property—so far, so good. But what outlets for violence *do* we provide for them? As a matter of fact, in regard to violence, we are so unreasonable that here is where the parent is apt to resort to violence himself. Few children of the educated middle class are slapped for masturbating any more, though they are not exactly raised in sexual freedom. But let the same parent meet with violence in his youngster, and as likely as not he will slap the child or thunder at him, thus demonstrating that violence is all right if one is older and stronger, and makes use of it under the guise of suppressing it. So we end by using violence to suppress violence, and in doing so teach our children that, in our opinion, there is just no other reasonable or intelligent way to deal with it. Yet the same parents, at another moment, would agree that suppression is the worst way to deal with the instincts. . . .

We have abolished the red-light districts and outlawed prostitution. I am all for such progress, mainly because it offers the girls more protection from being exploited. But for those who cannot afford the call girl, we have closed off an easy way to discharge both sexual and violent tendencies. Worse, by asserting that there is no place for sex outside of marriage, and none for violence in our society, we force each individual to suppress his violent tendencies till they build up to a pitch where he can no longer deny them or control them. Then they suddenly erupt in isolated acts of explosive violence.

These outbursts are conspicuous. By their spectacular nature they even give the impression that ours is an age of violence. So we clamor for still greater suppression of even small eruptions of violence that could act as safety valves, draining off small amounts and leaving a balance that the individual could assimilate. Even among psycho-analysts, Freud's death instinct is not quite respectable, because we decree that what is supposed not to exist cannot and does not exist; all evidence to the contrary is simply disregarded as nonexistent.

What I believe is needed, instead, is an intelligent recognition of "the nature of the beast." We shall not be able to deal intelligently with violence unless we are first ready to see it as part of human nature, until we have gotten so well acquainted with it, by learning to live with it, that through a slow and tenuous process we may one day domesticate it successfully. In short, we cannot say that because violence *should* not exist, we might as well proceed as if it did not.

52:13. Behold, my servant shall deal prudently, he shall be exalted and extolled, and be very high.

14. As many were astonied at thee; his visage was so marred more than any man, and his form more than the sons of men:

15. So shall he sprinkle many nations; the kings shall shut their mouths at him: for that which had not been told them shall they see; and that which they had not heard shall they consider.

53:1. Who hath believed our report? and to whom is the arm of the Lord revealed?

2. For he shall grow up before him as a tender plant, and as a root out of dry ground: he hath no form nor comeliness; and when we shall see him, there is no beauty that we should desire him.

3. He is despised and rejected of men; a man of sorrows, and acquainted with grief: and we hid as it were our faces from him; he was despised, and we esteemed him not.

4. Surely he hath borne our griefs, and carried our sorrows: yet we did esteem him stricken, smitten of God, and afflicted.

5. But he was wounded for our transgressions, he was bruised for our iniquities: the chastisement of our peace was upon him; and with his stripes we are healed.

6. All we like sheep have gone astray; we have turned every one to his own way; and the Lord hath laid on him the iniquity of us all.

7. He was oppressed, and he was afflicted, yet he opened not his mouth: he is brought as a lamb to the slaughter, and as a sheep before her shearers is dumb, so he openeth not his mouth.

8. He was taken from prison and from judgment: and who shall declare his generation? for he was cut off out of the land of the living: for the transgression of my people was he stricken.

9. And he made his grave with the wicked, and with the rich† in his death; because he had done no violence, neither was any deceit in his mouth.

10. Yet it pleased the Lord to bruise him; he hath put him to grief: when thou shalt make his soul an offering for sin, he shall see his seed, he shall prolong his days, and the pleasure of the Lord shall prosper in his hand.

11. He shall see the travail of his soul, and shall be satisfied: by his knowledge shall my righteous servant justify many; for he shall bear their iniquities.

12. Therefore will I divide him a portion with the great, and he shall divide the spoil with the strong; because he hath poured out his soul unto death: and he was numbered with the transgressors; and he bare the sin of many, and made intercession for the transgressors.

*Isaiah 52:13—53:12

†Some editors emend the Hebrew to give the meaning, "evildoers."

THE SCAPEGOAT

The word "scapegoat" is an invention of William Tindale's bible; it is not clear that the Old Testament word which it purports to translate is anything but a name. It was the name of one of a pair of sacrificial goats to which the community transferred its sins and so got rid of them. This custom was world-wide; the Jews were unusual only in being content to offer the life of an animal; for in many other places the scapegoat was human. The Athenians kept a reserve of such outcasts, and each spring drew from it one man and one woman and stoned them to death. On the Niger, the two victims were (and may still be) bought with the fines of those who had sinned; on this scale, grave sinners such as thieves and witches paid in 1858 about £2 apiece towards the cost of the human sacrifice. In Siam, the prostitute who was singled out to carry the sins of the community was not killed, but thrown on a dunghill beyond the walls and ever afterwards forbidden the city.

Many of these ceremonies are specific about the victim's sex, and in some of them sex is central to the sacrifice. The Asiatic Greeks began the murder of their human scapegoat to the sound of flutes, by beating him on his genitals with branches of the wild fig. Was this to expiate the universal sin of sex? Or was it to make their trees fertile? The Mexicans each year beheaded a girl at puberty so that her blood might be sprinkled in the temple of the goddess of maize. The Whitsun Mummers went dressed in leaves to their mock killing. In all this we catch in part a ritual in which the death of man makes nature fertile. . . .

J. BRONOWSKI

123

How can honorable men
cope with a ruthless enemy?

He is fanatical, diabolic, inhuman.

Stern measures are necessary. Fight fire with fire!

We must learn to
think as he thinks.

Plot and scheme
as he does.

125

Act as he acts. Hate as he hates.

WHOSE FACE IS THAT IN THE MIRROR?

The senseless murder of the President was a mirror we were forced to hold up to ourselves—and we did not like, or believe, the image that we saw.

"How could it happen here? In this day and age? In our country? I thought such things happened only in history. In Europe. Somewhere else and long ago."

These were the reactions of Americans. They bespoke a tremendous ignorance and delusiveness about ourselves. For, as I have written many times in the past (and have been assailed for so writing), we are a violent people who do not know the range and force of our primitive feelings.

Why should it not happen here? The last three Presidents out of four have had assassination attempts on their lives. Nowhere in Europe is this true; in most such countries, the chiefs of state walk about virtually unguarded.

In this day and age? This is the age of the most ferocious war the world has ever known, the most bloody dictatorships, the gas ovens, the concentration camps, the bombings of Hiroshima and Nagasaki by a "peace-loving" nation.

In our country? Why not, with our staggering homicide rate, our casual and callous auto fatalities, our shocking prevalence of firearms, our frontier relish for combat and conflict, our contempt for courts, our cynicism about the effectiveness of orderly processes.

If anyone still doubts this, consider the cry of applause that went up from the crowd gathered outside the Dallas jail when it learned that the presumed assassin of the President had himself been shot down.

This reaction is, to me, more appalling and more revealing than anything else in the whole nightmare of the weekend. Here was a man not known for sure to be the killer. He had not confessed, not been brought to trial, not defended, not sentenced. And he was killed while in the very hands of the police.

And the crowd outside shouted its approval of this bestial, stupid and irrational act. This is frightening, this is disgusting, this discloses the profound failure of our society to instill in its citizens any real sense of civilization, any idea of the meaning of law and justice. This is what turns our country into little better than a jungle.

If this dreadful murder of a President makes us see ourselves more clearly, makes us re-examine our feelings, makes us determined to purge the violence within each of us and all of us, it will not have been in vain.

Sydney Harris

THE MIRROR?

The senseless murder of the President was a mirror we were forced to hold up to ourselves—and we did not like, or believe, the image that we saw.

"How could it happen here? In this day and age? In our country? I thought such things happened only in history. In Europe. Somewhere else and long ago."

These were the reactions of Americans. They bespoke a tremendous ignorance and delusiveness about ourselves. For, as I have written many times in the past (and have been assailed for so writing), we are a violent people who do not know the range and force of our primitive feelings.

Why should it not happen here? The last three Presidents out of four have had assassination attempts on their lives. Nowhere in Europe is this true; in most such countries, the chiefs of state walk about virtually unguarded. In this day and age? This is the age of the most ferocious war the world has ever known, the most bloody dictatorships, the gas ovens, the concentration camps, the bombings of Hiroshima and Nagasaki by a "peace-loving" nation. In our country? Why not, with our staggering homicide rate, our casual and callous auto fatalities, our shocking prevalence of firearms, our frontier relish for combat and conflict, our contempt for courts, our cynicism about the effectiveness of orderly processes.

If anyone still doubts this, consider the cry of applause that went up from the crowd gathered outside the Dallas jail when it learned that the presumed assassin of the President had himself been shot down.

This reaction is, to me, more appalling and more revealing than anything else in the whole nightmare of the weekend. Here was a man not known for sure to be the killer. He had not confessed, not been brought to trial, not defended, not sentenced. And he was killed while in the very hands of the police. And the crowd outside shouted its approval of this bestial, stupid and irrational act. This is frightening, this is disgusting, this discloses the profound failure of our society to instill in its citizens any real sense of civilization, any idea of the meaning of law and justice. This is what turns our country into little better than a jungle.

If this dreadful murder of a President makes us see ourselves more clearly, makes us re-examine our feelings, makes us determined to purge the violence within each of us and all of us, it will not have been in vain

A Marine's Creed

I have lived and struggled my way through this life
Twisting and turning on its downward flight
Surmounting crises and overcoming strife
And hating demonstrators, our nation's blight.
I have travelled to countries and fought afar
Shooting at Slant-eyes in paddies of rice
Risking my life, but getting no cigar
Watching downed buddies is not very nice.
Dripping with cold sweat and covered with flies
Six course dinners in a C-ration can
Who can say wherein the real evil does lie?
At twenty feel like an eighty year old man.
I'm told I must be there then there I must be
For this is my duty, that we can be free.

John E. Dovale
Ed. Note: The author is a former
Marine Sergeant who saw action in Viet Nam.

128

A Lullaby

For wars his life and half a world away
The soldier sells his family and days.
He learns to fight for freedom and the State;
He sleeps with seven men within six feet.

He picks up matches and he cleans out plates;
Is lied to like a child, cursed like a beast.
They crop his head, his dog tags ring like sheep
As his stiff limbs shift wearily to sleep.

Recalled in dreams or letters, else forgot,
His life is smothered like a grave, with dirt;
And his dull torment mottles like a fly's
The lying amber of the histories.

Randall Jarrell

Department of State

BUREAU OF PUBLIC AFFAIRS

WHY WE ARE IN VIET-NAM

There is no doubt that our vital interests are deeply involved in Viet-Nam and in Southeast Asia. We are involved because the nation's word has been given that we would be involved. On February 1, 1955, by a vote of 82 to 1, the United States Senate passed the Southeast Asia Collective Defense Treaty. That Treaty stated that aggression by means of armed attack as defined in the Treaty would endanger our own peace and safety and, in that event, "we would act to meet the common danger." There is no question that an expanding armed attack by North Viet-Nam on South Viet-Nam has been under way in recent years; and six nations, with vital interests in the peace and security of the region, have joined South Viet-Nam in defense against that armed attack.

Behind the words and commitment of the Treaty lies the lesson learned in the tragic half century since the First World War. After that war our country withdrew from effective world responsibility. When aggressors challenged the peace in Manchuria, Ethiopia, and then Central Europe during the 1930's, the world community did not act to prevent their success. The result was a Second World War--which could have been prevented.

In short, we are involved in Viet-Nam because we know from painful experience that the minimum condition for order is that aggression must not be permitted to succeed. For when it does succeed, the consequence is not peace, it is the further expansion of aggression.

The leaders of free Asia have been heartened by our commitment to the defense of South Viet-Nam. The new vigor in Asia, the new hope and determination, are based in part on the conviction that the United States will continue to support the South Vietnamese in their struggle to build a new life of their own within the framework of the Geneva Accords of 1954 and 1962--that we shall see it through to an honorable peace.

We shall continue to do what is necessary--to protect the vital interests of the United States, to stand by our allies in Asia, and to work with all our energy for a peaceful, secure, and prosperous Southeast Asia. Only by meeting these commitments can we keep the minimum conditions for peace and order.

Race

NIGGER

And did ever a man go black with sun in a Belgian swamp,
On a feathery African plain where the sunburnt lioness lies,
And a coconut monkey grove where the cockatoos scratch the skies,
And the zebras striped with moonlight grasses gaze and stomp?

With a swatch of the baboon's crimson bottom cut for a lip,
And a brace of elephant ivories hung for a tusky smile,
With the muscles as level and lazy and long as the lifting Nile,
And a penis as loaded and supple and limp as the slaver's whip?

Are you beautiful still when you walk downtown in a knife-cut coat
And your yellow shoes dance at the corner curb like a brand new car,
And the buck with the arching pick looks over the new-laid tar
As you cock your eye like a cuckoo bird on a two-o'clock note?

When you got so little in steel-rim specks, when you taught that French,
When you wrote that book and you made that speech in the bottom south,
When you beat that fiddle and sang that role for Othello's mouth,
When you blew that horn for the shirt-sleeve mob and the snaky wench?

When you boxed that hun, when you raped that trash that you didn't rape,
When you caught that slug with a belly of fire and a face of gray,
When you felt that loop and you took that boot from a KKK,
Are you coming to peace, O Booker T. Lincoln Roosevelt of grape?

Did the Lord say yes, did the Lord say no, did you ask the Lord
When the jaw came down, when the cotton blossomed out of your bones?
Are you coming to peace, O Booker T. Lincoln Roosevelt Jones,
And is Jesus riding to raise your wage and cut that cord?

Karl Shapiro

134 /

"Trouble Every Day"

Well I'm about to get sick.
I was watchin' my T.V.
Just been checkin' out the news
That my eyeballs cannot see.
I've been sayin' everyday's a rotten mess.
And when it's gonna change is anybody's guess.
So I'm watchin' and a-waitin' and hopin' for the best.
You think I go astray when I hear them say
There is no other way than trouble comin' everyday.

Wednesday, I watched the riot.
I see cops out on the street,
Watchin' throwin' rocks and stuff and chokin' in the heat.
Listen to reports about the whiskey passin' round,
Seeing smoke and fire and the market burnin' down,
Watchin' while everybody on your street will take a turn.
They're stampin', mashin', crashin', bashin', bustin,' baby burn.

You can cool it, you can eat it, cause baby I don't need it.
Take your T.V. set and eat it.
All that phony stuff on sports
And all the unconfirmed reports.
And I watched that rotten box until my head began to hurt.
I've been checkin' out the way newsmen get the dirt before the guy on channel so and so.
If some woman driver gets machine gunned from the seat,
They say some joke about a Brownie,
And you see it all complete.
No way to delay that trouble comin' everyday.

And you know something people,
I'm not black, but there is a whole lot of times I wish I could say I'm not white.
When I see the fires burnin' and the lethal people turnin'
All the merchants and the shops who used to sell their brooms and mops
And every household item.
Watch 'em hard to turn and bite 'em.
And they say it served them right because a few of them are white.
It's the same across the nation,
Black and white discrimination
And the other you-can't-understand-me
And the other jazz they hand me
In the papers and T.V. and all that mass stupidity.
It seems to grow more everyday when you hear some nit-wit say
He must go and do you in for the color of your skin
Just don't appeal to him
No matter if it's black or white,
'Cause he's out for blood tonight.

You know we got to sit around at home and watch this thing begin,
And I bet there won't be many alive to see it really end.
'Cause the fire in the street ain't like the fire in the heart
And the eyes of all those people
Sayin', Don't you know that this could start
On any street of any town, in any state of any clown
Who decides that now's the time to fight
For some ideal that's "right."
And if a million more agree there ain't no great society
That applies to you and me, and our country isn't free.
And the law refuses to see
That all you'll ever be
Is a lousy janitor
Unless your brother owns the store.
You know, there are five in every four
Who are poor and nothing more.
So watch the rats go 'cross the floor,
And make up songs 'bout bein' poor.

Janis Ian

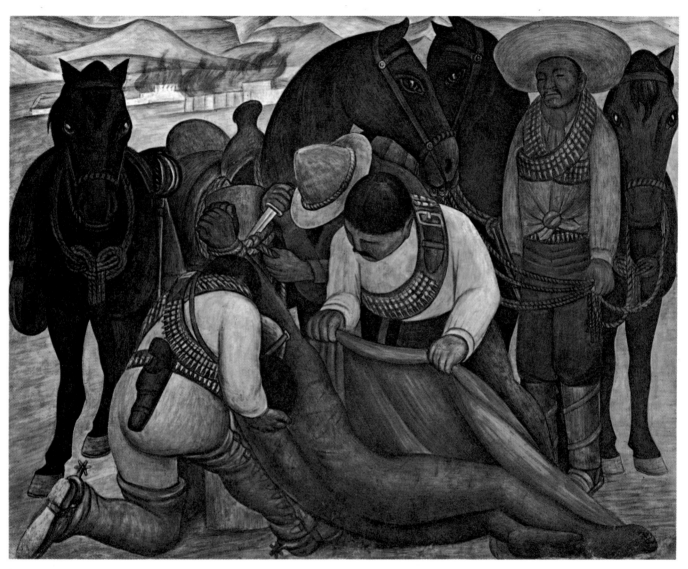

Diego Rivera: *Liberation of the Peon* 1931
Collection of the Philadelphia Museum of Art.

MIDDLE PASSAGE

1

Jesús, Estrella, Esperanza, Mercy:

> Sails flashing to the wind like weapons,
> sharks following the moans the fever and the dying;
> horror the corposant and compass rose.

Middle Passage:
> voyage through death
>   to life upon these shores.

> "10 April 1800—
> Blacks rebellious. Crew uneasy. Our linguist says
> their moaning is a prayer for death,
> ours and their own. Some try to starve themselves.
> Lost three this morning leaped with crazy laughter
> to the waiting sharks, sang as they went under."

Desire, Adventure, Tartar, Ann:

> Standing to America, bringing home
> black gold, black ivory, black seed.

> *Deep in the festering hold thy father lies,*
> *of his bones New England pews are made,*
> *those are altar lights that were his eyes.*

Jesus Saviour Pilot Me
Over Life's Tempestuous Sea

We pray that Thou wilt grant, O Lord,
safe passage to our vessels bringing
heathen souls unto Thy chastening.

Robert Hayden

Jesus Saviour

"8 bells. I cannot sleep, for I am sick
with fear, but writing eases fear a little
since still my eyes can see these words take shape
upon the page & so I write, as one
would turn to exorcism. 4 days scudding,
but now the sea is calm again. Misfortune
follows in our wake like sharks (our grinning
tutelary gods). Which one of us
has killed an albatross? A plague among
our blacks—Ophthalmia: blindness—& we
have jettisoned the blind to no avail.
It spreads, the terrifying sickness spreads.
Its claws have scratched sight from the Capt.'s eyes
& there is blindness in the fo'c'sle
& we must sail 3 weeks before we come
to port."

What port awaits us, Davy Jones'
or home? I've heard of slavers drifting, drifting,
playthings of wind and storm and chance, their crews
142 / *gone blind, the jungle hatred*
crawling up on deck.

Thou Who Walked On Galilee

"Deponent further sayeth *The Bella J*
left the Guinea Coast
with cargo of five hundred blacks and odd
for the barracoons of Florida:

"That there was hardly room 'tween-decks for half
the sweltering cattle stowed spoon-fashion there;
that some went mad of thirst and tore their flesh
and sucked the blood:

"That Crew and Captain lusted with the comeliest
of the savage girls kept naked in the cabins;
that there was one they called The Guinea Rose
and they cast lots and fought to lie with her:

"That when the Bo's'n piped all hands, the flames
spreading from starboard already were beyond
control, the negroes howling and their chains
entangled with the flames:

"That the burning blacks could not be reached,
that the Crew abandoned ship,
leaving their shrieking negresses behind,
that the Captain perished drunken with the wenches:

"Further Deponent sayeth not."

Pilot Oh Pilot Me

2

Aye, lad, and I have seen those factories,
Gambia, Rio Pongo, Calabar;
have watched the artful mongos baiting traps
of war wherein the victor and the vanquished

Were caught as prizes for our barracoons.
Have seen the nigger kings whose vanity
and greed turned wild black hides of Fellatah,
Mandingo, Ibo, Kru to gold for us.

And there was one—King Anthracite we named him—
fetish face beneath French parasols
of brass and orange velvet, impudent mouth
whose cups were carven skulls of enemies:

He'd honor us with drum and feast and conjo
and palm-oil-glistening wenches deft in love,
and for tin crowns that shone with paste,
red calico and German-silver trinkets

Would have the drums talk war and send
his warriors to burn the sleeping villages
and kill the sick and old and lead the young
in coffles to our factories.

Twenty years a trader, twenty years,
for there was wealth aplenty to be harvested
from those black fields, and I'd be trading still
but for the fevers melting down my bones.

3

Shuttles in the rocking loom of history,
the dark ships move, the dark ships move,
their bright ironical names
like jests of kindness on a murderer's mouth;
plough through thrashing glister toward
fata morgana's lucent melting shore,
weave toward New World littorals that are
mirage and myth and actual shore.

Voyage through death,
        voyage whose chartings are unlove.

A charnel stench, effluvium of living death
spreads outward from the hold,
where the living and the dead, the horribly dying,
lie interlocked, lie foul with blood and excrement.

Deep in the festering hold thy father lies,
the corpse of mercy rots with him,
rats eat love's rotten gelid eyes.

But, oh, the living look at you
with human eyes whose suffering accuses you,
whose hatred reaches through the swill of dark
to strike you like a leper's claw.

You cannot stare that hatred down
or chain the fear that stalks the watches
and breathes on you its fetid scorching breath;
cannot kill the deep immortal human wish,
the timeless will.

"But for the storm that flung up barriers
of wind and wave, *The Amistad,* señores,
would have reached the port of Príncipe in two,
three days at most; but for the storm we should
have been prepared for what befell.
Swift as the puma's leap it came. There was
that interval of moonless calm filled only
with the water's and the rigging's usual sounds,
then sudden movement, blows and snarling cries
and they had fallen on us with machete
and marlinspike. It was as though the very
air, the night itself were striking us.

Exhausted by the rigors of the storm,
we were no match for them. Our men went down
before the murderous Africans. Our loyal
Celestino ran from below with gun
and lantern and I saw, before the cane-
knife's wounding flash, Cinquez,
that surly brute who calls himself a prince,
directing, urging on the ghastly work.
He hacked the poor mulatto down, and then
he turned on me. The decks were slippery
when daylight finally came. It sickens me
to think of what I saw, of how these apes
threw overboard the butchered bodies of
our men, true Christians all, like so much jetsam.
Enough, enough. The rest is quickly told:
Cinquez was forced to spare the two of us
you see to steer the ship to Africa,
and we like phantoms doomed to rove the sea
voyaged east by day and west by night,
deceiving them, hoping for rescue,
prisoners on our own vessel, till
at length we drifted to the shores of this
your land, America, where we were freed
from our unspeakable misery. Now we
demand, good sirs, the extradition of
Cinquez and his accomplices to La
Havana. And it distresses us to know
there are so many here who seem inclined
to justify the mutiny of these blacks.
We find it paradoxical indeed
that you whose wealth, whose tree of liberty
are rooted in the labor of your slaves
should suffer the august John Quincy Adams
to speak with so much passion of the right
of chattel slaves to kill their lawful masters
and with his Roman rhetoric weave a hero's
garland for Cinquez. I tell you that
we are determined to return to Cuba
with our slaves and there see justice done. Cinquez—
or let us say 'the Prince'—Cinquez shall die."

The deep immortal human wish,
the timeless will:

        Cinquez its deathless primaveral image,
        life that transfigures many lives.

Voyage through death
                to life upon these shores.

THE MOJO

Abraham Taylor

There was always the time when the white man been ahead of the colored man. In slavery times John had done got to a place where the Marster whipped him all the time. Someone told him, "Get you a mojo, it'll get you out of that whipping, won't nobody whip you then."

John went down to the corner of the Boss-man's farm, where the mojo-man stayed, and asked him what he had. The mojo-man said, "I got a pretty good one and a very good one and a damn good one." The colored fellow asked him, "What can the pretty good one do?" "I'll tell you what it can do. It can turn you to a rabbit, and it can turn you to a quail, and after that it can turn you to a snake." So John said he'd take it.

Next morning John sleeps late. About nine o'clock the white man comes after him, calls him: "John, come on, get up there and go to work. Plow the taters and milk the cow and then you can go back home—it's Sunday morning." John says to him, "Get on out from my door, don't say nothing to me. Ain't gonna do nothing." Boss-man says, "Don't you know who this is? It's your Boss." "Yes, I know—I'm not working for you any more." "All right, John, just wait till I go home; I'm coming back and whip you."

White man went back and got his pistol, and told his wife, "John is sassy, he won't do nothing I tell him, I'm gonna whip him." He goes back to John, and calls, "John, get up there." John yells out, "Go on away from that door and quit worrying me. I told you once, I ain't going to work."

Well, then the white man he falls against the door and broke it open. And John said to his mojo, "Skip-skip-skip-skip." He turned to a rabbit, and run slap out the door by Old Marster. And he's a running son of a gun, that rabbit was. Boss-man says to his mojo, "I'll turn to a greyhound." You know that greyhound got running so fast his paws were just reaching the grass under the rabbit's feet.

Then John thinks, "I got to get away from here." He turns to a quail. And he begins sailing fast through the air—he really thought he was going. But the Boss-man says, "I will turn to a chicken hawk." That chicken hawk sails through the sky like a bullet, and catches right up to that quail.

Then John says, "Well, I'm going to turn to a snake." He hit the ground and begin to crawl; that old snake was natchally getting on his way. Boss-man says, "I'll turn to a stick and I'll beat your ass."

Two Worlds of One: Black and

My mind's segregation.
One must, one won't.
Two worlds of thought:
One will, one won't.

Two worlds of one,
One scared, one trust.
My mind's integration:
I can't. I must.

Jill Halley
(student)

First Little Rock.

Then Oxford.

We've had about enough from the South.

The Negro must be given his rights, now!   The South is his home.

And we can't have 'em up here, ruining real estate in Chicago.

From ON EDGE by Jim Crane; Copyright © M. E. Bratcher, 1965.
Reprinted by permission of John Knox Press.

"Just How Do You Relax Colored People at Parties?"

Lenny Bruce

The geography in this bit is unimportant, but I'm always searching for new areas, so I'll change it tonite to, ummm, Watertown, N.Y. That's a little ways from Buffalo and Niagara Falls.

Actually, it's eighty tract homes, and we are now in the "Medallion Model Home," with a formica ceiling. I'm a construction boss. I built all these pads. This pad I built for about eighteen thousand five hundred dollars, I dumped it for sixty thousand—lotta built-ins.

Now, they have a party—when I sell the pad, the people hold a big house-warming party, right? And who do they invite? They invite the guy who built the house, and the neighbors. Eric,* being colored, he would be a musician, which does not make the people who have the party bigoted in the least. Because many people do not know colored people, though to invite them to a party as a prop is Crow Jim. And there's a good book on Crow Jim: Ralph Ellison, *The Invisible Man,* man, which really lays it on the stick, man.

Now, the party is swinging, and the humor emanates from the now-becoming-obscure white person's concept of "Just How Do You Relax Colored People at Parties?" And in the bit, I play the white guy:

White Man [*rasping, aggressive voice*]: Oh, boy, what a hell of a party, eh?

Negro [*clear, well-educated*]: Yeah, I'm enjoying myself, having a wonderful time.

White: I really stuffed myself, boy, and I'm pissed to the ears, too, on top of it. Oh, boy . . . Before you drink you should take a tablespoonful of olive oil.

Negro: Is that right?

White: Thass the best . . .

Negro: Oh.

White: I didn't get your name.

Negro: Miller.

White: Miller, my name is Mr. Anderson.

Negro: Mr. Anderson, glad to know you.

White: Pleasure to know you indeed, sir.

[*Pause. Neither knows what to say next.*]

White: You know, that Joe Louis was a hell of a fighter.

*Eric Miller, a Negro guitarist who helped Bruce occasionally by taking The Negro's part in this bit.

Negro: Yeah, you can say that again. Joe Louis was a hell of a fighter.

White: What a man, boy.

Negro: Yeah, got right in there, right out.

White: He's a credit to your race. Don't you ever forget that, you sonofagun.

Negro: Well, thank you very much.

White: Thass awright, perfectly awright.

[*Pause*]

White: Well, here's to Henry Armstrong.

Negro: Yeah, here's to Henry Armstrong.

White: Awright . . .

[*Pause*]

White: You know, I did all the construction here, you know?

Negro: Oh, you did?

White: I did all except the painting, and these Hebes—[*whispers*] you're not Jewish, are you?

Negro: No, man, I'm not.

White: You know what I mean?

Negro: Yeah, I understand.

White: Someone calls me a Sheeney I'll knock em right on their ass . . . I wanna tell you sometin. I don't care what the hell a guy is so long as they keep in their place, you know?

Negro: Right.

White: So anyway, I tell all these Mochs—Jewish people, you know—I say, I'm gonna put up the lath. You know how they talk you know, "Vut tchou doink, dahlink"? You know? I'll tell you some Aby-and-Becky jokes later. So anyway, they say, "Vut tchou doink vit de paint," you know? That's Chinese—I do all the dialects. And, ah, then they pick out this color—themselves—isn't that a crappy color for ya?

Negro: No, I don't think so. I think that's very interesting, how they use the Dufy Blue with so many other pastels.

White: That sounds like alotta Commie horseshit to me—Du-fee blue.

Negro: Yeah, that's what it is, a Dufy blue.

White: Whatthehellissat?

Negro: Some French painter derived that color. I dunno.

White: Yeah? Du-Fee blue! I like that. That's pretty good. Du-fee blue. You didn't learn that in the back of the bus, you sonufagun! You're awright! Du-fee blue. How 'bout that. You know, you're a white Jew, you're O.K. You're really a good guy.

Negro: Thank you, thank you.

[*Pause*]

White: Well, here's to Stephen Fetcher.

Negro: Yeah, here's to Stephen Fetcher.

[*Pause*]

White: I guess you know alotta people in the show business, eh?

Negro: Yeah, I've met quite a few in my travels.

White: Aaaah, I'm bad on names, what the hell is that, aaaaah . . . You know Aunt Jemimah?

Negro: No, I don't know Aunt Jemimah. I'm sorry, I don't know her.

White: That guy on the—on the Cream of Wheat box?

Negro: No, I don't know him either.

[*Pause*]

White: Well, here's to Paul Robinson.

Negro: Yeah, here's to Paul Robinson.

White: Yeah, boy . . . . You get anything to eat yet?

Negro: No, I'm kinda hungry. I wish I had a sandwich or something.

White: I haven't got any fried chicken or watermelon, ahhh . . . raisins, or rice, whatever you people eat, but, aaahhhh, we'll get sometin up for you there . . .

You know sometin, you're awright, you know that? And I'm a good guy too—you see what I just did? *I touched ya.* Yeah! You're awright. Come over here. I like you, you sonofagun, you're awright.

Negro: Well, thank you . . .

White: I'd like to have you over the house.

Negro: Well, thank you very much. I'd like to come over.

White: Wouldja like that?

Negro: Umhum.

White: It'll be dark soon, aaahhh . . . I mean, what the hell, you know, aaahhh. . . . You gotta be careful they're all movin' in . . . you know? I mean, what the hell, I read some jerk overn the paper, *The Howard Star,* there, they're jus bein smart, you know—that first, the Indians were here, then when the white people came they said "Oh Christ the white people are moving in," you know, and they're gonna be all over, you know—but that's dangerous, that kinda talk, you know?

[*Pause*]

White: Here's to all colored people.

Negro: O.K.

White: Awright . . . Now, I wanya to comover the house, but I gotta tell ya somtin cause I know you people get touchy once in a while.

Negro: Oh, umhm?

White: Yeah, ahhh, I gotta sister, ya see?

Negro: Yeah?

White: Well now cummere. [*Whispers*] You wouldn't wanna Jew doin it to your sister, wouldja?

Negro: It doesn't make any difference to me, just as long as he's a nice guy.

White: *Whattayou, on the weed or somtin?* Look, nobody wants a Sheeney plowin' their sister, an I don't want no coon doin' it to my sister. What the hell, that makes sense. You can come over my house if you promise you don't do it to my sister. Promise?

Negro: O.K.

White: Awright.

Negro: Here's to the Mau Mau.

White: Awright.

The guy in this bit, we assume—see, that's the funny thing about indictment—we assume that this cat is all bad, then, and we destroy him. But you can't, man. He's bad in this sense, cause he has not matured, he has not been in a proper environment, cause if he were, to learn and to listen, he would swing, cause there are sensitive parts to him also, man. Cause the weird part we get hung up with, "I am pure and I am good, and those people are dirty and those murderers are bad and I am so pure, I'm so good that I have to murder those murderers." And then you end up getting screwed up. That's right.

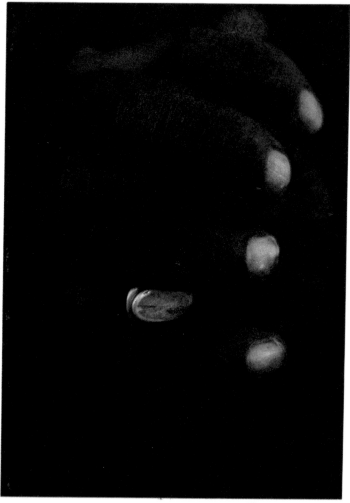

Photograph by Art Kane.

Soul is sass, man. Soul is arrogance. Soul is walkin' down the street in a way that says, "This is me, muh-fuh!" Soul is that nigger whore comin' along . . . ja . . . ja . . . ja, and walkin' like she's sayin', "Here it is, baby. Come an' git it." Soul is bein' true to yourself, to what is *you*. Now, hold on: soul is . . . that . . . uninhibited . . . no, *extremely* uninhibited self . . . expression that goes into practically every Negro endeavor. That's soul. And there's swagger in it, man. It's exhibitionism, and it's effortless. Effortless. You don't need to put it on; it just comes out.—*Claude Brown*

When I walk on Eighth Avenue, man, I see rhythms I don't see downtown. *Polyrhythms.* You look at one cat, he may be doin' bop, bop-bop bop, bop-bop, and another one goin' *bop*-de-bop, *de*-bop. Beautiful, man. Those are *beautiful* people. Yeah. But when I go downtown to Thirty-fourth Street, everybody's walkin' the same, you dig? They don't put themselves into it. Their walk tells you nothing about who they are. *Polyrhythms.* That's what it is. Like a flower garden in a breeze. The roses swing a little bit from side to side, kind of stiff, not too much. The lilacs swing wide, slow, lazy, not in a hurry. A blade of grass wiggles. It's 'cause they're all different and they're bein' themselves. Polyrhythms, like on Eighth Avenue. That's soul.—*Al Calloway*

The style of soul is about nurturing creativity, being aesthetic in thought and action as much as possible. It permeates one's entire existence. In Harlem, as in all of America's urban black communities, the style is seen in the way a soul brother selects and wears his vines (suit, coat, tie, shirt, etc.). The hat and shoes are most important. If they are *correct*, it is certain that his whole thing is beautiful. You know that he's a cat who cares about himself. His hat will be a soft beaver, felt or velour, blocked in whatever way he may feel at any given time. He buys the best hat and while he's in his crib playing tunes and laying with his woman he may just let his hands go all over the hat like a potter does his clay. Thus, he creates his thing. A soul brother's shoes are always pointy-toed and so shined that he can almost adjust his hat while looking at them. . . .

—*Al Calloway*

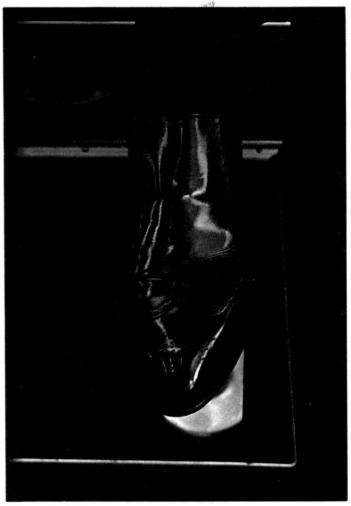

Photograph by Art Kane.

FROM CRISIS IN BLACK AND WHITE

Charles E. Silberman

. . . apathy appears to be the crux of the Negro's ''Negro problem.'' But apathy is itself just a cover for a more basic problem: self-hatred. ''The Negro,'' says Elijah Muhammad, titular head of the Black Muslims, ''wants to be everything but himself. He wants to be a white man. He processes his hair. Acts like a white man. He wants to integrate with the white man, but he cannot integrate with himself or his own kind. The Negro wants to lose his identity because he does not know his own identity.''

. . . Negro Americans have *always* had a problem of identity more serious than that faced by any white. James Baldwin has written movingly of the enormous toll extracted by the effort to discover his own identity, which required first that he escape from the traditional stereotype of the Negro in America. His father, Baldwin tells us, had ''had a terrible life; he was defeated long before he died because, at the bottom of his heart, he really believed what white people said about him.'' Young Jimmy tried terribly hard not to believe ''what the white people said,'' and so he struggled to avoid anything that might smack of the old stereotype—refusing to eat watermelon or to listen to Negro jazz. It was only when he began living the life of an American expatriate in Paris that Baldwin began to resolve the question of his own identity.

   As long as he lived in the United States, he writes, ''there was not, no matter where one turned, any acceptable image of oneself, no proof of one's existence. One had the choice, either of 'acting just like a nigger' or of *not* acting just like a nigger—and only those who have tried it know how impossible it is to tell the difference.''

   What makes the problem of Negro identity so complex and tortuous for both white and black is the fact that the ''nigger'' of whom Baldwin complains is not purely a figment of the white imagination. On the contrary, he was, and to a considerable degree still is, a reality—the end-product of the American system of slavery. To say this is not to accept the Southern view of inherent Negro inferiority, nor is it to insist that all Negroes are alike; obviously they are not. It is, rather, to insist that the problem of Negro personality and behavior be faced squarely and honestly.

   . . . Negroes *do* display less ambition than whites; as we have seen, apathy (with the self-hatred

that produces it) is the worst disease of the Negro slum. Negroes *do* have ''looser morals'': there is no belying the promiscuity of the Negro slumdweller or the high and apparently growing rate of illegitimacy. The Negro crime rate is substantially higher than the white. Negroes do ''care less for family''; the rate of separation is six times greater among Negro families than among the white. Negroes score lower on IQ tests than whites of comparable socio-economic status, and Negro children do poorer work in school.

   To acknowledge these unpleasant facts, however, does not imply that they are inherent characteristics or that they reflect intrinsic Negro inferiority. On the contrary, every one of them can be explained by the facts of Negro history in the United States. . . . The American Negro has been subject to a system designed to destroy ambition, prevent independence, and erode intelligence for the past three and a half centuries. Hence, nothing could be more foolish or more damaging to the Negro cause, than to refuse to face the harsh reality of what three hundred fifty years of white oppression have done to Negro personality and behavior. Uncomfortable as we all may find the truth, the truth is that the ''nigger'' with which Baldwin is obsessed, the ''Sambo'' of Southern folklore, was a reality and to a considerable extent still is. Not for all Negroes, certainly, and not in all places—but for enough Negroes, in enough places, over a long enough time, that the Negro cannot move into the main stream of American life unless he is able to destroy the image in his own mind and in the mind of the white. That image stems directly from slavery. A hundred years after its abolition, Negroes are still bound by its effects on their minds and spirits. . . .

Government Injunction Restraining
Harlem Cosmetic Co.

They say La Jac Brite Pink Skin Bleach avails not,
They say its Orange Beauty Glow does not glow,
Nor the face grow five shades lighter nor the heart
Five shades lighter. They say no.

They deny good luck, love, power, romance, and inspiration
From La Jac Brite ointment and incense of all kinds,
And Condemn in writing skin brightening and whitening
And whitening of minds.

There is upon the federal trade commission a burden of glory
So to defend the fact, so to impel
The plucking of hope from the hand, honor from the complexion,
Spirit from the spell.

Josephine Miles

Black is beautiful.

Naturally beautiful. But there's one requirement: naturally
beautiful skin. That's where Nadinola comes in.
Nadinola brings out the natural beauty of your complexion, gives
you a smooth, glowing skin tone that's even all over. No blotches.
No uneven dark areas. No blemishes. Just a beautiful you.
Black is beautiful. What makes it even more beautiful?
Nadinola. Naturally.

1. **Ultra Nadinola.** For blotchy skin. With special ingredient Dimatron® that
   searches out and fades dark areas and blotches caused by over-active
   skin pigment cells.
2. **Deluxe Nadinola.** For oily skin. Creams deeply into the skin, fights
   blemishes and leaves your skin wonderfully conditioned.
3. **Original Nadinola.** For dry skin. Creams and brightens to restore an even-
   all-over skin tone.
4. **Deluxe Nadinola Soap.** Creams, cleanses, conditions skin beautifully.

Nadinola • Chattanooga, Tennessee 37409

Nadinola smooths the way.

I HATE BLACK

I hate ants because they're black.
I hate toads because they're black.
I hate dirt because its black.
I hate the sea because its black.
I don't want to hate myself!
I'm black, I'm black, I'm ugly black.

Susan Drobac (*student*)

158 /

"All right, all right, class — now that we've had our little laugh . . ."

Wonders Never Cease

God's gift . . .

    tall, dark & ugly, with a
    mopped head and developed
    vocabulary of I'm hip and
    dig, stated that he was a
    lover . .

        big car
        forty suits
        no job
        "I" complex
        smooth line
        no line
        thinks positive
        hurts self
        recovered
        cool-
        sunglasses
        fixed smile
        no smile,
        his wife
        runrunrunGod'sgift

                . . . to women.

Don Lee

The Psychobiology of Racial Violence

LOUIS JOLYON WEST, MD

One man is very much like another. To a remarkable degree our brains and other organs look and work alike. Our blood can safely be transfused between "races." Type O blood from a Negro donor can save the life of a white man who would be killed by a transfusion of type A blood from his own brother. Matched for type, all men are blood brothers. Yet Dr. Charles Drew, the brilliant Negro physician who developed the blood bank, bled to death after a North Carolina highway accident when he was refused admission and transfusion at a segregated white hospital.

This was no less an act of racial violence than the assassination of Medgar Evers, or the murder of Mrs. Viola Liuzzo, or the group slaughter of three civil rights workers in Mississippi, or the bombing of a Birmingham church full of Negro Sunday-school children, or thousands of other acts of senseless savagery based on race alone.

Where does racial violence come from, and what does it mean? Biological differences—including surface features, bones, teeth, muscular attachments, and certain chemistries—are employed by anthropologists to classify racial types and subtypes. However, the range of individual differences *within* so-called major racial groups is far greater than mean differences be-

tween them in many respects, even with regard to such basic criteria for differentiation as skin color. Personality differences range even more widely. Blocs of standard whites and standard Negroes do not humanly exist. In this paper the terms "Negro" and "white" are therefore used as generalizations which are so far removed from human specificity as to be only marginally meaningful; but in the shadow of that margin lie the most violently destructive human passions.

Relatively few inquiries into the psychodynamics of racial prejudice in the United States have been undertaken since the original appearance in 1944 of Myrdal's classic monograph, *An American Dilemma.* Some have pointed out, as he did, the prominent relationship between violence toward Negroes by whites, and fear of sexual contact between Negro men and white women. However, most of these studies have raised the sexual issue only to dismiss it without exploring it in depth. Myrdal himself declared the white Southerner's preoccupation with intermarriage to be merely a rationalization for a more basic concern with social caste. *"What white people really want is to keep the Negroes in a lower status."*[1] Allport's treatise, *The*

1. Myrdal, G.: *An American Dilemma,* New York: Harper & Brothers, 1944.

Nature of Prejudice, also touches rather lightly on this issue. He postulates that the white woman's prejudice against Negroes is a defense against the projection of her own secret fascination. Allport relates the white man's prejudice to fear of retaliation because of his own crossracial sexual adventures, or to "anxiety concerning his own sexual adequacy."[2]

Psychiatry has addressed itself surprisingly little to the psychopathology of racial prejudice and violence, although there are a few case studies and commentaries by such on-the-spot students of the problem as Brody, Lief, Coles, Fishman, Solomon, Pierce and West.[3-9] Kubie has postulated that prejudice relates, among other things, to the child's hidden profound aversion to his own body (an aversion which oscillates with a secret guilty pride). The concept of "dirt" becomes deeply connected to this aversion so that the member of the rejected group is referred to as the *dirty* foreigner. But since dirt in our everyday mythology has a magic potential—sex is dirty—the dirty stranger of our fantasies is also bigger, stronger, and "endowed with a super potency which we fear and envy."[10]

My own observations on race and sex have been conducted over the past 15 years in a wide variety of situations, with primary concern for exploration of the irrational elements involved in generating violent emotions and violent behavior. Instinctual territoriality has been carefully considered and rejected as a major source of human conflict; I believe man is more like the elephant and the gorilla (mobile, nonterritorial) than he is like the wasp or the wolf.

Sexual and racial feelings and attitudes have been explored among more than 800 individuals, racially mixed couples, men and women who have had sexual experiences with partners of two or more races, civil rights demonstrators, and a variety of normal subjects, as well as psychiatric patients. Riots involving two or more ethnic groups, and recent riotous uprisings by Negroes in urban ghettos, while instructive, are considered secondary manifestations and have not figured significantly in my formulations of basic dynamics. Unjustified violent feelings and actions by whites against Negroes (on seeming racial grounds alone) are here taken as the major criteria. Although this work is naturalistic rather than experimental, and far from complete, some preliminary formulations may be useful to stimulate discussion and further inquiry by others.

2. Allport, G. W.: *The Nature of Prejudice,* Cambridge, Mass: Addison-Wesley Publishing Co., Inc. 1954, pp. 375–376.

3. Brody, E. B.: Color and Identity Conflict in Young Boys: Observations of Negro Mothers and Sons in Urban Baltimore, *Psychiatry* **26**:188–201, 1963.

4. Lief, H. I.: An Atypical Stereotype of the Negroes' Social Worlds, *Amer J Orthopsychiat* **32**:86–88, 1962.

5. Coles, R.: Observation or Participation: The Problem of Psychiatric Research on Social Issues, *J Nerv Ment Dis* **141**:274–284, 1965.

6. Fishman, J., and Solomon, F.: Youth and Social Action: I. Perspectives on Student Sit-In Movement, *Amer J Orthpsychiat* **33**:872–882, 1963.

7. Solomon, F., and Fishman, J. R.: Youth and Social Action: II. Action and Identity Formation in First Student Sit-In Demonstration, *J Soc Issues* **20**:36–45, 1964.

8. Pierce, C. M., and West, L. J.: Six Years of Sit-Ins: Psychodynamic Causes and Effects, *Int J Psychiat* **12**:29–34, 1966.

9. Solomon, F., et al: Civil Rights Activity and Reduction in Crime Among Negroes, *Arch Gen Psychiat* **12**:227–236, 1965.

10. Kubie, L. S.: The Ontogeny of Racial Prejudice, *J Nerv Ment Dis* **141**:265–273, 1965.

The Aftermath of Slavery

The United States continues to pay a penalty for its history of human slavery. Abolished more than a century ago, the curse of slavery seems destined to persist even beyond the seventh generation. Negroes are apprehensive of continued white exploitation; whites guiltily anticipate Negro revenge. As Clark points out, both groups are trapped in a human predicament from which they cannot escape without mutual aid. "Each one needs the other—the white to be free of his guilt, the Negro to be free of his fear."[11]

The Negro may react to feelings of inferiority (engendered by cultural influences from the day of his birth) in various ways, ranging from apathetic disclaimers of ambition to frenetic rebelliousness. The white man may react to feelings of guilt (engendered by empathy with the oppressed) in various ways, ranging from bitter denial of white culpability—and correspondingly violent antagonism toward the Negro—to the self-deceiving protestations of being wholly without prejudice that characterize Clark's *Delusions of the White Liberal.*[12]

Social, economic, cultural, educational, and political inequities persist in the wake of slavery. Such inequities are rapidly institutionalized by human society. The need to justify the inequity creates the shibboleths of prejudice, and the self-sustaining tendency of all social structures perpetuates both the discriminatory circumstance (e.g., the ghetto) and the prejudicial attitude (e.g., racial supremacy).

Under these conditions there develops a characteristic mythology, from which derivative secondary attitudes emerge. Thus the "master" group comes to view the "slave" group as being actually better off than they would be otherwise, really preferring their subjugated state, living like animals from choice, and not being truly human.

The Mythology of Blackness

The special mythology of the Negro in America has been highly color-bound. He is still called "black" no matter how light a shade of tan he may be, and the prejudice that goes with his color is peculiarly linked with his descent from slaves, since other dark-skinned people are not rejected in exactly the same way. The economic, social, political, and cultural aspects of the American Negro's persecution have been discussed extensively elsewhere. For the moment, however, in pursuit of the irrational, let us consider one point: blackness. Why should it make such a difference?

Human beings live by their eyesight. The global rhythm of light and dark, day and night, has a profound influence upon us. This diurnal cycle affects our most basic biological and psychological processes. For man daytime is the good time, the safe time, the healthy time, when he can see what's going on and make his way in the world. The *day*dream is happy aspiration; but the *night*mare is consummate terror. Even the air at night is bad (malaria), full of unhealthy influences (influenza). Night is the time of secrets, mystery, magic, danger, evil; and the man of the night is black.

11. Clark, K. B.: *Dark Ghetto,* New York: Harper & Row Publishers, 1965.
12. Clark, K. B.: *Delusions of the White Liberal, New York Times Magazine,* **27**:135–137, 1965.

164 /

The ignorant European peasants of the Middle (Dark!) Ages, who had never seen or heard of Negroes, invented black demons and devils. Sometimes at night they practiced the black mass and worshipped a phallic Satan—painted black. Even among the tribes of deepest Africa the word for black in many dialects is the same as the word for danger, evil, or threat. When an American Negro social scientist recently visited Central Africa, he was astonished to find that he was called "white" by the natives. His skin was dark as theirs, but he was known to be civilized, educated, *enlightened.*

There are many examples of the semantic "goodness" of white (e.g., fair, bright, unblemished, whitewashed, spotless, unsullied, immaculate, clean, illuminated, pure as the driven snow). Levin, in *The Power of Blackness,* quotes Jonathan Edwards to the effect that, "Since holiness comprehends all the other virtues, it is typified by white, which also represents purity because it signifies mother's milk and childish innocence . . . while sin, sorrow, and death are all represented in Scripture by darkness or the color black . . . ."[13]

Now consider blackening of character (denigration!), blackhearted blackguards, blackmail, blackball, blacklist, black marks, black looks, black words, black deeds. Black is the pit where the Prince of Darkness reigns. Magic is the black art (or at least black magic is the wicked kind). "They that touch pitch shall be defiled." Even the bad bile of melancholy is black.

Perhaps the light of reason, and extended personal contact, can be expected some day to alleviate the rejection of the "black" person in a "white" society, but the contact must be *human* if the myth is to be dispelled. Segregation stultifies human transactions and perpetuates interracial mythology.

The Myth of Negro Sexuality

One of the most profoundly distorted but emotionally explosive aspects of American racial mythology has to do with the sexuality of the Negro. The colored man is imagined to possess an enormous phallus, endless virility, and in addition, perhaps some woman-enslaving jungle magic. A common Southern tale has it that a white woman who mates with a Negro will never be satisfied with a white man again. As this superstition suggests, many whites hate the idea of contact between the Negro man and the white woman, a pair that might be termed "the dynamite dyad" because it is so explosive.

Much of the violence over school desegregation, and most of the racist "hate literature," is couched in terms of the danger to the purity of white womanhood, the horrors of miscegenation, and the like. The concern over sexual relations between white women and nonwhite men is apparently the primary emotional basis for the persistence of statutes forbidding racial intermarriage, often inaccurately termed antimiscegenation laws. Nineteen of our 50 states still list such clearly unconstitutional prohibitions in their legal codes. However, "mongrelization" is apparently perceived as a danger only when white women are involved.

In Oklahoma it is possible to consider this matter in crosscultural terms involving

13. Levin, H.: *Power of Blackness,* New York: Vintage Books, Inc., 1958, p. 32.

both Negroes and Indians. Some Indian blood is considered an honor: politicians boast of being 1/64 Cherokee. Some Negroes try to "pass" as Indians; a white woman marries an Indian without giving a thought to the anti-miscegenation law. In spite of the historical fact that for more than 250 years in North America whites were often raped, enslaved, and slain by Indians while the Negro was the white man's helper, it is still the Negro who appears in the white Oklahoma maiden's dream as the ominous rapist, and the sight of a Negro boy dancing with a white girl still moves Oklahomans to feelings and acts of violence. For the Indian was never enslaved, so he remains "the noble *red* man" (dark brown though he may be); while the former slave—whose black feelings every nonslave secretly understands—is feared for his universally comprehended revenge. In one version did not Oedipus, when his father whipped him aside on the road, slay him and rape his mother on his father's corpse?

In point of fact the Negro man is far from the potent black beast of the white man's fantasies. Broken homes, dependency, and intimidation have been shown to cause frequent passivity and impotence in Negro men, among whom homosexuality is also a growing problem. The Negro boy, racked with frustration and ravaged by poverty and deprivation, may turn against society through the losing game of crime, or turn away through the futile escape of drugs, or drop out of school (twice as many Negro girls as boys are in college), or succumb to tuberculosis or malignant hypertension or just plain malnutrition to die, on the average, seven years younger than his white counterpart.[14] The extent to which caste sanctions and the threat of

violence adversely affect the entire personality development of the Negro has been precisely documented by Karon,[15] who shows with chilling objectivity how (especially in the South) deprivation of hope can be the most crushing consequence of the Negro's struggle with an overwhelming negative identity.

What, then, makes the Negro man such a special sexual threat? No anthropometric data show that mean racial differences in adult erect genital size approach the great range of individual differences catalogued centuries ago in the Kama Sutra. But suppose the average Negro phallus were larger than that of the white. What would this mean? The clinical experience of psychiatrists and marriage counselors clearly reveals that a large penis does not correlate at all with virility or the ability to give special satisfaction in coitus, and it is now evident from studies of sexual physiology, such as those of Masters and Johnson,[16] that a small penis is a most unlikely basis for sexual incompatibility. In fact, "too large" rather than "too small" is the much more common complaint of the allegedly maladjusted woman. We know these things, but I hear no sighs of, "Alas, the poor Negro, his penis is too large!"

Like the white man's other "compliments" to the Negro (for his childish good nature, primitive rhythmicity, toiler's songfulness, etc.) there is an ancient insult in being caricatured as genitally oversized. This might be called the myth of "Good-

14. Young, W. M., Jr.: *To Be Equal,* New York: McGraw-Hill Book Co., Inc., 1964, pp. 182–211.
15. Karon, B. P.: *The Negro Personality*, New York: Springer Publishers, 1958.
16. Masters, W. H., and Johnson, V.: *Human Sexual Response*, Boston: Little, Brown, & Co., 1966.

Natured Dick," after the feebleminded fellow (in *Fanny Hill*) on whose prodigious penis "you might have trolled dice securely." For in him the folklore held true, that "Nature . . . had done so much for him in those parts, that she . . . held herself acquitted in doing so little for his head."[17]

The concern with penis size is a well-known masculine foible experienced by every boy who looks at his father and then at himself. The aspiration to manhood and the association of man's estate with the phallus has caused the small boy in every culture to brood over the seemingly insurpassable difference between his own tiny nozzle and his father's mighty hose. In point of fact, the Negro has many of the same sexual concerns that the white man has, and tends to fear the white man as a sexual competitor for colored women with much greater basis in historical reality than the reverse obsession.

Since the fear of the Negro as an automatic sexual threat is irrational, it is to be understood only through consideration of psychodynamic mechanisms that can be found to play a role in studies involving interviews of both patients and normal subjects. These studies also help us to understand how such myths can become self-fulfilling prophecies.

Many whites apparently deny their own "black" sexual and associated violent instinctual strivings, and project them onto the Negro. Would the Southern white boy wish to overthrow paternal authority, grow a penis larger than his father's, possess his mother, and even have her prefer him? Such unacceptable wishes and powers, denied in one's self, are easily attributed to the nearby numerous black men.

However, with the projection of these feelings and attributes, there also tends to develop an unconscious identification with the Negro. Put into him these parts of yourself, and you become a part of him as you now imagine him to be. Thus arises the secret erotic wish that Negro men will actually transgress successfully against white women (a well-known pornographic "best seller" in a thousand guises), and from this derives the necessity for a most violent conscious denial. The greater a man's insecurity regarding his own masculinity (i.e., unconscious passive strivings or latent homosexuality), the more strenuously these mechanisms must be called into play.

When ego defenses break down in psychiatric illness the repressed wish may be acted out, with the psychotic or pathologically intoxicated white husband dragging home a Negro to set upon his wife. Within emancipated circles in the North more subtle examples are not infrequent, wherein the Negro friend is literally maneuvered and unconsciously invited to cuckold him by the white man—who might be truly termed a liberal under these circumstances.

It is not hard to see how this mythology can dovetail with the fantasies of underprivileged, frustrated Negro boys who enjoy an endless variety of tales of being invited to bed by white "Miz Ann," perhaps while "Mister Charlie" peeks around the corner, so that the myth becomes biracially perpetuated. It may be complicated by the competition between white and Negro children for the attention and affection of the Negro woman serving as a domestic helper or "mammy." It is further compli-

17. Cleland, J.: *Fanny Hill*, New York: G. Putnam & Sons, 1963, pp. 183–186.

cated by the endless variety of genuine sexual experience. The realities of interracial sexual transactions—self-fulfilling prophecies and all—are in themselves a fascinating and instructive study and will be reported elsewhere.[18] Nevertheless, racial violence is not related to genital sex in reality, but to the fantasy of the forbidden.

The Universal Stranger

Important as the complex symbolization of black and white in America may be, however, and comprehensible as the sexual-racial matrix becomes under psychodynamically sophisticated scrutiny, in the end we find that none of the foregoing suffices to account for the whole of racial violence as it has been known here and elsewhere throughout history. A deeper understanding can only come from the study of the Universal Stranger.

Men have always identified certain *Strangers* as being significantly different from themselves, labeling them as a different race even if they were the same color. Once the Stranger is defined, all of the familiar myth-engendered taboos and warnings are heard: forbid intermarriage; avoid close contact; suspect their motives; beware of their degraded practices and mysterious treacheries; remember that they are beneath us, they are sexually dangerous, they want to displace us, overcome us, drag us down. Tribes, city-states, nations, and entire cultures have designated particular groups, domestic and foreign, as the Strangers to be feared and hated. Today, in Ruanda-Urundi, the tall Watusi are threatened with extermination by their erstwhile serfs among the short Bahutu in a racial massacre, while nearby in Kenya and Tanzania the Masai are similarly threatened by the Kikuyu. On Cyprus recently we have seen Turks and Greeks slaughter each other, still Strangers after living together for generations. The same suspicions can be found between Moslem and Hindu in India, between "colored" and Negro in Guyana, between Malay and Chinese in Indonesia and throughout the Orient; the examples are endless. Even the interminable Arab-Israeli conflict—presumably nationalistic and religious—has been sometimes couched in racial terms, while both groups continue to acknowledge their descent from the same man, Abraham, father of all.

The definition of the Stranger may change with time and treaty, but attitudes, feelings, and prejudices shift with peculiar ease from the old Stranger to the new. Man appears to need some outsider that he can identify as a source of great and continuing danger to his country, community, womenfolk, home, and way of life. Herein lies a substantial facet of organized human violence.[19]

To understand this tendency and its near universality, we must examine man as he grows and develops. In almost every society a high degree of frustration is a universal experience during the growing up of children. It is a peculiarly human attribute that the brain matures much more rapidly than the body as a whole, so that for many years as children we are helpless and dependent for survival on the adult world, while mental capacity, imagination, learning, and emotions are relatively well-

18. West, L. J.: *The Color of Tears,* to be published.
19. West, L. J.: The Act of Violence, *Sooner Magazine* **36:**2–5, (Dec) 1963.

developed functions. During these years the myriad impulses, wishes, and desires of the child are frustrated again and again. Frustration leads to aggression; but aggression is not tolerated—the child must learn to control and repress it. He must accept and even love the adult institutions, activities, and individuals who frustrate him, but upon whom his survival depends.

In childish fantasies or dreams he may wreak his vengeance: a bomb drops on the town and kills everybody but himself (and maybe a friend); or a tidal wave swamps the village and everyone else drowns, while he is washed up on a new and lovelier island, uninhabited except for a beautiful maiden. But with age and responsibility come identification with, and pride in, his family, city, state, country, and race. Aggressive and taboo feelings toward his own kind are denied and—to insure that they do not reappear to plague him—they are attributed instead to the Stranger.

Thus it is not I who would slay my father, rape the family womenfolk, devastate the community, and destroy my own society, whose taboos and frustrating restrictions so infuriated me when I was a child. It is not I, it is the Stranger! He is of another race or nation or religion or political persuasion. The important thing is that he is different from me, and I must be sure that he *remains* a Stranger so that I cannot find out the truth: that he is as much like me as I am like myself. So deep-seated is this inner conflict that it permeates the unconscious mind; in a recent study of thousands of dream narratives (of both Negroes and whites) the Stranger was found to stalk with great frequency as a threatening, attacking figure (Calvin Hall: personal communication to the author).

Above all, the Stranger must contain elements of our secret self. Levin reminds us of the insights provided by some of America's classical literary greats in this connection. In one novel, Henry James' abandoned house conceals the missing man, who finally turns out to be "the self that might have been: A black stranger"![13] Inevitably, when we unconsciously invest our hidden sexual and violent feelings in the Stranger, an important part of ourselves becomes ensconced within his skin; insofar as we hate, fear, and secretly relish that part of ourselves, we shall hate, fear, and secretly relish it in him.

Thus, most people, when they would isolate or destroy the Stranger, are feeling or acting the very sense of righteousness that motivates the struggle against their own unacceptable sexual and violent impulses, against that "negative identity" so vividly described by Erikson.[20] The Stranger threatens us, so we must crush him (or segregate him) for the safety of ourselves and the group with which we identify ourselves. Thus we construct defenses to deal with our unconscious hostile feelings toward our own kind. We labor to maintain repression of the unacceptable, and thus prevent self-betrayal; and so in our conflict with the Stranger we detest most of all someone who is like ourselves, but who becomes a traitor. For those who are moved to hate and fear the Negro (because he has been selected as their Stranger), the white "nigger-lover" who would aid the Negro is a renegade and therefore becomes the object of supreme hostility and contempt.

20. Erikson, E. H.: The Concept of Identity in Race Relations: Note and Queries, *Daedalus* **94**:155–156, 1965.

In some severe character disorders the identification with the Stranger is conscious, and the individual may act out the Stranger's role, say, by killing a universal father figure such as a president, or otherwise pursuing a strenuously antisocial life directed against the society from which he feels profoundly alienated. In certain psychotic episodes, with sweeping disruption of ego defenses, the Stranger bursts out, as it were, and slaughters without apparent motive a group of kindly nurses, or shoots randomly at strangers happening to pass within gunshot range, even though their only relationship to the frustrating parents is that they belong to the same society onto which the entire burden of hatred has become displaced and generalized.

It is true that most normal individuals are unlikely to act directly in response to the violent impulses deriving from the forces described above. But these same forces in disguised forms are responsible for perpetuating injustices, inequities, ghettoes, and other social violences that lead to the secondary elaboration of violent interpersonal consequences. This is particularly true in cities, where the emotional forces are more intensified by overcrowding and enforced proximity. Last year in the United States, Negroes, who comprise slightly over 10% of the population and who accounted for only 10% of all arrests in rural areas, were arrested for more than half of all murders, rapes, robberies, and aggravated assaults in the cities. In spite of the fact that the large majority of victims were also Negroes, this nonspecific violence cannot be separated from precursive racial violence, which is more clearly related to prejudice and antagonism toward Negroes by whites. Forcing the minority group to live under jungle conditions thus breeds other violence from which the whole society suffers; and the Negro, as usual, suffers most.

Summary and Conclusions

Beneath inculcated prejudice, socio-economic anxieties, organized hostility as rationalized justification for past and present oppression (i.e., slavery and its aftermath), and the symbolic meaning of blackness, are found the sexual roots of racial violence. Among American whites they stem largely from fears of contact between Negro men and white women. The elaborate mythology surrounding this subject can be found to have origins in such well-known psychodynamic shorthand formulations as the oedipal conflict, castration anxiety, preoccupation with penis size, and unconscious passive strivings or latent homosexuality. Case studies reveal that the irrational conscious *hate* (toward Negroes) is a reaction against a preconscious *fear* (of Negroes), which in turn is a violent denial of the unconscious *wish* brought about by projection of unacceptable sexual impulses onto the Negro and the linked identification with him.

The taproot of organized violent behavior among humankind everywhere, including racial strife, group conflict, and war, emerges as a biosocial product of normal human growth and development. It relates to the prolonged physical helplessness of the child, whose brain develops so much faster than his body, and his inevitable frustration by—and hostility toward—those on whom he is most dependent. This promotes his unconscious identification with the Stranger (often defined in racial terms, regardless of color) onto whom he projects his unacceptable aggressive, sexual, and destructive feelings toward his own family and community. The ubiquity of this inner conflict makes one wonder, if the American Negro is redefined as a familiar and accepted brunette citizen, where we shall turn to nominate his successor in the Stranger's role!

The inescapable tendency to develop ambivalence toward those who are closest raises questions regarding the unavoidability of racial conflict, or the universality of violence in human affairs. With Erikson, I believe that such social pathology should not be accepted as inevitable. Whatever else Americans do to solve the racial problem (and there is a tremendous amount that can be done), we must also work toward a healthier resolution of these myth-engendered hates, fears, and inner conflicts. A fruitful approach to this emotional disease of society might well employ the same basic technique utilized by dynamic psychotherapy to promote awareness and understanding of the irrational nature of the prejudicial attitudes and emotions involved, and of the unconscious roots from which they spring and by behavioral psychotherapy to induce and then systematically reinforce the desired behavior—racial integration—with negative reinforcement for undesired behavior—racial discrimination. To this great challenge the growing discipline of social psychiatry should dedicate itself.

By Malone for Negro Digest.

Society's Child

Janis Ian

Come to my door, Baby
Face as clean and shining, black as night.
My mother went to answer you know
And you looked so fine
Now I could understand your tears and your shame.
She called you Boy instead of your name.
When she wouldn't let you inside
When she turned and said,
"But Honey he's not our kind."
She says I can't see you anymore, baby,
Can't see you anymore.

Walk me down to school Baby.
Everybody's acting deaf and blind,
Until they turn and say,
"Why don't you stick to your own kind?"
My teachers laugh, their smirking stares
Cutting deep in our affairs.
They're preaching equality.
If they believe it,
Why won't they just let us be?
They say I can't see you anymore, Baby,
Can't see you anymore.

They wonder why you're taking me.
Now wouldn't you prefer your own kind?
They say there can be just one thing on your mind.
That's what they want you to do,
Just so they can say
They were right about you.
I'm old enough to make up my mind,
But they'll do the making for me this one time.
They say I can't see you anymore, Baby,
Can't see you anymore.

One of these days I'm gonna stop my listening
Going to raise my head up high
One of these days I'm gonna raise my glistening wings and fly.
But that day will have to wait for a while.
Baby, I'm only society's child.
When we're older, things may change.
But for now this is the way they must remain.
They say I can't see you anymore, baby,
Can't see you anymore, no. . .
I don't wanna see you anymore baby.

SOUL HEROES.

At Forty-third Street and Langley Avenue, on Chicago's South Side, amid the many storefront churches and dilapidated tenements, stands a soulful monument to African-American folk heroes past and present. Last summer, Billy Abernathy, his wife, and at least a score of other artists and draftsmen within the black community formed the Organization of Black American Culture (O.B.A.C.) and got the building's owner, who happens to be black, to consent to the creation of the revolutionary and historical hand-painted mural. Folk heroes who have made great contributions to the worlds of music, sports and literature adorn the Wall: men like Marcus Garvey, Malcolm X and Stokely Carmichael; men who have steered large masses of black people away from the "assimilation complex" bag that DuBois talked about and guided them to the positive course of *digging* themselves. The Wall is blessed with Dr. DuBois' image too. The great innovators of American music, Charlie Parker, Thelonious Monk, Max Roach, Ornette Coleman and the late John Coltrane, share a large portion of the Wall, along with Sassy Sarah Vaughn and Nina Simone. The mighty men, Muhammad Ali and Wilt Chamberlain, are there because they do their thing with a lot of style, and that's important. The real genius of the Wall is that it generates African-American self-pride. No matter what happens to Chicago, the Wall is sure to stand.

Back Again, Home

(confessions of an ex-executive)

Pains of insecurity surround me;
shined shoes,
conservative suits,
button down shirts with silk ties.
bi-weekly payroll.

Ostracized, but not knowing why;
executive haircut,
clean shaved,
"yes" instead of "yeah" and "no" instead of "naw;"
hours, nine to five. (after five he's alone)

"Doing an excellent job, keep it up;"
promotion made—semi-monthly payroll,
very quiet—never talks,
budget balanced—saved the company money,
quality work—production tops.
He looks sick. (but there is a smile in his eyes)

He resigned, we wonder why;
let his hair grow—a mustache too,
out of a job—broke and hungry,
friends are coming back—bring food,
not quiet now—trying to speak,
what did he say?

"Back Again,

BLACK AGAIN,

Home."

Don Lee   Don Lee   Don Lee   Don Lee   Don Lee   Don Lee   Don Lee   Don Lee

AWARENESS

BLACK   PEOPLE   THINK
PEOPLE   BLACK   PEOPLE
THINK   PEOPLE   THINK
BLACK   PEOPLE   THINK—
THINK   BLACK.

the great straights

Now you can wear them! The great, straight "in" hairstyles! Because now your hairdresser has Epic ... a new, truly different curl relaxer. It's cool! Really cool! So cool your hairdresser needn't wear gloves. So "relaxing" it smooths even extra-tight curls. So gentle, color-treated hair can trust it completely. So thoughtful it leaves just enough body to hold the "Great Straight" style you like best. Hear this! Your new Epic won't revert in heat or rain! Skeptical? Would you believe your hairdresser? Call. Make an appointment. Ask for Epic Curl Relaxer. It's the Cool one! It's at better beauty salons right now.

The Epic Professional Products Co., Division ◄Gillette► Chicago, Ill.

The Winds of Change

Loyle Hairston

It was my big day and I was so hopped up I woke up before the alarm went off. Geez. The house was quiet except for Sis hummin' out in the kitchen. I set my watch by the clock and gauged my time; then laid out my vine, a clean shirt and things on the bed. After I brushed my kicks, I looked my wig over in the mirror. My stockin' cap slipped off my head when I was sleepin' and the waves in my hair done unstrung and was all tangled up.

"Damn!"

I mean I wouldn't make my *own* funeral without my *wig* bein' in shape. So I went into the livin' room and called Sonny for an appointment; I *had* to have a marcel! He said he could take me on round ten o'clock. Whew! Glancin' at my watch I seen I had plenty of time; so I went back in my room and took out my bongos and worked out a while.

And just when the licks was comin' good, she opens up on me again. I mean if she wasn't my sister——

"Waddell."

At eight o'clock in the *a.m.*! And pa's tryin' to cop a snooze in the next room.

"Waddell!"

I locked my door, bolted it. She's way out in the kitchen but her voice it busts t'rough the walls like a truck. I didn't say nothin'; the name I had for her was burnin' the tip of my tongue—but I didn't say nothin'. I just kept on workin' out on my bongos, tryin' to think about that audition gig I had to make at one o'clock. My big chance to cop a show, a off-Broadway show; my chance to make enough long bread to put her down—and she wanta heat me up and make me blow it——

"Waddell Wilkins!"

"Goddam it, Sis, leave me alone—*please!*"

"Don't you know papa's tryin' to sleep . . . !"

Don't *I* know it; she's blastin' like a H-bomb and askin' me don't *I* know pa's tryin' to sleep. Geez! I mean I couldn't bear it no longer; so I t'rowed my bongos on the bed and went and run some water in the bathtub.

"You takin' a *bath?*" she said as I went in the kitchen where she was washin' dishes. Her hair was undone, curlin' over her forehead from under her kerchief; and her slip was showin' t'rough her loose robe.

"I'm gon wash my head."

She dropped her towel in the dishwater and gaped at me like I just said I was gon commit a murder.

"Aw naw! Don't tell me that wavy-wigged-Waddell's gonna wash out his beauty tresses!"

"Lay off me, Sis; goddam it, lay off!"

"'Lay off me, Sis; . . . lay off!'" she mocked back at me. "You slick-headed ditty-bop, if you spent half as much time tryin' to put something *inside* that worthless hat-rack as you did havin' your brains fryed——"

"Goddam it, Sis . . . Aw go to hell."

I took a cake of soap from the cabinet and went back to the bathroom.

I mean what'd she know. She think I'm gon make a audition lookin' like a creep. You think they're lookin' for talent in the raw; appearance is half the game. A block-head knows that. If you ain't pressed and got the right spiel, you ain't sayin' *nothin'* to the silks; it's the only language they can dig.

". . . If you had any backbone you'd be outlookin' for a job . . ."

A job! What she think I'm knockin' myself out to make this audition gig for—my old-age pension; I asked her that!

"Hah! You'll never have to worry about old-age pension; at the rate you're goin', you'll starve to death before you're twenty-one."

Dig her; I mean just dig *her*. Like them Nationalists always say: black folks is like crabs in a barrel—try to climb out and they'll snatch you right back ever' time.

"You know what you are, Sis; you're a creep—that's what you are!"

Then she really exploded. I wrapped my towel round my ears and went on in my room and put my old clothes back on, then hung my *vine* on a hanger, figurin' I'd dress when I got finished at the barbershop. Sis was hammerin' away through the walls like she was in a stone fit; until I couldn't take no more.

I blasted her, "Shut your trap a minute and take a look at this dump you're livin' in. The walls is cracked; the ceilin's busted; the pipes leak; there ain't no heat; no hot water mosta the time; no fresh air. The only thing expensive here is your goddam rent. Geez.

"You want me to grow up a sap like pa—knockin' hisself out on a mail-handler gig at the Post Office where the pay is so lousy he's gotta work a part-time gig to keep the finance company from bustin' the door down . . . I mean are you a damn fool, Sis?"

Sometimes I have to ask myself how come ma had to die and leave me saddled with *her*. Geez . . .

I copped a hack to Ray's Barbershoppe. The joint was already hummin' with cats talkin' about "broads," the numbers they *missed*, integration, the silks, and the figure they was gon play *today*. Half of the chairs was full; there was a few squares *actual'* takin' regular haircuts. Five cats was settin' under the dryers in back diggin' the NEWS. I set down and tried to think about the audition; I mean what them gigs was really like and how many cats I had to compete with, and wonderin' how good I really was on the bongos. My man, Sonny, dug me.

"You ready, Baby."

"Yeah," I winked and took the resumé scratch-sheet he mapped out for me: background; how long I been studyin'; where at; workin' experience; and such particulars. It was boss, the way he faked it. After goin' over it I put it back in my pocket, checked the time, and watched Sonny put the finish on the cat he was workin' on. His wig was shinin' like black satin; and Sonny was layin' in the waves with his hands, rollin' a big one in front and workin' the others in, soft and delicate like they growed natural. It was a swingin' job.

When my turn come I told him I wanted one just like he laid on that cat. Sonny rubbed the process in so thick with his rubber gloves, it started stingin' a little t'rough the heavy layer of grease he packed in my scalp.

"Damn, Baby!"

"Cool it, Mamma," Sonny said, combin' the process into my hair. "The secret to this business is to burn it so close to the scale, it'll look natural all the way to the roots."

When he finished I dug my wig in the mirror.

"That's boss, Baby—the best I ever seen."

"Wow!" the cat in the next chair said. "You been transformed, daddy-o; if you was a shade lighter, you could pass for a silk!"

"The only way you'll ever get your mop to grow natural again, Mamma," Sonny boasted, "is to have you head *shaved*!"

"Shee-it," I said, t'rowed my man a five-spot, and told him to bank the change.

After I put on my vine and they all wished me good luck, I went over to St. Nick's and took the A-train down to Fifty-ninth Street. It was only twelve o'clock, so I set in a Brass Rail on Eighth Avenue and tightened my nerves with a few slugs of Imperial. Then I boated it down to Forty-sixth' where the joint was, took a deep breath, and went inside.

They was runnin' off a dance number on the stage; only some cat in shirt sleeves and a cigar stump stuck in his teeth kept interruptin' 'em ever'time they got started. They was all in a sweat and I was tryin' to dig what was happenin' when this little blade-nosed cat switched over and told me to wait outside.

There was a settin' room on the left, full of silk broads settin' round a old table, smokin' and yackin' away about nothin'; so I set on a chair against the wall in the corridor. From another part of the building I heard all sorts of drums beatin' and feet stompin' and a sad chorus that couldn't find the beat. They must be *silks*, I thought; and just to ease my nerves I tried to pick up the beat on my bongos. That huddle of old silk broads stopped yackin' and *dug* me, their eyes slidin' over me and stoppin' on my hair, where they lit up and they whispered somethin' to one another. I played it cool.

Then this tall one, with green eyes and faded blond hair, eased out of the door with a cigarette in her mouth, lookin' round like she was pickin' out somebody to cop a light from. She asked one of the greys in the settin' room, lit up, then leaned against the wall by the dressin' room door. And daddy she was *built!* Without lookin' at her face, I knowed she was buzzin' me with her pearls. Not bad at all—for a silk.

And you could tell she thought I was a big-shot entertainer like Harry Belafonte or somebody from the way she was diggin' me. Geez! I mean, soon's they think you're famous and pullin' down that long bread they're ready to integrate the hell outa you——

"Hi."

I played a freeze; like my thoughts had me up-tight. But she was standin' right in front of me now; and I'm diggin' the way them leotogs was spellin' the truth out to me the way they was huggin' her. I mean I ain't no stone.

"Hello," I said, playin' it straight; silks think you can't talk nothin' but slang.

"Excuse me, but aren't you Doug Ward?"

See what I mean. Like I'm psychic, I dig silks.

"No," I said and t'rowed her a sympathetic smile. Then three more, one of 'em a member, bolted out of the dressin' room and sailed over to where we was. Miss Fine said she was sorry and introduced herself to me, then the three others. I nodded to 'em and told 'em my name and dug 'em where they was sayin' the most. I mean they all was stacked; and they was friendly as hell. But this member—daddy, she was a real fox! Her big nut-shaped eyes was so bright it made you squint when you looked straight at 'em; and she musta been playin' the part of a African in the play because she wore her hair short and natural, like Miriam Makeba. But the way her big gold-looped earrings gleamed against her long satin-smooth neck, she looked like a African *princess!* Without comin' outa my freeze, I dug her the most.

We struck up a conversation, and Colleen—the bold one—was tellin' me that they was all students with the American Ballet outfit when I was called for my gig. I rushed off, hopin' I'd get back before they left so I could put the sound on the princess.

When I got inside and seen five cats in the middle of the floor, stripped down to tights, squattin' behind them long-bellied African drums, I got a feelin' in my gut that I didn't like. In nothin' flat, the cat in charge let me know what the feelin' was. They done changed the "locale" to a African settin' and when I told him that I never done no primitive dancin', he told me, with a lotta friggin' double-talk—to blow! I could see Sis's face, mockin' and laughin' at me, so clear, I walked into the door.

I was gettin' on the elevator when I heard this Colleen's voice. I turned and she gave *me* a sympathetic smile like she knowed straight off what happened. She was dressed and said she was waitin' for the others; then she asked me where I was goin'. I shrugged my shoulders, tryin' to pull myself together.

"Want to come with us?"

". . . Ah . . . I mean—where?"

"To the UN, We're——"

"The UN . . .?"

"Oh, come on. It'll take you mind off this. Okay?"

And before I give her an answer, she told me to wait for the girls while she took her car outa the parkin' lot. After I seen the princess, I forgot ever'thing—but *her!* All the way across town I'm tryin' to figure how I'm gon get her alone so I can sound her, and they're busy yackin' about the UN. It floored 'em when I told 'em I ain't never been there. So I remembered what the NEWS always said about the joint and told 'em I didn't go because I thought the place was run by the commies. They bust laughin' on me. And that's when I learnt that Oleta, the princess, was a *pure* African; and that her brother was a member of her country's UN delegation. Geez! I mean I coulda hid in the ash tray on the armrest.

Colleen parked the car and we all strolled up the boulevard to the UN. Out in front a long row of flags was wavin' in the bright breeze, showin' off dazzlin' colors in all sorts of patterns; and I couldn't take my eye off that tall buildin' juttin' against the pale blue as we climbed the steps and went across the stone court to the "General Assembly Building."

Inside it was a boss lay-out; streamlined down to the carpets, with a soft bluish light streamin' in from the glass walls openin' on a side garden-court splashed with green and bright-colored flowers. But when I got upstairs and seen all them African cats settin' round the tables on the main floor, I damn near flipped! Some of 'em wore reg'lar blue-serge; some showed off their native styles. Papers was stacked neat on their desks alongside pitchers of water. And they kept leanin' over to one another, talkin' confidential—puttin' the *ig'* on the silks scattered amongs' 'em.

The gallery was buzzin' about "Lumumba" and "Tshombe" and the "Belgium mercenaries" and "Kasavuba" and some "resolution" the "Afro-Asian" delegations done put to the floor. Oleta pointed her brother out to me, settin' with a lotta young cats with smooth black round faces and woolly hair cropped even all over. They all was beamin' like they had Charley's number; and Charley was settin' there fussin' with his notes like he *knowed* it. I mean it was all I could do to keep from jumpin' up on my seat and bust out clappin'. No wonder the NEWS say the joint's run by Reds!

If Sis could see this, she'd flip—for certain, I thought, sittin' there between princess Oleta and Colleen, with my earphones on, and listenin' to this African talkin' in *French*. And it's comin' t'rough my earphones in *English!* Geez. I mean—*damn!*

By the time they got done hasslin' over that resolution and blastin' the silks until they buckled, me and Oleta was hittin' it off fine. And she was lookin' foxier by the minute. I copped her address when we got downstairs. Colleen had to pick her ol' lady up downtown and said that she didn't have time to drive us back across town. We walked her to her car, where she said she was very glad to meet me, shook my hand, wished me luck in show business, and give me the nicest smile you could get from a "silk broad." I mean it moved me.

"Now don't forget my party Friday night." She said to her gal friends, while I was makin' some sounds to Oleta. "You too, Oleta."

"Colleen, you know I have a class Friday night."

"Oh, posh with your class—I insist that you be there!"

"Oh, alright, we'll see," Oleta give in with a smile bright as a rose. Colleen got in her car, then called me:

". . . Why don't *you* come too, Mr. Wilkins?"

"Well——"

"Here, I'll give you my address. We'd love to have you," she said, winkin' at Oleta as she scribbled her address on the back of a card.

All the way uptown, Princess Oleta and makin' that party Friday night was the only thing on my mind. It was only Monday and by Friday my process'd need retouchin'; so I went by Ray's and made an appointment with Sonny for Friday. I was hongry, but after blowin' my audition, I wasn't in no mood for Sis's abuse; so I copped a sandwich and took in a flick.

Marilyn Monroe was playin' at the Loew's; only soon's I got comfortable I went to sleep and dreamt I was with Oleta by the lake in Central Park, playin' my bongos, and she was dancin' for me; and I was watchin' her Fine Brown reflectin' in the water shinin' with golden moonlight. Then she'd come over and stroke my hair; and in the gleamin' pools of her eyes I seen myself holdin' her close; only I was stripped down like a African warrior and my hair was woolly like them cats at the UN. I woke up then. I mean the dream was gettin' outa hand!

All week long there was something about them Africans that was buggin' me. I mean without even tryin'—they was *sayin'* something. I told Sis about 'em before I left for the barbershop.

"You mean they ain't brown-nosin' to the white folks like some of our 'leaders.'"

I cut out then and there. Geez. You ask her a question and she gotta make a speech. After gettin' my kicks shined and my fingernails honed and polished, I set down in the barber chair, rubbin' the fuzz on my chin and thinkin' about Oleta and how fine she was in a way I ain't never seen in a girl, member or silk. Sonny stopped gassin' with some guys in the back and put the cloth round my neck. I told him to give me a shave. And he started crankin' the chair back.

"Not my face, daddy—my *head!*"

It shook the cat so, he dropped his clippers. I just grinned and laid back and shut my eyes, wonderin' where I could cop myself a deuce of African drums . . .

YOWZAH

Shel Silverstein

Well, it wasn't too very long ago, y'know,
Some folks walked with a hi-de-ho,
And other folks walked around kinda low
Sayin' "Yowzah" and "Sho' nuff" and "Yazzuh, boss."

Now it was ashes to ashes and dust to dust
They didn't believe in makin' a fuss
So, they just moved to the back of the bus
And said "Yowzah" and "Sho' nuff" and "Yazzuh, boss."

Yeah, they perspired and they expired
And still they never got no higher
Till finally at last they just got sorta tired
Of sayin' "Yowzah" and "Sho'nuff" and "Yazzuh, boss."

So they went out and they did a little prayin',
Little arm wavin' and a little bit of swayin'
Still and all, everybody just kept right on sayin'
"Yowzah," "Sho' nuff" and "Yazzuh, boss."

They were shinin' shoes, fryin' chicken,
Washin' floors, watermelon pickin'
Well finally at last they got damn sick
of sayin' "Yowzah," "Sho'nuff" and "Yazzuh, boss."

So they went out, they did a little standin'
Little less askin' and a lot more demandin'
Little more thinkin' and demonstratin'
Little less hoping and a little less waitin'
Little less liftin' and a little less totin'

A lot more thinkin' an a lot more votin'
A lot less hopin', a lot less waitin'
Whole lot more demonstratin'
Whole lot less Pearly-gatin'
Lot more screamin' and a lot more walkin'
Till finally, hardly anybody at all
Was talkin' like "Yowsah," "Sho'nuff" and "Yazzuh, boss."

Now the moral of the story is plain to see
They finally achieved equality
And now like you and me
They can stand up strong and free
And say "Yessir" and "Of course, sir," and "Anything you say, J.B."

DEATH

Painting by Bob Amft

190

Golden Falcon

He sees the circle of the world
  Alive with wings that he
Was born to rend; his eyes are stars
  Of amber cruelty.

God lit the fires in his eyes
  And bound swords on his feet,
God fanned the furnace of his heart
  To everlasting heat.

His two eyes take in all the sky,
  East, west, north, and south,
Opposite as poles they burn;
  And death is in his mouth.

Death because his Maker knew
  That death is last and best,
Because he gives to those he loves
  The benison of rest.

Golden, cruel word of God
  Written on the sky!
Living things are lovely things,
  And lovely things must die.

ROBERT TRISTRAM COFFIN

COMMUNION

Gentle the deer with solicitude
Solace them with salt
Comfort them with apples
Prepare them for the rectitude
Of Man who will come
A stranger with the unfamiliar gun.
The watcher calls. In trust the head turns.
Between the antlers St. Hubert's cross burns.
No conversion today—but quick shot.
The buck falls to his knees
In decent genuflection to death.
                              The doe flees.
He is not dead. He will arise.
In three weeks, the head
Will look through the wall
But with changed eyes.

But what of the body of swiftness
And litheness. Oh. Witness
Ground heart and muscle
Intestinal cased, tied with gristle,
The sausage sacrament of communion.
So that all may be one
Under the transplanted eyes
    of the watcher.

EUGENE McCARTHY

191

THE DAY OF THE HUNTER

Fred Myers

In these United States, any criticism of the tradition-hallowed sport of hunting is likely to bring down on one's head as much abuse as an attack upon motherhood, the Fourth of July, or the New York Mets. It is part of our folk-myth that all red-blooded American men live in a state of suspended animation during most of the year, awaiting impatiently the day when they can put a gun and a Bowser into the family car, stuff their corn-cob pipes with Old Shagbark, and sally forth to kill, kill, kill. The same myth has it that this lustful obsession is highly commendable—essential, even, to a claim of normality.

192

The statistics on American hunting indicate that either the folk-myth is founded upon fact, or it has a powerful propaganda effect. Figures prepared by the U. S. Department of the Interior show that this year there are more than 20 million licensed hunters in the country. But in many states farmers don't bother to get licenses to hunt on their own and neighboring lands. No state requires children under 16 to get licenses. Add the unlicensed hunters in, and we have about 30 million hunters loose in the land this season.

A single voice raised to say that 30 million Americans can be and are wrong, and that most hunters ought to be ashamed of themselves, may sound like King Canute bidding the waves of the sea to stop advancing. Nevertheless, a few adverse comments on hunting and hunters may be interesting—and might even reduce the number of hunters next year from 30 million to 29,999,999.

Let it be clear, before any indictment of hunting is presented, that this is no wholesale condemnation of *hunters*. The power of the hunting tradition is great, and the motives that take men to field and forest with gun in hand are complex. Hunters include many humanitarians—men and women who may have this moral blind-spot, but who in no sense are consciously inhumane. One of the most damning counts against the sport of hunting, in fact, is precisely that its excitement, its genuine tests of skill, and its moments of beauty, make good men participants in evil.

The reasons why hunting as a sport should be abolished from our civilization are twofold:

1. Every year, every month, every day, and every minute, hunters are inflicting unspeakable agonies upon living creatures—unnecessarily.

2. Because this cruelty is propagandized as a *sport*, hunting distorts moral judgments and corrupts the public conscience.

It is hard to comprehend the enormity of the slaughter and torture that hunters perpetrate every year. Statistics on this subject are like excerpts from a book on astronomy. In Missouri alone, for example, according to the Wildlife Management Institute, sportsmen killed 3.5 million rabbits during one 6-month period. In Maine, in 1 year, hunters killed 41,730 deer—not counting those killed by poachers. When Pennsylvania, some years ago, declared a 1-day open season on antlerless deer, hunters shot 84,000 of them in 10 hours.

A writer in a national hunting-fishing magazine recently reported that in one day he shot 34 woodchucks, "and probably hit at least 9 others, although they got into their holes." In another magazine of the same sort, a writer tells with relish of the slaughter of 46 crows by him and one companion in a single morning.

It's anybody's guess, but it is probably conservative to estimate that no less than a half-billion animals are killed in the United States in the name of "fun."

The animals cleanly killed, of course, are the lucky ones. Millions upon millions of less fortunate animals, from elk and bear to the lowly wood-chuck, are "merely" wounded by the sportsmen. An explosive, soft-nosed .30-30 bullet can tear a chunk of flesh as big as a football out of a leg or even the soft belly of a deer, without dropping it. Ten or fifteen pellets from a shotgun blast can penetrate a rabbit, or break the wing of a duck, without immediately causing death. Eventually the animal or bird dies—but perhaps not until it has suffered for days the agony of a gangrenous wound or broken bone, the pangs of starvation, and finally a death-dealing fever or a helpless end under the fang and claw of a predator.

One game warden of an Eastern state, who spends most of every hunting season in the field watching hunters, estimates that for every game animal and bird killed by hunters' guns, at least two others are wounded and escape to suffer an agonized, slow death.

To imagine the staggering total of physical suffering inflicted upon animals by hunters, one has only to see a cottontail rabbit with its entrails blasted out of its body by a shotgun blast, but still crawling desperately over icy ground for cover; or find in the spring thaw-time the skeleton of a deer with its shoulder-bone shattered to splinters by the explosion of a .30-calibre rifle bullet. Multiply the agony of the one rabbit or the one deer by millions upon millions—if you can—and that is what hunters are doing every year.

* * *

Yet the most damning indictment of sport-hunters is *not* the suffering they inflict.

After all, the majority of us implicitly condone the killing of animals as necessary to provide us with meat, leather, furs, and other animal products. Most of us find it logically impossible to cast stones at hunters who are seeking food—because most of us live in glass houses. The rabbit shot by a Missouri farmer for his family's table suffers no more (and probably less) than does the steer that was branded, castrated, reared on a range, shipped a thousand miles, and slaughtered in a packing house to produce steaks or hamburgers for our own tables and shoes for our feet.

No, the worst aspect of sport-hunting is that its devotees are not seeking food, they are not fighting pests, they are under no necessity of any kind. They kill and cripple for *pleasure*.

Whenever this charge is made, apologists for the sport-hunter are likely to react with a more-in-sorrow-than-in-anger attitude.

"The true sportsman doesn't go hunting for the *kill*," the defender of the faith will say. "The *real* sportsman goes to enjoy the beauty of the woods, the good companionship with other sportsmen, the thrill of matching skill and wits with the game."

194

Granted that a lot of sport-hunters have genuinely convinced themselves, or been convinced by the rivers of propaganda for hunting, that they go afield for noble reasons. The defense is made no more valid, however, just because some hunters sincerely believe it. And the fact is that the defense holds no water.

Doubtless it is true that many hunters enjoy the glories of the forest and field. But that enjoyment could be fully savored without killing or maiming an animal. By definition, a hunter is one who goes out to *kill*. A hunter, therefore, is one who is not satisfied by nature's beauty; to complete his joy, he must extinguish a life or make some other living thing suffer.

The same inexorable logic disposes of the contention that the "real" sportsman is more interested in companionship than in the kill. The defense ignores the fact that companionship can be obtained in many other ways, that millions of hunters prefer to hunt alone, and that the hunter's pleasure is not complete until he has killed or maimed.

Most ridiculous of all the common defenses of sport-hunting is the assertion that hunting's appeal lies in the contest of wits with the wild animals. A photograph of an animal would record a human triumph in the "contest of wits" just as effectively as a carcass, but there is no indication that "sportsmen" are switching from gun to camera—despite efforts by many agencies to achieve that end.

Townsend Miller, the genuinely humane editor of *Texas Game and Fish*, once published an editorial deploring the "lust to kill." Mr. Miller's editorial seemed to imply that there are good hunters and bad hunters. The dividing line seems to be, in Mr. Miller's mind, that "bad" hunters do a lot of killing, while "good" hunters do less.

"However," Mr. Miller goes on, "we have lost, maybe not sleep, but a lot of time wondering about those individuals who seem to want to kill everything that moves. What is the force that persuades them without reason or need to end the stay on this good earth of so many harmless creatures?"

A psychiatrist, Dr. Karl A. Menninger, has answered that such "joy of killing or inflicting pain" is a product of an "erotic sadistic motivation." Most other psychiatrists would agree. But one need not explore the subconscious of the hunter to arrive at the simple conclusion that the whole point, purpose, essence, and *sine qua non* of sport-hunting is "without reason or need to end the stay on this good earth of so many harmless creatures."

* * *

195

The "educational" effect upon each generation of children and young people of the propaganda for sport-hunting is incalculable—one can only say, sadly, that it certainly is infinitely more powerful than the humane education that the organized humane movement can afford. There is the example, always before the young, of the 20 million adults who every year go out to kill. The children see that in most circles the killing is applauded. Magazines, motion pictures, newspapers, radio, television—all foster the impression that hunting is romantic, pleasurable, admirable. Even the churches very often bless hunting.

The child is being educated, by all this, to be callous to suffering. He is being conditioned to inflict suffering without remorse. He is being taught that religion does not mean what it says—or, even worse, being taught to work out a subconscious hypocrisy to justify violation of a faith. He is being made blind to the kindred nature of all living things. He is being taught to kill and inflict cruelty for pleasure.

The direction in which our children are led by the institution of sport-hunting is opposite to the direction in which the peoples of the world must go if they are to arrive someday at a realization of brotherhood—of a warless world in which the Golden Rule is a universal law. Cruelty, like kindness, is indivisible. Children and men cannot be taught to take pleasure from cruelty to some living things, and simultaneously to abhor cruelty to others.

The great crime of the sport-hunter is not that he kills—necessity may justify killing, perhaps even in a manner that causes suffering. The great crime of the sport-hunter is that he *enjoys* killing—and that with his obscene pleasure he pollutes our whole civilization.

The Groundhog

In June, amid the golden fields,
I saw a groundhog lying dead.
Dead lay he; my senses shook,
And mind outshot our naked frailty.
There lowly in the vigorous summer
His form began its senseless change,
And made my senses waver dim
Seeing nature ferocious in him.
Inspecting close his maggots' might
And seething cauldron of his being,
Half with loathing, half with a strange love,
I poked him with an angry stick.
The fever arose, became a flame
And Vigour circumscribed the skies,
Immense energy in the sun,
And through my frame a sunless trembling.
My stick had done nor good nor harm.
Then stood I silent in the day
Watching the object, as before;
And kept my reverence for knowledge
Trying for control, to be still,
To quell the passion of the blood;
Until I had bent down on my knees
Praying for joy in the sight of decay.
And so I left; and I returned
In Autumn strict of eye, to see
The sap gone out of the groundhog,
But the bony sodden hulk remained.
But the year had lost its meaning,
And in intellectual chains
I lost both love and loathing,
Mured up in the wall of wisdom.
Another summer took the fields again
Massive and burning, full of life,
But when I chanced upon the spot
There was only a little hair left,
And bones bleaching in the sunlight
Beautiful as architecture;
I watched them like a geometer,
And cut a walking stick from a birch.
It has been three years, now.
There is no sign of the groundhog.
I stood there in the whirling summer,
My hand capped a withered heart,
And thought of China and of Greece,
Of Alexander in his tent;
Of Montaigne in his tower,
Of Saint Theresa in her wild lament.

Richard Eberhart

Photograph by May Mirin.

AS THE GENERATION OF LEAVES, SO IS THAT OF MEN.
Homer

SPRING AND FALL:
TO A YOUNG CHILD

Margaret, are you grieving
Over Goldengrove unleaving?
Leaves, like the things of man, you
With your fresh thoughts care for, can you?
Ah! As the heart grows older
It will come to such sights colder
By and by, nor spare a sigh
Though worlds of wanwood leafmeal lie;
And yet you will weep and know why.
Now no matter, child, the name:
Sorrow's springs are the same.
Nor mouth had, no nor mind expressed
What heart heard of, ghost guessed:
It is the blight man was born for,
It is Margaret you mourn for.

GERARD MANLEY HOPKINS

Giovanni di Paolo: *The Triumph of Death*
Communal Library, Siena: SCALA/New York/Florence.

DIRGE

1-2-3 was the number he played but today the number came 3-2-1;
Bought his Carbide at 30 and it went to 29; had the favorite at Bowie but
    the track was slow—

O executive type, would you like to drive a floating-power, knee-action,
    silk-upholstered six? Wed a Hollywood star? Shoot the course in 58? Draw
    to the ace, king, jack?
O fellow with a will who won't take no, watch out for three cigarettes on
    the same, single match; O democratic voter born in August under Mars,
    beware of liquidated rails—

Denouement to denouement, he took a personal pride in the certain, certain
    way he lived his own, private life,
But nevertheless, they shut off his gas; nevertheless, the bank foreclosed;
    nevertheless, the landlord called; nevertheless, the radio broke,

And twelve o'clock arrived just once too often,
Just the same he wore one gray tweed suit, bought one straw hat, drank
    one straight Scotch, walked one short step, took one long look, drew
    one deep breath,
Just one too many,

And wow he died as wow he lived,
Going whop to the office and blooie home to sleep and biff got married and
    bam had children and oof got fired,
Zowie did he live and zowie did he die,

With who the hell are you at the corner of his casket, and where the hell're
    we going on the right hand silver knob, and who the hell cares walking
    second from the end with an American Beauty wreath from why the hell
    not,

Very much missed by the circulation staff of the New York Evening Post;
    deeply, deeply mourned by the B. M. T.,

Wham, Mr. Roosevelt; pow, Sears Roebuck; awk, big dipper; bop, summer rain;
Bong, Mr., bong, Mr., bong, Mr., bong.

Kenneth Fearing

From the Rubaiyat of Omar Khayyam

XVI

Think, in this batter'd Caravanserai
Whose Doorways are alternate Night and Day,
*   How Sultan after Sultan with his Pomp*
Abode his Hour or two, and went his way.

XXXIII

Then to the rolling Heav'n itself I cried,
Asking, "What Lamp had Destiny to guide
*   Her little Children stumbling in the Dark?"*
And—"A blind understanding!" Heav'n replied.

XXXVII

One Moment in Annihilation's Waste,
One moment, of the Well of Life to taste—
*   The Stars are setting, and the Caravan*
Starts for the dawn of Nothing—Oh, make haste!

Edward FitzGerald

Ozymandias

I met a traveler from an antique land
Who said: "Two vast and trunkless legs of stone
Stand in the desert. Near them, on the sand,
Half sunk, a shattered visage lies, whose frown,
And wrinkled lip, and sneer of cold command,
Tell that its sculptor well those passions read
Which yet survive, stamped on these lifeless things,
The hand that mocked them, and the heart that fed:
And on the pedestal these words appear:
'My name is Ozymandias, King of Kings:
Look on my works, ye Mighty, and despair!'
Nothing beside remains. Round the decay
Of that colossal wreck, boundless and bare
The lone and level sands stretch far away."

Percy Bysshe Shelley

SLEEPERS

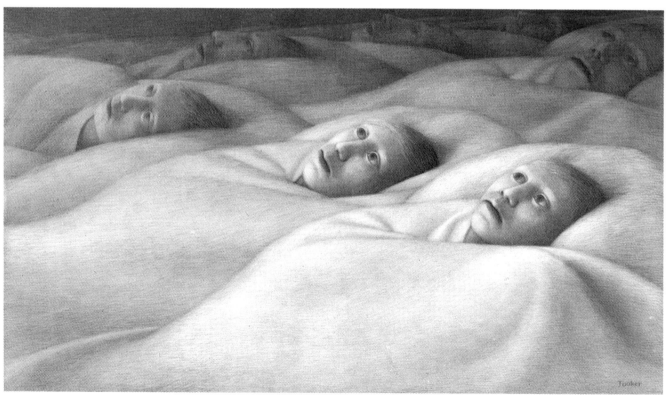

TOOKER, George *Sleepers, II.* (1959)
Collection, The Museum of Modern Art, New York.
Larry Aldrich Foundation Fund.

"In a rut, men? . . . Discouraged? . . . Life look hopeless?"

• •

RICHARD CORY

Whenever Richard Cory went down town,
  We people on the pavement looked at him:
He was a gentleman from sole to crown,
  Clean favored, and imperially slim.

And he was always quietly arrayed,
  And he was always human when he talked;
But still he fluttered pulses when he said,
  "Good-morning," and he glittered when he walked.

And he was rich—yes, richer than a king—
  And admirably schooled in every grace:
In fine, we thought that he was everything
  To make us wish that we were in his place.

So on we worked, and waited for the light,
  And went without the meat, and cursed the bread;
And Richard Cory, one calm summer night,
  Went home and put a bullet through his head.

E. A. Robinson

A UTOPIAN JOURNEY

"In a minute the doctor will find out what is wrong
And cure me," the patients think as they wait.
They are as patient as their name, and look childishly
And religiously at the circumstances of their hope,
The nurse, the diplomas, the old magazines.

And their childishness is natural; here in this office
The natural perplexities of their existence,
The demands they can neither satisfy nor understand,
Are reduced to the child's, "I hurt," the bare
Intention of any beast: to go on being.

And they go in to the doctor at last
And go out to the hospitals, sanatoria, or graves
He prescribes—look into the masked unnoticing
Faces of their saviors, smell the sick
Sweet smell of nothing, leave, send back their checks;

But what was it? What am I?
The convalescent stitched up with black thread,
His pains withering, his uneasy head
Quieted with enemas and orange-juice, the inconclusive
Evasive silence—remembers, silently, a sweet,

Evasive, and conclusive speech . . . Goes back to his living,
Day and Night ask, *Child, have you learned anything?*
He answers, *Nothing*—walled in these live ends,
In these blind blossoming alleys of the maze
That lead, through a thousand leaves, to the beginning

Or that lead at last into—dark, leaved—a door.

RANDALL JARRELL

THAT WHICH
I SHOULD HAVE DONE
I DID NOT DO

207

A Refusal to Mourn the Death, by Fire, of a Child in London

Never until the mankind making
Bird beast and flower
Fathering and all humbling darkness
Tells with silence the last light breaking
And the still hour
Is come of the sea tumbling in harness

And I must enter again the round
Zion of the water bead
And the synagogue of the ear of corn
Shall I let pray the shadow of a sound
Or sow my salt seed
In the least valley of sackcloth to mourn

The majesty and burning of the child's death.
I shall not murder
The mankind of her going with a grave truth
Nor blaspheme down the stations of the breath
With any further
Elegy of innocence and youth.

Deep with the first dead lies London's daughter,
Robed in the long friends,
The grains beyond age, the dark veins of her mother,
Secret by the unmourning water
Of the riding Thames.
After the first death, there is no other.

Dylan Thomas

 HEAVEN

Fish (fly-replete, in depth of June
Dawdling away their wat'ry noon)
Ponder deep wisdom, dark or clear,
Each secret fishy hope or fear.
Fish say, they have their Stream and Pond;
But is there anything Beyond?
This life cannot be All, they swear,
For how unpleasant, if it were!
One may not doubt that, somehow, good
Shall come of Water and of Mud;
And, sure, the reverent eye must see
A purpose in Liquidity.
We darkly know, by Faith, we cry,
The future is not Wholly Dry.
Mud unto Mud!—Death eddies near—
Not here the appointed end, not here!
But somewhere beyond Space and Time,
Is wetter water, slimier slime!
And there (they trust) there swimmeth One
Who swam ere rivers were begun,
Immense, of fishy form and mind,
Squamous, omnipotent and kind;
And under that Almighty Fin
The littlest fish may enter in.
Oh! never fly conceals a hook,
Fish say, in that Eternal Brook,
But more than mundane weeds are there,
And mud, celestially fair;
Fat caterpillars drift around,
And Paradisal grubs are found;
Unfading moths, immortal flies,
And the worm that never dies.
And in that Heaven of all their wish,
There shall be no more land, say fish.

Rupert Brooke

 210

WE FANCY NOW HE'D
WISH TO LIVE AGAIN
COULD HE BUT KNOW
WHAT HIS FUNERAL COST

TOMBSTONE
IN ST. GILES' CHURCHYARD
Norwich, Eng.

Reprint permission granted by
RIPLEY ENTERPRISES, INC.

ON CASKETS

Chambers' caskets are just fine,
Made of sandalwood and pine.
If your loved ones have to go
Call Columbus 690.
If your loved ones pass away,
Have them pass the Chambers way.
Chambers' customers all sing:
"Death, oh death, where is thy sting?"

Casket Commercial, sung to tune of Rock of Ages.

FROM THE AMERICAN WAY OF DEATH

JESSICA MITFORD

How long, I would ask, are we to be subjected to the tyranny of custom and undertakers? Truly, it is all vanity and vexation of spirit—a mere mockery of woe, costly to all, far, far beyond its value; and ruinous to many; hateful, and an abomination to all; yet submitted to by all, because none have the moral courage to speak against it and act in defiance of it.
—LORD ESSEX

O DEATH, where is thy sting? O grave, where is thy victory? Where, indeed. Many a badly stung survivor, faced with the aftermath of some relative's funeral, has ruefully concluded that the victory has been won hands down by a funeral establishment—in disastrously unequal battle.

Much has been written of late about the affluent society in which we live, and much fun poked at some of the irrational "status symbols" set out like golden snares to trap the unwary consumer at every turn. Until recently, little has been said about the most irrational and weirdest of the lot, lying in ambush for all of us at the end of the road—the modern American funeral.

If the Dismal Traders (as an eighteenth-century English writer calls them) have traditionally been cast in a comic role in literature, a universally recognized symbol of humor from Shakespeare to Dickens to Evelyn Waugh, they have successfully turned the tables in recent years to perpetrate a huge, macabre and expensive practical joke on the American public. It is not consciously conceived of as a joke, of course; on the contrary, it is hedged with admirably contrived rationalizations.

Gradually, almost imperceptibly, over the years the funeral men have constructed their own grotesque cloud-cuckooland where the trappings of Gracious Living are transformed, as in a nightmare, into the trappings of Gracious Dying. The same familiar Madison Avenue language, with its peculiar adjectival range designed to anesthetize sales resistance to all sorts of products, has seeped into the funeral industry in a new and bizarre guise. The emphasis is on the same desirable qualities that we have all been schooled to look for in our daily search for excellence: comfort, durability, beauty, craftsmanship. The attuned ear will recognize too the convincing quasi-scientific language, so reassuring even if unintelligible.

So that this too, too solid flesh might not melt, we are offered "solid copper—a quality casket which offers superb value to the client seeking long-lasting protection," or "the Colonial Classic Beauty—18 gauge lead coated steel, seamless top, lap-jointed welded body construction." Some are equipped with foam rubber, some with innerspring mattresses. Elgin offers "the revolutionary 'Perfect-Posture' bed." Not every casket need have a silver lining, for one may choose between "more than 60 color matched shades, magnificent and unique masterpieces" by the Cheney casket-lining people. Shrouds no longer exist. Instead, you may patronize a grave-wear couturière who promises "handmade original fashions—styles from the best in life for the last memory—dresses, men's suits, negligees, accessories." For the final, perfect grooming: "Nature-Glo—the ultimate in cosmetic embalming." And, where have we heard that phrase "peace of mind protection" before? No matter. In funeral advertising, it is applied to the Wilbert Burial Vault, with its $\frac{3}{8}$-inch precast asphalt inner liner plus extra-thick, reinforced concrete—all this "guaranteed by Good Housekeeping." Here again the Cadillac, status symbol par excellence, appears in all its gleaming glory, this time transformed into a pastel-colored funeral hearse.

You, the potential customer for all this luxury, are unlikely to read the lyrical descriptions quoted above, for they are culled from *Mortuary Management* and *Casket and Sunnyside*, two of the industry's eleven trade magazines. For you there are ads in your daily newspaper, generally found on the obituary page, stressing dignity, refinement, high-caliber professional service and that intangible quality, *sincerity*. The trade advertisements are, however, instructive, because they furnish an important clue to the frame of mind into which the funeral industry has hypnotized itself.

A new mythology, essential to the twentieth-century American funeral rite, has grown up—or rather has been built up step by step—to justify the peculiar customs surrounding the disposal of our dead. And, just as the witch doctor must be convinced of his own infallibility

in order to maintain a hold over his clientele, so the funeral industry has had to "sell itself" on its articles of faith in the course of passing them along to the public.

The first of these is the tenet that today's funeral procedures are founded in "American tradition." The story comes to mind of a sign on the freshly sown lawn of a brand-new Midwest college: "There is a tradition on this campus that students never walk on this strip of grass. This tradition goes into effect next Tuesday." The most cursory look at American funerals of past times will establish the parallel. Simplicity to the point of starkness, the plain pine box, the laying out of the dead by friends and family who also bore the coffin to the grave—these were the hallmarks of the traditional funeral until the end of the nineteenth century.

Secondly, there is the myth that the American public is only being given what it wants—an opportunity to keep up with the Joneses to the end. "In keeping with our high standard of living, there should be an equally high standard of dying," says the past president of the Funeral Directors of San Francisco. "The cost of a funeral varies according to individual taste and the niceties of living the family has been accustomed to." Actually, choice doesn't enter the picture for the average individual, faced, generally for the first time, with the necessity of buying a product of which he is totally ignorant, at a moment when he is least in a position to quibble. In point of fact the cost of a funeral almost always varies, not "according to individual taste" but according to what the traffic will bear.

Thirdly, there is an assortment of myths based on half-digested psychiatric theories. The importance of the "memory picture" is stressed—meaning the last glimpse of the deceased in open casket, done up with the latest in embalming techniques and finished off with a dusting of makeup. A newer one, impressively authentic-sounding, is the need for "grief therapy," which is beginning to go over big in mortuary circles. A historian of

213

American funeral directing hints at the grief-therapist idea when speaking of the new role of the undertaker—"the dramaturgic role, in which the undertaker becomes a stage manager to create an appropriate atmosphere and to move the funeral party through a drama in which social relationships are stressed and an emotional catharsis or release is provided through ceremony."

Lastly, a whole new terminology, as ornately shoddy as the satin rayon casket liner, has been invented by the funeral industry to replace the direct and serviceable vocabulary of former times. Undertaker has been supplanted by "funeral director" or "mortician." (Even the classified section of the telephone directory gives recognition to this; in its pages you will find "Undertakers—see Funeral Directors.") Coffins are "caskets"; hearses are "coaches," or "professional cars"; flowers are "floral tributes"; corpses generally are "loved ones," but mortuary etiquette dictates that a specific corpse be referred to by name only—as, "Mr. Jones"; cremated ashes are "cremains." Euphemisms such as "slumber room," "reposing room," and "calcination—the *kindlier* heat" abound in the funeral business.

214

If the undertaker is the stage manager of the fabulous production that is the modern American funeral, the stellar role is reserved for the occupant of the open casket. The decor, the stagehands, the supporting cast are all arranged for the most advantageous display of the deceased, without which the rest of the paraphernalia would lose its point—*Hamlet* without the Prince of Denmark. It is to this end that a fantastic array of costly merchandise and services is pyramided to dazzle the mourners and facilitate the plunder of the next of kin.

Grief therapy, anyone? But it's going to come high. According to the funeral industry's own figures, the *average* undertaker's bill in 1961 was $708 for casket and "services," to which must be added the cost of a burial vault, flowers, clothing, clergy and musician's honorarium, and cemetery charges. When these costs are added to the undertaker's bill, the total average cost for an adult's funeral is, as we shall see, closer to $1,450.

The question naturally arises, *is* this what most people want for themselves and their families? For several reasons, this has been a hard one to answer until recently. It is a subject seldom discussed. Those who have never had to arrange for a funeral frequently shy away from its implications, preferring to take comfort in the thought that sufficient unto the day is the evil thereof. Those who have acquired personal and painful knowledge of the subject would often rather forget about it. Pioneering "Funeral Societies" or "Memorial Associations," dedicated to the principle of dignified funerals at reasonable cost, have existed in a number of communities throughout the country, but their membership has been limited for the most part to the more sophisticated element in the population—university people, liberal intellectuals—and those who, like doctors and lawyers, come up against problems in arranging funerals for their clients.

Some indication of the pent-up resentment felt by vast numbers of people against the funeral interests was furnished by the astonishing response to an article by Roul Tunley, titled "Can You Afford to Die?" in *The Saturday Evening Post* of June 17, 1961. As though a dike had burst, letters poured in from every part of the country to the *Post*, to the funeral societies, to local newspapers. They came from clergymen, professional people, old-age pensioners, trade unionists. Three months after the article appeared, an estimated six thousand had taken pen in hand to comment on some phase of the high cost of dying. Many recounted their own bitter experiences at the hands of funeral directors; hundreds asked for advice on how to establish a consumer organization in communities where none exists; others sought information about pre-need plans. The membership of the funeral societies skyrocketed. The funeral industry, finding itself in the glare of public spotlight, has begun to engage in serious debate about its own future course—as well it might.

Is the funeral inflation bubble ripe for bursting? A few years ago, the United States public suddenly rebelled against the trend in the auto industry towards ever more showy cars, with their ostentatious and nonfunctional fins, and a demand was created for compact cars patterned after European models. The all-powerful auto industry, accustomed to *telling* the customer what sort of car he wanted, was suddenly forced to *listen* for a change. Overnight, the little cars became for millions a new kind of status symbol. Could it be that the same cycle is working itself out in the attitude towards the final return of dust to dust, that the American public is becoming sickened by ever more ornate and costly funerals, and that a status symbol of the future may indeed be the simplest kind of "funeral without fins"?

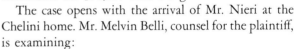

THE THEME that the American public, rather than the funeral industry, is responsible for our funeral practices, because it demands "the best" in embalming and merchandise for the dead, is one often expounded by funeral men. "We are merely giving the public what it wants," they say.

This is an interesting thought. It is a little hard to conceive of how this public demand is expressed and made known in practice to the seller of funeral service. Does the surviving spouse, for example, go into the funeral establishment and say, "I want to be sure my wife is thoroughly disinfected and preserved. Her casket must be both comfortable and eternally durable. And—oh yes, do be sure her burial footwear is really practical"?

Perhaps it does not often happen just like that. Yet it has been known to happen, and in fairness to the undertaking trade, an example should be given of a case in which the funeral buyer, of sound mind and deeply aware of his own desires, wanted and demanded the best.

The case involves Mr. August Chelini, fifty-seven-year-old mechanic, sometime scrap dealer and garage owner. His monthly earnings averaged $300 to $400. Mr. Chelini, an only child, lived with his aged mother, who died in 1943 at the age of ninety-nine years and seven months. It then became incumbent upon Mr. Chelini to arrange for the funeral, which he did by calling in Mr. Silvio Nieri, an undertaker and family friend.

What developed is best recounted by quoting from the transcript of the case of August Chelini, plaintiff, versus Silvio Nieri, defendant, in the Superior Court of San Mateo County, California.

Mr. August Chelini comes to life for us in the pages of a court reporter's typescript. We learn to know his hopes and fears, something of his history, something of his philosophy, his way of life, his motives and methods. He was in some respects an undertaker's dream person, a materialization of that man of sentiment and true feeling for the dead so often encountered in funeral trade magazines. Only the fact that he was suing an undertaker for $50,000 casts a slight shadow.

The case opens with the arrival of Mr. Nieri at the Chelini home. Mr. Melvin Belli, counsel for the plaintiff, is examining:

Q. [Mr. Belli] When he came to the house, did you have a conversation with him?

A. [Mr. Chelini] Well, he come in and he asked me if he should move the body, and I told him I wanted to talk things over with him first.

Q. Did you have a conversation there?

A. So I talked to him out in the kitchen, and explained to him what I wanted, and the conversation was that I told him what my mother requested.

Q. What did you tell him in this regard?

A. Well, I told him that my mother wanted to be buried where there was no ants or any bugs could get at her.

Q. Had your mother made that request?

A. She made that request.

Q. By the way, was your mother of sound mentality at the time?

A. Oh, yes, very sound. Pretty bright.

Q. Did you tell him anything else?

A. Well, I told him that she had $1500 of her own money, and that I intended to put all that into her funeral, and she had other moneys coming, and I wanted a hermetically sealed casket, because—

Q. You told him that, that you wanted—

A. I told him I wanted the best kind of embalming, and I wanted her put in a hermetically sealed casket.

Q. Did you know what a hermetically sealed casket was at that time?

A. Well, I know that it was a casket that no air or no water could get into.

Q. All right, did you tell him anything else?

A. I told him that is what I wanted. I didn't care what the cost was going to be, but I did have the $1500 on hand that belonged to her, and these other moneys were coming in that I could put into it later.

216

Q. All right. Did you tell him anything else at that time?

A. Also told him that I was anticipating making a lead box to eventually put her in, after the war was over; that lead couldn't be had at that time, and I am a mechanic. I intended to construct a lead box.

Q. You were going to do it yourself?

A. Yes, I have a sample of the box, the design of it, and I told him that I was going to figure to put her in a crypt until the war was over, and so that I could get the necessary things, and put her away in accordance with her wishes.

Q. By the way, you lived with your mother all her life?

A. There was times she lived out in South City, but we were with her pretty near every day.

Q. So, after you told him that you were going to make this lead coffin, after the war, did you have any further conversation with him?

A. Well, we talked about the embalming, how long he could preserve it, he says, "Practically forever," he says, "We got a new method of embalming that we will put on her, and she will keep almost forever."

Q. Pardon me. Go ahead.

A. I says, "That is a pretty long period, isn't it?" Well, he says, "They embalmed Caruso, and they embalmed Lincoln, that way, and they have these big candles near Caruso, and we have a new method of embalming. We have a new method of embalming. We can do a first-class job, and she will keep almost forever." . . .

Q. Then, the next day, did you have another conversation with him?

A. Then the next day he told me that I would have to come down to his establishment, and pick out a casket. . . .

Q. And you went down there?

A. My wife and I went down there.

Q. And when you got down there, did you have a further conversation with him?

A. Well, yes, he took me down in the basement there where he had all these caskets, and he told me to look them all over, and we picked out what we thought was the best casket in the house. . . . First I looked around, and my wife looked around. We both decided on the same casket. So, I asked him if that was a hermetically sealed job, he says, "Oh, yes, that is the finest thing there is, that is a bronze casket." . . . He told me this was a casket, it was a bronze casket, and was a hermetically sealed casket, and he said that that is the finest thing that is made, and he says, "This is pre-war stuff," and he says, "As a matter of fact, this is—I am going to keep one of these myself, in case anything happens to me, I am going to be buried in one of these myself." . . . He quoted me a price, then he says, "Well, that will be $875, that will include everything, everything in connection with the whole funeral," he says, "That will be completely everything in connection with the whole funeral, $875."

Q. Yes.

A. So, from what he told me, this casket was the best—it seemed very reasonable, so I told him that we would select that.

(Later that day, Chelini's mother was brought back to his house.)

Q. Was there any conversation in the house?

A. Well, by the time I got there, she was up there, the wife and I decided to put her in the dining room, originally, and when I got up there, he had her in the living room.

Q. Did you have some conversation with him at that time?

A. So, he said, "Well, I think it will be better to have her here, because there is a window here, she'll get lots of air." . . . He said he would have to put this body here in the front room on account of the window was here.

Q. Yes.

A. And he said it would be better to have a breeze, a flow of fresh air come in there.

Q. All right, did you have a conversation about the funeral with him to hurry over this?

A. Let's see. I don't think there was very much spoken about the funeral right then. I was feeling pretty bad. He spoke of this new embalming. He picked up her cheeks and skin on her and showed me how nice it was, pliable, it was—

Q. Did he tell you that that was a new method of embalming?

A. Yes, and her cheek was very pliable, her skin was especially.

Q. Is that what he said?

A. Well, that is the way he said that is the way it felt, and he told me that is a new type of embalming that they have, pliable. . . .

Q. All right, then you had a discussion with him at that time about paying him the money?

A. I asked him how much it was. He says, "it was $875." So I says, "Well, I want mother's ring back on her finger," I says, "when she is removed from the crypt to her final resting place. I want that ring put back on her finger," and I says, "I want some little slippers put on her that I can't get at this time," I says, "I want her all straightened up, and cleaned off nice," and I says "I will add another $25 for that service, for doing that," so he says, "All right," he says, "if that is the way you want it, we will do it, I would have done it for nothing," so I gave him that extra check for $25. . . . Oh, I also reminded him to be sure that when they put her finally into the cemetery, to see that she was properly secured, and he says, "Don't worry about it," he says, "I will see that everything is done properly." So, he took the check, and I asked him if he would go out and have a little drink with me, which he consented to, and which we did, in the kitchen.

217

(Probably, seldom was a little drink more needed than at that moment and by these principals. The scene now shifts to Cypress Lawn Cemetery):

Q. Did you go out there when your mother was taken out there?

A. Yes, I went out to the funeral, and she had the services there. Why, she left here on one of those little roller affairs, and we all walked out. Mr. Nieri—I came out to the car and asked him if he would go in there and see that she was properly adjusted from any shifting, or anything, and make sure that she was well sealed in, so he went in there, and he come out, and I asked him, I says, "Did you get her all sealed in nice?" Did you straighten her all up nice?" He says, "Don't be worrying about that, Gus," he says, "I will take care of everything."

Mr. Chelini was, it appears, the exceptional—nay, perfect—funeral customer. Not only did he gladly and freely choose the most expensive funeral available in the Nieri establishment; he also contracted for a $1,100 crypt in the Cypress Lawn mausoleum. He appreciated and endorsed every aspect of the funeral industry's concept of the sort of care that should be accorded the dead. An ardent admirer of the embalmer's art, he insisted on the finest receptacle in which to display it; indeed, he thought $875 a very reasonable price and repeatedly intimated his willingness to go higher.

At first glance, it seems like a frightful stroke of bad luck that Mr. Chelini, of all people, should be in court charging negligence and fraud against his erstwhile friend the undertaker, asserting that "the remains of the said Caroline Chelini were permitted to and did develop into a rotted, decomposed and insect and worm infested mess." Yet the inner logic of the situation is perhaps such that *only* a person of Mr. Chelini's persuasion in these matters would ever find himself in a position to make such a charge; for who else would be interested in ascertaining the condition of a human body after its interment?

It was not until two months after the funeral that Mr. Chelini was first assailed by doubts as to whether all was well within the bronze casket.

Mr. Chelini was in the habit of making frequent trips to his mother's crypt—he was out at the cemetery as many as three, four, or even five times a week. Sometimes he went to pay what he referred to as his vaultage; more often, merely to visit his mother. On one of these visits, he noticed a lot of ants "kind of walking around the crypt." He complained to the cemetery attendants, who promised to use some insect spray; he complained to Mr. Nieri, who assured him there was nothing to worry about.

Over the next year and a half, the ant situation worsened considerably, in spite of the spraying: "I could see more ants than ever, and there is a lot of little hideous black bugs jumping around there. Well, I had seen these hideous black bugs before, like little gnats, instead of flying they seemed to jump like that."

This time, he had a long, heart-to-heart talk with Mr. Nieri. The latter insisted that the body would still be just as perfect as the day it was buried, except for perhaps a little mold on the hands. Ants would never "tackle" an embalmed body, Mr. Nieri said. To prove his point, he produced a bottle of formaldehyde; he averred that he could take a piece of fresh horse meat of the best kind, or steak, or anything, saturate it with formaldehyde, and "nothing will tackle it."

The idea had evidently been growing in Mr. Chelini's mind that he must investigate the situation at first hand. With his wife, his family doctor and an embalmer from Nieri's establishment, he went to Cypress Lawn Cemetery and there caused the casket to be opened; upon which the doctor exclaimed, "Well, this is a hell of a mess, and a hell of a poor job of embalming, in my opinion."

In court, the undertaking fraternity rushed to the defense of their embattled colleague. Defense expert witnesses included several practicing funeral directors and Mr. Donald Ashworth, then dean of the San Francisco College of Mortuary Science. They were in an undeniably difficult position, for in order to build a case for Mr. Nieri they were forced to reveal some truths ordinarily concealed from the public. The defense theory—perhaps the only possible one in the circumstances—was that there is no such thing as "eternal preservation," that the results of embalming are always unpredictable; that, therefore, Mr. Nieri could not have entered into the alleged agreement with Mr. Chelini. Before the case was over, the theory of "everlasting security for your loved one," an advertising slogan gleefully flung at them by Mr. Belli, was thoroughly exploded by the reluctant experts. They also conceded that the expensive metal "sealer type" caskets, if anything, hasten the process of decomposition. The jury awarded damages to Mr. Chelini in the sum of $10,900.

218

219

Coq Guerrier

JANET WAKING

Beautifully Janet slept
Till it was deeply morning. She woke then
And thought about her dainty-feathered hen,
To see how it had kept.

One kiss she gave her mother,
Only a small one gave she to her daddy
Who would have kissed each curl of his shining baby;
No kiss at all for her brother.

"Old Chucky, Old Chucky!" she cried,
Running on little pink feet upon the grass
To Chucky's house, and listening. But alas,
Her Chucky had died.

It was a transmogrifying bee
Came droning down on Chucky's old bald head
And sat and put the poison. It scarcely bled,
But how exceedingly

And purply did the knot
Swell with the venom and communicate
Its rigor! Now the poor comb stood up straight
But Chucky did not.

So there was Janet
Kneeling on the wet grass, crying her brown hen
(Translated far beyond the daughters of men)
To rise and walk upon it.

And weeping fast as she had breath
Janet implored us, "Wake her from her sleep!"
And would not be instructed in how deep
Was the forgetful kingdom of death.

John Crowe Ransom

TORCH SONG

AFTER JACK LOREY had known Joan Harris in New York for a few years, he began to think of her as The Widow. She always wore black, and he was always given the feeling, by a curious disorder in her apartment, that the undertakers had just left. This impression did not stem from malice on his part, for he was fond of Joan. They came from the same city in Ohio and had reached New York at about the same time in the middle thirties. They were the same age, and during their first summer in the city they used to meet after work and drink Martinis in places like the Brevoort and Charles', and have dinner and play checkers at the Lafayette.

Joan went to a school for models when she settled in the city, but it turned out that she photographed badly, so after spending six weeks learning how to walk with a book on her head she got a job as a hostess in a Longchamps. For the rest of the summer she stood by the hatrack, bathed in an intense pink light and the string music of heartbreak, swinging her mane of dark hair and her black skirt as she moved forward to greet the customers. She was then a big, handsome girl with a wonderful voice, and her face, her whole presence, always seemed infused with a gentle and healthy pleasure at her surroundings, whatever they were. She was innocently and incorrigibly convivial, and would get out of bed and dress at three in the morning if someone called her and asked her to come out for a drink, as Jack often did. In the fall, she got some kind of freshman executive job in a department store. They saw less and less of each other and then for quite a while stopped seeing each other altogether. Jack was living with a girl he had met at a party, and it never occurred to him to wonder what had become of Joan.

Jack's girl had some friends in Pennsylvania, and in the spring and summer of his second year in town he often went there with her for weekends. All of this—the shared apartment in the Village, the illicit relationship, the Friday-night train to a country house—were what he had imagined life in New York to be, and he was intensely happy. He was returning to New York with his girl one Sunday night on the Lehigh line. It was one of those trains that move slowly across the face of New Jersey, bringing back to the city hundreds of people, like the victims of an immense and strenuous picnic, whose faces are blazing and whose muscles are lame. Jack and his girl, like most of the other passengers, were overburdened with vegetables and flowers. When the train stopped in Pennsylvania Station, they moved with the crowd along the platform, toward the escalator. As they were passing the wide, lighted windows of the diner, Jack turned his head and saw Joan. It was the first time he had seen her since Thanksgiving, or since Christmas. He couldn't remember.

Joan was with a man who had obviously passed out. His head was in his arms on the table, and an overturned highball glass was near one of his elbows. Joan was shaking his shoulders gently and speaking to him. She seemed to be vaguely troubled, vaguely amused. The waiters had cleared off all the other tables and were standing around Joan, waiting for her to resurrect her escort. It troubled Jack to see in these straits a girl who reminded him of the trees and the lawns of his home town, but there was nothing he could do to help. Joan continued to shake the man's shoulders, and the crowd pressed Jack past one after another of the diner's windows, past the malodorous kitchen, and up the escalator.

He saw Joan again, later that summer, when he was having dinner in a Village restaurant. He was with a new girl, a Southerner. There were many Southern girls in the city that year. Jack and his belle had wandered into the restaurant because it was convenient, but the food was terrible and the place was lighted with candles. Halfway through dinner, Jack noticed Joan on the other side of the room, and when he had finished eating, he crossed the room and spoke to her. She was with a tall man who was wearing a monocle. He stood, bowed stiffly from the waist, and said to Jack, "We are very pleased to meet you." Then he excused himself and headed for the toilet. "He's a count, he's a Swedish count," Joan said. "He's on the radio, Friday afternoons at four-fifteen. Isn't it exciting?" She seemed to be delighted with the count and the terrible restaurant.

Sometime the next winter, Jack moved from the Village to an apartment in the East Thirties. He was crossing Park Avenue one cold morning on his way to the office when he noticed, in the crowd, a woman he had met a few times at Joan's apartment. He spoke to her and asked about his friend. "Haven't you heard?" she said. She pulled a long face. "Perhaps I'd better tell you. Perhaps you can help." She and Jack had breakfast in a drugstore on Madison Avenue and she unburdened herself of the story.

The count had a program called "The Song of the Fiords," or something like that, and he sang Swedish folk songs. Everyone suspected him of being a fake, but that didn't bother Joan. He had met her at a party and, sensing a soft touch, had moved in with her the following night. About a week later, he complained of pains in his back and said he must have some morphine. Then he needed morphine all the time. If he didn't get morphine, he was abusive and violent. Joan began to deal with those doctors and druggists who peddle dope, and when they wouldn't supply her, she went down to the bottom of the city. Her friends were afraid she would be found some morning stuffed in a drain. She got pregnant. She had an abortion. The count left her and moved to a flea bag near Times Square, but she was so impressed by then with his helplessness, so afraid that he would die without her, that she followed him there and shared his room and continued to buy his narcotics. He abandoned her again, and Joan waited a week for him to return before she went back to her place and her friends in the Village.

It shocked Jack to think of the innocent girl from Ohio having lived with a brutal dope addict and traded with criminals, and when he got to his office that morning, he telephoned her and made a date for dinner that night. He met her at Charles'. When she came into the bar, she seemed as wholesome and calm as ever. Her voice was sweet, and reminded him of elms, of lawns, of those glass arrangements that used to be hung from porch ceilings to tinkle in the summer wind. She told him about the count. She spoke of him charitably and with no trace of bitterness, as if her voice, her disposition, were incapable of registering anything beyond simple affection and pleasure. Her walk, when she moved ahead of him toward their table, was light and graceful. She ate a large dinner and talked enthusiastically about her job. They went to a movie and said goodbye in front of her apartment house.

That winter, Jack met a girl he decided to marry. Their engagement was announced in January and they planned to marry in July. In the spring, he received, in his office mail, an invitation to cocktails at Joan's. It was for a Saturday when his fiancée was going to Massachusetts to visit her parents, and when the time came and he had nothing better to do, he took a bus to the Village. Joan had the same apartment. It was a walkup. You rang the bell above the mailbox in the vestibule and were answered with a death rattle in the lock. Joan lived on the third floor. Her calling card was in a slot on the mailbox, and above her name was written the name Hugh Bascomb.

Jack climbed the two flights of carpeted stairs, and when he reached Joan's apartment, she was standing by the open door in a black dress. After she greeted Jack, she took his arm and guided him across the room. "I want you to meet Hugh, Jack," she said.

Hugh was a big man with a red face and pale-blue eyes. His manner was courtly and his eyes were inflamed with drink. Jack talked with him for a little while and then went over to speak to someone he knew, who was standing

223

by the mantelpiece. He noticed then, for the first time, the indescribable disorder of Joan's apartment. The books were in their shelves and the furniture was reasonably good, but the place was all wrong, somehow. It was as if things had been put in place without thought or real interest, and for the first time, too, he had the impression that there had been a death there recently.

As Jack moved around the room, he felt that he had met the ten or twelve guests at other parties. There was a woman executive with a fancy hat, a man who could imitate Roosevelt, a grim couple whose play was in rehearsal, and a newspaperman who kept turning on the radio for news of the Spanish Civil War. Jack drank Martinis and talked with the woman in the fancy hat. He looked out of the window at the back yards and the ailanthus trees and heard, in the distance, thunder exploding off the cliffs of the Hudson.

Hugh Bascomb got very drunk. He began to spill liquor, as if drinking, for him, were a kind of jolly slaughter and he enjoyed the bloodshed and the mess. He spilled whiskey from a bottle. He spilled a drink on his shirt and then tipped over someone else's drink. The party was not quiet, but Hugh's hoarse voice began to dominate the others. He attacked a photographer who was sitting in a corner explaining camera techniques to a homely woman. "What did you come to the party for if all you wanted to do was to sit there and stare at your shoes?" Hugh shouted. "What did you come for? Why don't you stay at home?"

The photographer didn't know what to say. He was not staring at his shoes. Joan moved lightly to Hugh's side. "Please don't get into a fight now, darling," she said. "Not this afternoon."

"Shut up," he said. "Let me alone. Mind your own business." He lost his balance, and in struggling to steady himself he tipped over a lamp.

"Oh, your lovely lamp, Joan," a woman sighed.

"Lamps!" Hugh roared. He threw his arms into the air and worked them around his head as if he were bludgeoning himself. "Lamps. Glasses. Cigarette boxes. Dishes. They're killing me. They're killing me, for Christ's sake. Let's all go up to the mountains, for Christ's sake. Let's all go up to the mountains and hunt and fish and live like men, for Christ's sake."

People were scattering as if a rain had begun to fall in the room. It had, as a matter of fact, begun to rain outside. Someone offered Jack a ride uptown, and he jumped at the chance. Joan stood at the door, saying goodbye to her routed friends. Her voice remained soft, and her manner, unlike that of those Christian women who in the face of disaster can summon new and formidable sources of composure, seemed genuinely simple. She appeared to be oblivious of the raging drunk at her back, who was pacing up and down, grinding glass into the rug, and haranguing one of the survivors of the party with a story of how he, Hugh, had once gone without food for three weeks.

In July, Jack was married in an orchard in Duxbury, and he and his wife went to West Chop for a few weeks. When they returned to town, their apartment was cluttered with presents, including a dozen after-dinner coffee cups from Joan. His wife sent her the required note, but they did nothing else.

Later in the summer, Joan telephoned Jack at his office and asked if he wouldn't bring his wife to see her; she named an evening the following week. He felt guilty about not having called her, and accepted the invitation. This made his wife angry. She was an ambitious girl who liked a social life that offered rewards, and she went unwillingly to Joan's Village apartment with him.

Written above Joan's name on the mailbox was the name Franz Denzel. Jack and his wife climbed the stairs and were met by Joan at the open door. They went into her apartment and found themselves among a group of people for whom Jack, at least, was unable to find any bearings.

Franz Denzel was a middle-aged German. His face was pinched with bitterness or illness. He greeted Jack and his wife with that elaborate and clever politeness that is intended to make guests feel that they have come too early or too late. He insisted sharply upon Jack's sitting in the chair in which he himself had been sitting, and then went and sat on a radiator. There were five other Germans sitting around the room, drinking coffee. In a corner was another American couple, who looked uncomfortable. Joan passed Jack and his wife small cups of coffee with whipped cream. "These cups belonged to Franz's mother," she said. "Aren't they lovely? They were the only things he took from Germany when he escaped from the Nazis."

225

Franz turned to Jack and said, "Perhaps you will give us your opinion on the American educational system. That is what we were discussing when you arrived."

Before Jack could speak, one of the German guests opened an attack on the American educational system. The other Germans joined in, and went on from there to describe every vulgarity that had impressed them in American life and to contrast German and American culture generally. Where, they asked one another passionately, could you find in America anything like the Mitropa dining cars, the Black Forest, the pictures in Munich, the music in Bayreuth? Franz and his friends began speaking in German. Neither Jack nor his wife nor Joan could understand German, and the other American couple had not opened their mouths since they were introduced. Joan went happily around the room, filling everyone's cup with coffee, as if the music of a foreign language were enough to make an evening for her.

Jack drank five cups of coffee. He was desperately uncomfortable. Joan went into the kitchen while the Germans were laughing at their German jokes, and he hoped she would return with some drinks, but when she came back, it was with a tray of ice cream and mulberries.

"Isn't this pleasant?" Franz asked, speaking in English again.

Joan collected the coffee cups, and as she was about to take them back to the kitchen, Franz stopped her.

"Isn't one of those cups chipped?"

"No, darling," Joan said. "I never let the maid touch them. I wash them myself."

"What's that?" he asked, pointing at the rim of one of the cups.

"That's the cup that's always been chipped, darling. It was chipped when you unpacked it. You noticed it then."

"These things were perfect when they arrived in this country," he said.

Joan went into the kitchen and he followed her.

Jack tried to make conversation with the Germans. From the kitchen there was the sound of a blow and a cry. Franz returned and began to eat his mulberries greedily. Joan came back with her dish of ice cream. Her voice was gentle. Her tears, if she had been crying, had dried as quickly as the tears of a child. Jack and his wife finished their ice cream and made their escape. The wasted and unnerving evening enraged Jack's wife, and he supposed that he would never see Joan again.

Jack's wife got pregnant early in the fall, and she seized on all the prerogatives of an expectant mother. She took long naps, ate canned peaches in the middle of the night, and talked about the rudimentary kidney. She chose to see only other couples who were expecting children, and the parties that she and Jack gave were temperate. The baby, a boy, was born in May, and Jack was very proud and happy. The first party he and his wife went to after her convalescence was the wedding of a girl whose family Jack had known in Ohio.

226

The wedding was at St. James', and afterward there was a big reception at the River Club. There was an orchestra dressed like Hungarians, and a lot of champagne and Scotch. Toward the end of the afternoon, Jack was walking down a dim corridor when he heard Joan's voice. "Please don't, darling," she was saying. "You'll break my arm. *Please* don't, darling." She was being pressed against the wall by a man who seemed to be twisting her arm. As soon as they saw Jack, the struggle stopped. All three of them were intensely embarrassed. Joan's face was wet and she made an effort to smile through her tears at Jack. He said hello and went on without stopping. When he returned, she and the man had disappeared.

When Jack's son was less than two years old, his wife flew with the baby to Nevada to get a divorce. Jack gave her the apartment and all its furnishings and took a room in a hotel near Grand Central. His wife got her decree in due course, and the story was in the newspapers. Jack had a telephone call from Joan a few days later.

"I'm awfully sorry to hear about your divorce, Jack," she said. "She seemed like *such* a nice girl. But that wasn't what I called you about. I want your help, and I wondered if you could come down to my place tonight around six. It's something I don't want to talk about over the phone."

He went obediently to the Village that night and climbed the stairs. Her apartment was a mess. The pictures and the curtains were down and the books were in boxes. "You moving, Joan?" he asked.

"That's what I wanted to see you about, Jack. First, I'll give you a drink." She made two Old-Fashioneds. "I'm being evicted, Jack," she said. "I'm being evicted because I'm an immoral woman. The couple who have the apartment downstairs—they're charming people, I've always thought—have told the real-estate agent that I'm a drunk and a prostitute and all kinds of things. Isn't that fantastic? This real-estate agent has always been so nice to me that I didn't think he'd believe them, but he's cancelled my lease, and if I make any trouble, he's threatened to take the matter up with the store, and I don't want to lose my job. This nice real-estate agent won't even talk with me any more. When I go over to the office, the receptionist leers at me as if I were some kind of dreadful woman. Of course, there have been a lot of men here and we sometimes are noisy, but I can't be expected to go to bed at ten every night. Can I? Well, the agent who manages this building has apparently told all the other agents in the neighborhood that I'm an immoral and drunken woman, and none of them will give me an apartment. I went in to talk with one man—he seemed to be such a nice old gentleman—and he made me an indecent proposal. Isn't it fantastic? I have to be out of here on Thursday and I'm literally being turned out into the street."

Joan seemed as serene and innocent as ever while she described this scourge of agents and neighbors. Jack listened carefully for some sign of indignation or bitterness or even urgency in her recital, but there was none. He was reminded of a torch song, of one of those forlorn and touching ballads that had been sung neither for him nor for her but for their older brothers and sisters by Marion Harris. Joan seemed to be singing her wrongs.

"They've made my life miserable," she went on quietly. "If I keep the radio on after ten o'clock, they telephone the agent in the morning and tell him I had some kind of orgy here. One night when Phillip—I don't think you've met Phillip; he's in the Royal Air Force; he's gone back to England—one night when Phillip and some other people were here, they called the police. The police came bursting in the door and talked to me as if I were I don't know what and then looked in the bedroom. If they think there's a man up here after midnight, they call me on the telephone and say all kinds of disgusting things. Of course, I can put my furniture into storage and go to a hotel, I guess. I guess a hotel will take a woman with my kind of reputation, but I thought perhaps you might know of an apartment. I thought—"

It angered Jack to think of this big, splendid girl's being persecuted by her neighbors, and he said he would do what he could. He asked her to have dinner with him, but she said she was busy.

Having nothing better do to, Jack decided to walk uptown to his hotel. It was a hot night. The sky was overcast. On his way, he saw a parade in a dark side street off Broadway near Madison Square. All the buildings in the neighborhood were dark. It was so dark that he could not see the placards the marchers carried until he came to a street light. Their signs urged the entry of the United States into the war, and each platoon represented a nation that had been subjugated by the Axis powers. They marched up Broadway, as he watched, to no music, to no sound but their own steps on the rough cobbles. It was for the most part an army of elderly men and women—Poles, Norwegians, Danes, Jews, Chinese. A few idle people like himself lined the sidewalks, and the marchers passed between them with all the self-consciousness of enemy prisoners. There were children among them dressed in the costumes in which they had, for the newsreels, presented the Mayor with a package of tea, a petition, a protest, a constitution, a check, or a pair of tickets. They hobbled through the darkness of the loft neighborhood like a mortified and destroyed people, toward Greeley Square.

In the morning, Jack put the problem of finding an apartment for Joan up to his secretary. She started phoning real-estate agents, and by afternoon she had found a couple of available apartments in the West Twenties. Joan called Jack the next day to say that she had taken one of the apartments and to thank him.

Jack didn't see Joan again until the following summer. It was a Sunday evening; he had left a cocktail party in a Washington Square apartment and had decided to walk a few blocks up Fifth Avenue before he took a bus. As he was passing the Brevoort, Joan called to him. She was with a man at one of the tables on the sidewalk. She looked cool and fresh, and the man appeared to be respectable. His name, it turned out, was Pete Bristol. He invited Jack to sit down and join in a celebration. Germany had invaded Russia that weekend, and Joan and Pete were drinking champagne to celebrate Russia's changed position in the war. The three of them drank champagne until it got dark. They had dinner and drank champagne with their dinner. They drank more champagne afterward and then went over to the Lafayette and then to two or three other places. Joan had always been tireless in her gentle way. She hated to see the night end, and it was after three o'clock when Jack stumbled into his apartment. The following morning he woke up haggard and sick, and with no recollection of the last hour or so of the previous evening. His suit was soiled and he had lost his hat. He didn't get to his office until eleven. Joan had already called him twice, and she called him again soon after he got in. There was no hoarseness at all in her voice. She said that she had to see him, and he agreed to meet her for lunch in a seafood restaurant in the Fifties.

He was standing at the bar when she breezed in, looking as though she had taken no part in that calamitous night. The advice she wanted concerned selling her jewelry. Her grandmother had left her some jewelry, and she wanted to raise money on it but didn't know where to go. She took some rings and bracelets out of her purse and showed them to Jack. He said that he didn't know anything about jewelry but that he could lend her some money. "Oh, I couldn't borrow money from you, Jack," she said. "You see, I want to get the money for Pete. I want to help him. He wants to open an advertising agency, and he needs quite a lot to begin with." Jack didn't press her to accept his offer of a loan after that, and the project wasn't mentioned again during lunch.

He next heard about Joan from a young doctor who was a friend of theirs. "Have you seen Joan recently?" the doctor asked Jack one evening when they were having dinner together. He said no. "I gave her a checkup last week," the doctor said, "and while she's been through enough to kill the average mortal—and you'll never know what she's been through—she still has the constitution of a virtuous and healthy woman. Did you hear about the last one? She sold her jewelry to put him into some kind of a business, and as soon as he got the money, he left her for another girl, who had a car—a convertible."

Jack was drafted into the Army in the spring of 1942. He was kept at Fort Dix for nearly a month, and during this time he came to New York in the evening whenever he could get permission. Those nights had for him the intense keenness of a reprieve, a sensation that was heightened by the fact that on the train in from Trenton women would often press upon him dog-eared copies of *Life* and half-eaten boxes of candy, as though the brown clothes he wore were surely cerements. He telephoned Joan from Pennsylvania Station one night. "Come right over, Jack," she said. "Come right over. I want you to meet Ralph."

She was living in that place in the West Twenties that Jack had found for her. The neighborhood was a slum. Ash cans stood in front of her house, and an old woman was there picking out bits of refuse and garbage and stuffing them into a perambulator. The house in which Joan's apartment was located was shabby, but the apartment itself seemed familiar. The furniture was the same. Joan was the same big, easy-going girl. "I'm so glad you called me," she said. "It's so good to see you. I'll make you a drink. I was having one myself. Ralph ought to be here by now. He promised to take me to dinner." Jack offered to take her to Cavanagh's, but she said that Ralph might come while she was out. "If he doesn't come by nine, I'm going to make myself a sandwich. I'm not really hungry."

Jack talked about the Army. She talked about the store. She had been working in the same place for—how long was it? He didn't know. He had never seen her at her desk and he couldn't imagine what she did. "I'm terribly sorry Ralph isn't here," she said. "I'm sure you'd like him. He's not a young man. He's a heart specialist who loves to play the viola." She turned on some lights, for the summer sky had got dark. "He has this dreadful wife on Riverside Drive and four ungrateful children. He—"

The noise of an air-raid siren, lugubrious and seeming to spring from pain, as if all the misery and indecision in the city had been given a voice, cut her off. Other sirens, in distant neighborhoods, sounded, until the dark air was full of their noise. "Let me fix you another drink before I have to turn out the lights," Joan said, and took his glass. She brought the drink back to him and snapped off the lights. They went to the windows, and, as children watch a

229

thunderstorm, they watched the city darken. All the lights nearby went out but one. Air-raid wardens had begun to sound their whistles in the street. From a distant yard came a hoarse shriek of anger. "Put out your lights, you Fascists!" a woman screamed. "Put out your lights, you Nazi Fascist Germans. Turn out your lights. Turn out your lights." The last light went off. They went away from the window and sat in the lightless room.

In the darkness, Joan began to talk about her departed lovers, and from what she said Jack gathered that they had all had a hard time. Nils, the suspect count, was dead. Hugh Bascomb, the drunk, had joined the Merchant Marine and was missing in the North Atlantic. Franz, the German, had taken poison the night the Nazis bombed Warsaw. "We listened to the news on the radio," Joan said, "and then he went back to his hotel and took poison. The maid found him dead in the bathroom the next morning." When Jack asked her about the one who was going to open an advertising agency, she seemed at first to have forgotten him. "Oh, Pete," she said after a pause. "Well, he was always very sick, you know. He was supposed to go to Saranac, but he kept putting it off and putting it off and—" She stopped talking when she heard steps on the stairs, hoping, he supposed, that it was Ralph, but whoever it was turned at the landing and continued to the top of the house. "I wish Ralph would come," she said, with a sigh. "I want you to meet him." Jack asked her again to go out, but she refused, and when the all-clear sounded, he said goodbye.

Jack was shipped from Dix to an infantry training camp in the Carolinas and from there to an infantry division stationed in Georgia. He had been in Georgia three months when he married a girl from the Augusta boarding-house aristocracy. A year or so later, he crossed the continent in a day coach and thought sententiously that the last he might see of the country he loved was the desert towns like Barstow, that the last he might hear of it was the ringing of the trolleys on the Bay Bridge. He was sent into the Pacific and returned to the United States twenty months later, uninjured and apparently unchanged. As soon as he received his furlough, he went to Augusta. He presented his wife with the souvenirs he had brought from the islands, quarrelled violently with her and all her family, and, after making arrangements for her to get an Arkansas divorce, left for New York.

Jack was discharged from the Army at a camp in the East a few months later. He took a vacation and then went back to the job he had left in 1942. He seemed to have picked up his life at approximately the moment when it had been interrupted by the war. In time, everything came to look and feel the same. He saw most of his old friends. Only two of the men he knew had been killed in the war. He didn't call Joan, but he met her one winter afternoon on a crosstown bus.

Her fresh face, her black clothes, and her soft voice instantly destroyed the sense—if he had ever had such a sense—that anything had changed or intervened since their last meeting, three or four years ago. She asked him up for cocktails and he went to her apartment the next Saturday afternoon. Her room and her guests reminded him of the parties she had given when she had first come to New York. There was a woman with a fancy hat, an elderly doctor, and a man who stayed close to the radio, listening for news from the Balkans. Jack wondered which of the men belonged to Joan and decided on an Englishman who kept coughing into a handkerchief that he pulled out of his sleeve. Jack was right. "Isn't Stephen brilliant?" Joan asked him a little later, when they were alone in a corner. "He knows more about the Polynesians than anyone else in the world."

Jack had returned not only to his old job but to his old salary. Since living costs had doubled and since he was paying alimony to two wives, he had to draw on his savings. He took another job, which promised more money, but it didn't last long and he found himself out of work. This didn't bother him at all. He still had money in the bank, and anyhow it was easy to borrow from friends. His indifference was the consequence not of lassitude or despair but rather of an excess of hope. He had the feeling that he had only recently come to New York from Ohio. The sense that he was very young and that the best years of his life still lay before him was an illusion that he could not seem to escape. There was all the time in the world. He was living in hotels then, moving from one to another every five days.

In the spring, Jack moved to a furnished room in the badlands west of Central Park. He was running out of money. Then, when he began to feel that a job was a desperate necessity, he got sick. At first, he seemed to have only a bad cold, but he was unable to shake it and he began to run a fever and to cough blood. The fever kept him drowsy most of the time, but he roused himself occasionally and went out to a cafeteria for a meal. He felt sure that none of his friends knew where he was, and he was glad of this. He hadn't counted on Joan.

Late one morning, he heard her speaking in the hall with his landlady. A few moments later, she knocked on his door. He was lying on the bed in a pair of pants and a soiled pajama top, and he didn't answer. She knocked again and walked in. "I've been looking everywhere for you, Jack," she said. She spoke softly. "When I found out that you were in a place like this I thought you must be broke or sick. I stopped at the bank and got some money, in case you're broke. I've brought you some Scotch. I thought a little drink wouldn't do you any harm. Want a little drink?"

Joan's dress was black. Her voice was low and serene. She sat in a chair beside his bed as if she had been coming there every day to nurse him. Her features had coarsened, he thought, but there were still very few lines in her face. She was heavier. She was nearly fat. She was wearing black cotton gloves. She got two glasses and poured Scotch into them. He drank his whiskey greedily. "I didn't get to bed until three last night," she said. Her voice had once before reminded him of a gentle and despairing song, but now, perhaps because he

231

was sick, her mildness, the mourning she wore, her stealthy grace, made him uneasy. "It was one of those nights," she said. "We went to the theatre. Afterward, someone asked us up to his place. I don't know who he was. It was one of those places. They're so strange. There were some meat-eating plants and a collection of Chinese snuff bottles. Why do people collect Chinese snuff bottles? We all autographed a lampshade, as I remember, but I can't remember much."

Jack tried to sit up in bed, as if there were some need to defend himself, and then fell back again, against the pillows. "How did you find me, Joan?" he asked.

"It was simple," she said. "I called that hotel. The one you were staying in. They gave me this address. My secretary got the telephone number. Have another little drink."

"You know you've never come to a place of mine before—never," he said. "Why did you come now?"

"Why did I come, darling?" she asked. "What a question! I've known you for thirty years. You're the oldest friend I have in New York. Remember that night in the Village when it snowed and we stayed up until morning and drank whiskey sours for breakfast? That doesn't seem like twelve years ago. And that night—"

"I don't like to have you see me in a place like this," he said earnestly. He touched his face and felt his beard.

232

"And all the people who used to imitate Roosevelt," she said, as if she had not heard him, as if she were deaf. "And that place on Staten Island where we all used to go for dinner when Henry had a car. Poor Henry. He bought a place in Connecticut and went out there by himself, one weekend. He fell asleep with a lighted cigarette and the house, the barn, everything burned. Ethel took the children out to California." She poured more Scotch into his glass and handed it to him. She lighted a cigarette and put it between his lips. The intimacy of this gesture, which made it seem not only as if he were deathly ill but as if he were her lover, troubled him.

"As soon as I'm better," he said, "I'll take a room at a good hotel. I'll call you then. It was nice of you to come."

"Oh, don't be ashamed of this room, Jack," she said. "Rooms never bother me. It doesn't seem to matter to me where I am. Stanley had a filthy room in Chelsea. At least, other people told me it was filthy. I never noticed it. Rats used to eat the food I brought him. He used to have to hang the food from the ceiling, from the light chain."

"I'll call you as soon as I'm better," Jack said. "I think I can sleep now if I'm left alone. I seem to need a lot of sleep."

"You really *are* sick, darling," she said. "You must have a fever." She sat on the edge of his bed and put a hand on his forehead.

"How is that Englishman, Joan?" he asked. "Do you still see him?"

"What Englishman?" she said.

"You know. I met him at your house. He kept a handkerchief up his sleeve. He coughed all the time. You know the one I mean."

"You must be thinking of someone else," she said. "I haven't had an Englishman at my place since the war. Of course, I can't remember everyone." She turned and, taking one of his hands, linked her fingers in his.

"He's dead, isn't he?" Jack said. "That Englishman's dead." He pushed her off the bed, and got up himself. "Get out," he said.

"You're sick, darling," she said. "I can't leave you alone here."

"Get out," he said again, and when she didn't move, he shouted, "What kind of an obscenity are you that you can smell sickness and death the way you do?"

"You poor darling."

"Does it make you feel young to watch the dying?" he shouted. "Is that the lewdness that keeps you young? Is that why you dress like a crow? Oh, I know there's nothing I can say that will hurt you. I know there's nothing filthy or corrupt or depraved or brutish or base that the others haven't tried, but this time you're wrong. I'm not ready. My life isn't ending. My life's beginning. There are wonderful years ahead of me. There are, there are wonderful, wonderful, wonderful, wonderful years ahead of me, and when they're over, when it's time, then I'll call you. Then, as an old friend, I'll call you and give you whatever dirty pleasure you take in watching the dying, but until then, you and your ugly and misshapen forms will leave me alone."

She finished her drink and looked at her watch. "I guess I'd better show up at the office," she said. "I'll see you later. I'll come back tonight. You'll feel better then, you poor darling." She closed the door after her, and he heard her light step on the stairs.

Jack emptied the whiskey bottle into the sink. He began to dress. He stuffed his dirty clothes into a bag. He was trembling and crying with sickness and fear. He could see the blue sky from his window, and in his fear it seemed miraculous that the sky would be blue, that the white clouds should remind him of snow, that from the sidewalk he could hear the shrill voices of children shrieking, "I'm the king of the mountain, I'm the king of the mountain, I'm the king of the mountain." He emptied the ashtray containing his nail parings and cigarette butts into the toilet, and swept the floor with a shirt, so that there would be no trace of his life, of his body, when that lewd and searching shape of death came there to find him in the evening.

John Cheever

233

RELIGION

GOD IS DEAD IN GEORGIA

Eminent Deity Succumbs During Surgery—Succession in Doubt As All Creation Groans

LBJ ORDERS FLAGS AT HALF STAFF

Special to The New York Times

ATLANTA, GA., Nov. 9—God, creator of the universe, principal deity of the world's Jews, ultimate reality of Christians, and most eminent of all divinities, died late yesterday during major surgery undertaken to correct a massive diminishing influence. His exact age is not known, but close friends estimate that it greatly exceeded that of all other extant beings. While he did not, in recent years, maintain any fixed abode, his house was said to consist of many mansions.

The cause of death could not be immediately determined, pending an autopsy, but the deity's surgeon, Thomas J. J. Altizer, 38, of Emory University in Atlanta, indicated possible cardiac insufficiency. Assisting Dr. Altizer in the unsuccessful surgery were Dr. Paul van Buren of Temple University, Philadelphia; Dr. William Hamilton of Colgate-Rochester, Rochester, N. Y.; and Dr. Gabriel Vahanian of Syracuse University, Syracuse, N. Y.

Word of the death, long rumored, was officially disclosed to reporters at five minutes before midnight after a full day of mounting anxiety and the comings and going of ecclesiastical dignitaries and members of the immediate family. At the bedside, when the end came, were, in addition to the attending surgeons and several nurses, the Papal Nuncio to the United States, representing His Holiness, Pope Paul VI, Vicar of Christ on Earth and Supreme Pontiff of the Roman Catholic Church; Iakovos, Archbishop of North and South America, representing the Orthodox Churches; Dr. Eugene Carson Blake, Stated Clerk of the Presbyterian Church in the USA, representing the World Council of Churches, predominantly a Protestant institution; Rabbi Mark Tannenbaum of New York City, representing the tribes of Israel, chosen people, according to their faith, of the deceased; The Rev. William Moyers, Baptist minister, representing President Johnson; the 3rd Secretary of the Soviet embassy in Trinidad, representing the Union of Soviet Socialist Republics; and a number of unidentified curious bystanders.

Unable to be in Atlanta owing to the pressure of business at the second Vatican Council, now in session, the Pope, in Rome, said, in part: "We are deeply distressed for we have suffered an incalculable loss. The contributions of God to the Church cannot be measured, and it is difficult to imagine how we shall proceed without Him." Rumors swept through the Council, meeting under the great vaulted dome of St. Peter's, that, before adjourning the Council in December, the Pope will proclaim God a saint, an action, if taken, that would be wholly without precedent in the history of the Church. Several aged women were reported to have come forward with claims of miraculous cures due to God's intervention. One woman, a 103 year old Bulgarian peasant, is said to have conceived a son at the very instant God expired. Proof of miracles is a precondition for sanctification according to ancient tradition of the Roman Catholic faith.

In Johnson City, Texas, President Johnson, recuperating from his recent gall bladder surgery, was described by aides as "profoundly upset." He at once directed that all flags should be at half-staff until after the funeral. The First Lady and the two presidential daughters, Luci and Lynda, were understood to have wept openly. Luci, 18, the younger daughter, whose engagement has been lately rumored, is a convert to Roman Catholicism. It is assumed that the President and his family, including his cousin, Oriole, will attend the last rites, if the international situation permits. Both houses of Congress met in Washington at noon today and promptly adjourned after passing a joint resolution expressing "grief and great respect for the departed spiritual leader." Sen. Wayne Morse, Dem. of Oregon, objected on the grounds that the resolution violated the principle of separation of church and state, but he was overruled by Vice President Hubert Humphrey, who remarked that "this is not a time for partisan politics."

Plans for the deity's funeral are incomplete. Reliable sources suggested that extensive negotiations may be necessary in order to select a church for the services and an appropriate liturgy. Dr. Wilhelm Pauck, theologian, of Union Seminary in New York City proposed this morning that it would be "fitting and seemly" to inter the remains in the ultimate ground of all being, but it is not known whether that proposal is acceptable to the family. Funerals for divinities, common in ancient times, have been exceedingly rare in recent centuries, and it is understood that the family wishes to review details of earlier funerals before settling upon rites suitable for God.

(In New York, meanwhile, the stock market dropped sharply in early trading. Volume was heavy. One broker called it the most active market day since the assassination of President Kennedy, Nov. 22, 1963. The market rallied in late trading, after reports were received that Jesus—see 'Man in the News,' p. 36, col. 4—who survives, plans to assume a larger role in management of the universe.)

Reaction from the world's great and from the man in the street was uniformly incredulous. "At least he's out of his misery," commented one housewife in an Elmira, N. Y., supermarket. "I can't believe it," said the Right Reverend Horace W. B. Donegan, Protestant Episcopal Bishop of New York, who only last week celebrated the 15th anniversary of his installation as Bishop. In Paris, President de Gaulle, in a 30 second appearance on national television, proclaimed: "God is dead! Long live the republic! Long live France!" Mrs. Jacqueline Kennedy, widow of the late President, was reported "in seclusion" in her Fifth Avenue

apartment. "She's had about all she can take," a close friend of the Kennedy family said. News of the death was included in a one sentence statement, without comment, on the 3rd page of Pravda, official organ of the Soviet government. The passing of God has not been disclosed to the 800 million Chinese who live behind the bamboo curtain.

Public reaction in this country was perhaps summed up by an elderly retired streetcar conductor in Passaic, New Jersey, who said: "I never met him, of course. Never even saw him. But from what I heard I guess he was a real nice fellow. Tops." From Independence, Mo., former President Harry S. Truman, who received the news in his Kansas City barbershop, said: "I'm always sorry to hear somebody is dead. It's a damn shame." In Gettysburg, Pa., former President Dwight D. Eisenhower, released, through a military aide, the following statement: "Mrs. Eisenhower joins me in heartfelt sympathy to the family and many friends of the late God. He was, I always felt, a force for moral good in the universe. Those of us who were privileged to know him admired the probity of his character, the breadth of his compassion, the depth of his intellect. Generous almost to a fault, his many acts of kindness to America will never be forgotten. It is a very great loss indeed. He will be missed."

From Basel, Switzerland, came word that Dr. Karl Barth, venerable Protestant theologian, informed of the death of God, declared: "I don't know who died in Atlanta, but whoever he was he's an imposter." Dr. Barth, 79, with the late Paul Tillich, is widely regarded as the foremost theologian of the 20th Century.

(There have been unconfirmed reports that Jesus of Nazareth, 33, a carpenter and reputed son of God, who survives, will assume the authority, if not the title, of the deceased deity. Jesus, sometimes called the Christ, was himself a victim of death, having succumbed some 1932 years ago in Palestine, now the state of Israel, purportedly on orders of a Roman governor, Pontius Pilate, and at the behest of certain citizens of Jerusalem. This event, described by some as 'deicide,' has lately occupied the deliberations of the Vatican Council, which has solemnly exonerated the Jews generally of responsibility for the alleged crime. The case is complicated by the fact that Jesus, although he died, returned to life, and so may not have died at all. Diplomats around the world were speculating today on the place the resurrected Jesus will occupy in the power vacuum created by the sudden passing of God.)

Dr. Altizer, God's surgeon, in an exclusive interview with the Times, stated this morning that the death was "not unexpected." "He had been ailing for some time," Dr. Altizer said, "and lived much longer than most of us thought possible." He noted that the death of God had, in fact, been prematurely announced in the last century by the famed German surgeon, Nietzsche. Nietzsche, who was insane the last ten years of his life, may have confused "certain symptoms of morbidity in the aged patient with actual death, a mistake any busy surgeon will occasionally make," Dr. Altizer suggested. "God was an excellent patient, compliant, cheerful, alert. Every comfort modern science could provide was made available to him. He did not suffer—he just, as it were, slipped out of our grasp." Dr. Altizer also disclosed that plans for a memorial to God have already been discussed informally, and it

is likely a committee of eminent clergymen and laymen will soon be named to raise funds for use in "research into the causes of death in deities, an area of medicine many physicians consider has been too long neglected." Dr. Altizer indicated, finally, that he had great personal confidence that Jesus, relieved of the burdens of divinity, would, in time, assume a position of great importance in the universe. "We have lost," he said, "a father, but we have gained a son."

(Next Sunday's New York Times will include, without extra charge, a 24-page full-color supplement with many photographs, reviewing the major events of God's long reign, the circumstances of his sudden and untimely death, and prospects for a godless future. The editors will be grateful for pertinent letters, photographs, visions and the like.)

There has been as yet no statement from Jesus, but a close associate, the Holy Ghost, has urged prayer and good works. He also said that it is the wish of the family that in lieu of flowers contributions be made to the Building Fund for the Cathedral of St. John the Divine in New York City so that the edifice may be finished.

—Anthony Towne

239

Raphael: *God Separating Land and Water*
The Bettmann Archive

TOWARD A HIDDEN GOD

Is God dead? It is a question that tantalizes both believers, who perhaps secretly fear that he is, and atheists, who possibly suspect that the answer is no.

Is God dead? The three words represent a summons to reflect on the meaning of existence. No longer is the question the taunting jest of skeptics for whom unbelief is the test of wisdom and for whom Nietzsche is the prophet who gave the right answer a century ago. Even within Christianity, now confidently renewing itself in spirit as well as form, a small band of radical theologians has seriously argued that the churches must accept the fact of God's death, and get along without him.

How does the issue differ from the age-old assertion that God does not and never did exist? Nietzsche's thesis was that striving, self-centered man had killed God, and that settled that. The current death-of-God group* believes that God is indeed absolutely dead, but proposes to carry on and write a theology without *theos*, without God. Less radical Christian thinkers hold that at the very least God in the image of man, God sitting in heaven, is dead, and—in the central task of religion today—they seek to imagine and define a God who can touch men's emotions and engage men's minds.

If nothing else, the Christian atheists are waking the churches to the brutal reality that the basic premise of faith—the existence of a personal God, who created the world and sustains it with his love—is now subject to profound attack. "What is in question is God himself," warns German Theologian Heinz Zahrnt, "and the churches are fighting a hard defensive battle, fighting for every inch." "The basic theological problem today," says one thinker who has helped define it, Langdon Gilkey of the University of Chicago Divinity School, "is the reality of God."

---

* Principally Thomas J. J. Altizer of Emory University, William Hamilton of Colgate Rochester Divinity School, and Paul Van Buren of Temple University.

A Time of No Religion. Some Christians, of course, have long held that Nietzsche was not just a voice crying in the wilderness. Even before Nietzsche, Sören Kierkegaard warned that "the day when Christianity and the world become friends, Christianity is done away with." During World War II, the anti-Nazi Lutheran martyr Dietrich Bonhoeffer wrote prophetically to a friend from his Berlin prison cell: "We are proceeding toward a time of no religion at all."

For many, that time has arrived. Nearly one of every two men on earth lives in thralldom to a brand of totalitarianism that condemns religion as the opiate of the masses—which has stirred some to heroic defense of their faith but has also driven millions from any sense of God's existence. Millions more, in Africa, Asia and South America, seem destined to be born without any expectation of being summoned to the knowledge of the one God.

Princeton Theologian Paul Ramsey observes that "ours is the first attempt in recorded history to build a culture upon the premise that God is dead." In the traditional citadels of Christendom, grey Gothic cathedrals stand empty, mute witnesses to a rejected faith. From the scrofulous hobos of Samuel Beckett to Antonioni's tired-blooded aristocrats, the anti-heroes of modern art endlessly suggest that waiting for God is futile, since life is without meaning.

For some, this thought is a source of existential anguish: the Jew who lost his faith in a providential God at Auschwitz, the Simone de Beauvoir who writes: "It was easier for me to think of a world without a creator than of a creator loaded with all the contradictions of the world." But for others, the God issue—including whether or not he is dead—has been put aside as irrelevant. "Personally, I've never been confronted with the question of God," says one such politely indifferent atheist, Dr. Claude Lévi-Strauss, professor of social anthropology at the Collège de France. "I find it's perfectly possible to spend my life knowing that we will never explain the universe." Jesuit Theologian John Courtney Murray points to another variety of unbelief: the atheism of distraction, people who are just "too damn busy" to worry about God at all.

Johannine Spirit. Yet, along with the new atheism has come a new reformation. The open-window spirit of Pope John XXIII and Vatican II have revitalized the Roman Catholic Church. Less spectacularly but not less decisively, Protestantism has been stirred by a flurry of experimentation in liturgy, church structure, ministry. In this new Christianity, the watchword is witness: Protestant faith now means not intellectual acceptance of an ancient confession, but open commitment—perhaps best symbolized in the U. S. by the civil rights movement—to eradicating the evil and inequality that beset the world.

The institutional strength of the churches is nowhere more apparent than in the U. S., a country where public faith in God seems to be as secure as it was in medieval France. According to a survey by Pollster Lou Harris last year, 97% of the American people say they believe in God. Although clergymen agree that the postwar religious revival is over, a big majority of believers continue to display their faith by joining churches. In 1964, reports the National Council of Churches, denominational allegiance rose about 2%, compared with a population gain of less than 1.5%. More than 120 million Americans now claim a religious affiliation; and a recent Gallup survey indicated that 44% of them report that they attend church services weekly.

For uncounted millions, faith remains as rock-solid as Gibraltar. Evangelist Billy Graham is one of them. "I know that God exists because of my personal experience," he says. "I know that I know him. I've talked with him and walked with him. He cares about me and acts in my everyday life." Still another is Roman Catholic Playwright William Alfred, whose off-Broadway hit, *Hogan's Goat*, melodramatically plots a turn-of-the-century Irish immigrant's struggle to achieve the American dream. "People who tell me there is no God," he says, "are like a six-year-old boy saying that there is no such thing as passionate love—they just haven't experienced it."

Practical Atheists. Plenty of clergymen, nonetheless, have qualms about the quality and character of contemporary belief. Lutheran Church Historian Martin Marty argues that all too many pews are filled on Sunday with practical atheists—disguised nonbelievers who behave during the rest of the week as if God did not exist. Jesuit Murray qualifies his conviction that the U.S. is basically a God-fearing nation by adding: "The great American proposition is 'religion is good for the kids, though I'm not religious myself.'" Pollster Harris bears him out: of the 97% who said they believed in God, only 27% declared themselves deeply religious.

Christianity and Judaism have always had more than their share of men of little faith or none. "The fool says in his heart, 'there is no God,'" wrote the Psalmist, implying that there were plenty of such fools to be found in ancient Judea. But it is not faintness of spirit that the churches worry about now: it is doubt and bewilderment assailing committed believers.

Particularly among the young, there is an acute feeling that the churches on Sunday are preaching the existence of a God who is nowhere visible in their daily lives. "I love God," cries one anguished teen-ager, "but I hate the church." Theologian Gilkey says that "belief is the area in the modern Protestant church where one finds blankness, silence, people not knowing what to say or merely repeating what their preachers say." Part of the Christian mood today, suggests Christian Atheist William Hamilton, is that faith has become not a possession but a hope.

Anonymous Christianity. In search of meaning, some believers have desperately turned to psychiatry, Zen or drugs. Thousands of others have quietly abandoned all but token allegiance to the churches, surrendering themselves to a life of "anonymous Christianity" dedicated to civil rights or the Peace Corps. Speaking for a generation of young Roman Catholics for whom the dogmas of the church have lost much of their power, Philosopher Michael Novak of Stanford writes: "I do not understand God, nor the way in which he works. If, occasionally, I raise my heart in prayer, it is to no God I can see, or hear, or feel. It is to a God in as cold and obscure a polar night as any non-believer has known."

Even clergymen seem to be uncertain. "I'm confused as to what God is," says no less a person than Francis B. Sayre, the Episcopal dean of Washington's National Cathedral, "but so is the rest of America." Says Marty's colleague at the Chicago Divinity School, the Rev. Nathan Scott, who is also rector of St. Paul's Episcopal Church in Hyde Park: "I look out at the faces of my people, and I'm not sure what meaning these words, gestures and rituals have for them."

Hydrogen & Carbon. To those who do formulate a God, he seems to be everything from a celestial gas to a kind of invisible honorary president "out there" in space, well beyond range of the astronauts. A young Washington scientist suggests that "God, if anything, is hydrogen and carbon. Then again, he might be thermonuclear fission, since that's what makes life on this planet possible." To a streetwalker in Tel Aviv, "God will get me out of this filth one day. He is a God of mercy, dressed all in white and sitting on a golden throne." A Dutch charwoman says: "God is a ghost floating in space." Screenwriter Edward Anhalt (*Becket*) says that "God is an infantile fantasy, which was necessary when men did not understand what lightning was. God is a cop-out." A Greek janitor thinks that God is "like a fiery flame, so white that it can blind you." "God is all that I cannot understand," says a Roman seminarian. A Boston scientist describes God as "the totality of harmony in the universe." Playwright Alfred muses: "It is the voice which says, 'It's not good enough'—that's what God is."

Even though they know better, plenty of Christians find it hard to do away with ideas of God as a white-bearded father figure. William McCleary of Philadelphia, a Roman Catholic civil servant, sees God "a lot like he was explained to us as children. As an older man, who is just and who can get angry at us. I know this isn't the true picture, but it's the only one I've got."

Invisible Supermen. Why has God become so hard to believe in, so easy to dismiss as a nonbeing? The search for an answer begins in the complex—and still unfinished—history of man's effort to comprehend the idea that he might have a personal creator.

No one knows when the idea of a single god became part of mankind's spiritual heritage. It does seem certain that the earliest humans were religious. Believing the cosmos to be governed by some divine power, they worshiped every manifestation of it: trees, animals, earth and sky. To the more sophisticated societies of the ancient world, cosmological mystery was proof that there were many gods. Ancient Babylonia, for example, worshiped at least 700 deities. Yet even those who ranked highest in the divine hierarchies were hardly more than invisible supermen. The Zeus of ancient Greece, although supreme on Olympus, was himself subject to the whims of fate—and besides that was so afflicted by fits of lust that he was as much the butt of dirty jokes as an object of worship.

Much closer to the deity of modern monotheism was the Egyptian sun god Aten, which the Pharaoh Amenophis IV forced on his polytheistic people as "the only god, beside whom there is no other." But the Pharaoh's heresy died out after his death, and the message to the world that there was but one true God came from Egypt's tiny neighbor, Israel. It was not a sudden revelation. Some scholars believe that Yahweh was originally a tribal deity—a god whom the Hebrews worshiped and considered superior to the pagan gods adored by other nations. It is even questionable to some whether Moses understood Yahweh to be mankind's only God, the supreme lord of all creation. Even after the emergence of Israel's faith, there is plenty of Biblical evidence that the Hebrews were tempted to abandon it: the prophets constantly excoriate the chosen people for whoring after strange gods.

The God of Israel was so utterly beyond human comprehension that devout Jews neither uttered nor wrote his sacred name.* At the same time, Judaism has a unique sense of God's personal presence. Scripture records that he walked in the Garden of Eden with Adam, spoke familiarly on Mount Sinai with Moses, expressed an almost human anger and joy. Christianity added an even more mystifying dimension to the belief that the infinitely distant was infinitely near: the doctrine that God came down to earth in the person of a Jewish carpenter named Jesus, who died at Jerusalem around 26 A.D.

It was not an easy faith to define or defend, and the early church, struggling to rid itself of heresy, turned to an intellectual weapon already forged and near at hand: the metaphysical language of Greece. The alliance of Biblical faith and Hellenic reason culminated in the Middle Ages. Although they acknowledged that God was ultimately unknowable, the medieval scholastics devoted page after learned page of their *summas* to discussions of the divine attributes—his omnipotence, immutability, perfection, eternity. Although infinitely above men, God was seen as the apex of a great pyramid of being that extended downward to the tiniest stone, the ultimate ruler of an ordered cosmos cooperatively governed by Christian church and Christian state.

Undermining Faith. Christians are sometimes inclined to look back nostalgically at the medieval world as the great age of faith. In his book, *The Death of God*, Gabriel Vahanian of Syracuse University suggests that actually it was the beginning of the divine demise. Christianity, by imposing its faith on the art, politics and even economics of a culture, unconsciously

245 ♠

---

* Almost impossible to translate, the name Yahweh means roughly "I am who I am" or "He causes to be."

made God part of that culture—and when the world changed, belief in this God was undermined. Now "God has disappeared because of the image of him that the church used for many, many ages," says Dominican Theologian Edward Schillebeeckx.

At its worst, the image that the church gave of God was that of a wonder worker who explained the world's mysteries and seemed to have somewhat more interest in punishing men than rewarding them. Life was a vale of tears, said the church; men were urged to shun the pleasure of life if they would serve God, and to avoid any false step or suffer everlasting punishment in hell. It did little to establish the credibility of this "God" that medieval theologians categorized his qualities as confidently as they spelled out different kinds of sin, and that churchmen spoke about him as if they had just finished having lunch with him.

The Secular Rebellion. The rebellion against this God of faith is best summed up by the word secularization. In *The Secular City*, Harvey Cox of the Harvard Divinity School defines the term as "the loosing of the world from religious and quasi-religious understandings of itself, the dispelling of all closed world views, the breaking of all supernatural myths and sacred symbols." Slowly but surely, it dawned on men that they did not need God to explain, govern or justify certain areas of life.

The development of capitalism, for example, freed economics from church control and made it subject only to marketplace supply and demand. Political theorists of the Enlightenment proved that law and government were not institutions handed down from on high, but things that men had created themselves. The 18th century deists argued that man as a rational animal was capable of developing an ethical system that made as much sense as one based on revelation. Casting a cold eye on the complacency of Christianity before such evils as slavery, poverty and the factory system, such 19th century atheists as Karl Marx and Pierre Joseph Proudhon declared that the churches and their God would have to go if ever man was to be free to shape and improve his destiny.

But the most important agent in the secularizing process was science. The Copernican revolution was a shattering blow to faith in a Bible that assumed the sun went round the earth and could be stopped in its tracks by divine intervention, as Joshua claimed. And while many of the pioneers of modern science—Newton and Descartes, for example—were devout men, they assiduously explained much of nature that previously seemed godly mysteries. Others saw no need for such reverential lip service. When he was asked by Napoleon why there was no mention of God in his new book about the stars, the French astronomer Laplace coolly answered: "I had no need of the hypothesis." Neither did Charles Darwin, in uncovering the evidence of evolution.

Prestige of Science. Faith in God survived scientific attack only when the churches came to realize that the religious language of the Bible is what Theologian Krister Stendahl calls "poetry-plus, rather than science-minus." Nowadays not even fundamentalists are upset by the latest cosmological theories of astronomers. Quasars, everyone agrees, neither prove nor disprove divine creation; by pushing back the boundaries of knowledge 8 billion light years without finding a definite answer, they do, in a way, admit its possibility. Nonetheless, science still presents a challenge to faith—in a new and perhaps more dangerous way.

Anglican Theologian David Jenkins points out that the prestige of science is so great that its standards have seeped into other areas of life; in effect, knowledge has become that which can be known by scientific study—and what cannot be known that way somehow seems uninteresting, unreal. In previous ages, the man of ideas, the priest or the philosopher was regarded as the font of wisdom. Now, says Jenkins, the sage is more likely to be an authority "trained in scientific methods of observing phenomena, who bases what he says on a corpus of knowledge built up by observation and experiment and constantly verified by further processes of practice and observation." The prestige of science has been helped along by the analytic tradition of philosophy, which tends to limit "meaningful" ideas and statements to those that can be verified. It is no wonder, then, that even devout believers are empirical in outlook, and find themselves more at home with visible facts than unseen abstractions.

247

Socialization has immunized man against the wonder and mystery of existence, argues Oxford Theologian Ian Ramsey. "We are now sheltered from all the great crises of life. Birth is a kind of discontinuity between the prenatal and post-natal clinics, while death just takes somebody out of the community, possibly to the tune of prerecorded hymns at the funeral parlor." John Courtney Murray suggests that man has lost touch with the transcendent dimension in the transition from a rural agricultural society to an urbanized, technological world. The effect has been to veil man from what he calls natural symbols—the seasonal pattern of growth—that in the past reminded men of their own finiteness. The question is, says Murray, "whether or not a contemporary industrial civilization can construct symbols that can help us understand God."

Teach-In for God. Secularization, science, urbanization—all have made it comparatively easy for the modern man to ask where God is, and hard for the man of faith to give a convincing answer, even to himself. It is precisely to this problem—how do men talk of God in the context of a culture that rejects the transcendent, the beyond?—that theologians today are turning. In part, this reflects popular demand and pastoral need. "God is the question that interests laymen the most," says David Edwards, editor of the Anglican SCM Press. Last month the University of Colorado sponsored a teach-in on God, featuring William Hamilton and Dr. George Forell of the University of Iowa's School of Religion; more than 1,700 people showed up for the seven-hour session—a greater turnout than for a recent similar talkfest on Viet Nam. At the University of California at Santa Barbara, students and faculty jammed two lecture halls to hear Harvey Cox talk on "The 'Death of God' and the Future of Theology."

"If you want to have a well-attended lecture," says Rabbi Abraham Heschel, a visiting professor at Manhattan's Union Theological Seminary, "discuss God and faith." Ministers have found that currently there is no easier way to boost Sunday attendance than to post "Is God Dead?" as the topic of their next sermon.

The new theological approach to the problem of God is not that of the ages when solid faith could be assumed. No serious theologian today would attempt to describe the qualities of God as the medieval scholastic did with such assurance. Gone, too, is any attempt to prove God by reason alone.* For one thing, every proof seems to have a plausible refutation; for another, only a committed Thomist is likely to be spiritually moved by the realization that there is a self-existent Prime Mover. "Faith in God is more than an intellectual belief," says Dr. John Macquarrie of Union Theological Seminary. "It is a total attitude of the self."

Four Options. What unites the various contemporary approaches to the problem of God is the conviction that the primary question has become not what God is, but how men are justified in using the word. There is no unanimity about how to solve this problem, although theologians seem to have four main options: stop talking about God for awhile, stick to what the Bible says, formulate a new image and concept of God using contemporary thought categories, or simply point the way to areas of human experience that indicate the presence of something beyond man in life.

It is not only the Christian Atheists who think it pointless to talk about God. Some contemporary ministers and theologians, who have no doubts that he is alive, suggest that the church should stop using the word for awhile, since it is freighted with unfortunate meanings. They take their clue from Bonhoeffer, whose prison-cell attempt to work out a "nonreligious interpretation of Biblical concepts" focused on Jesus as "the man for others." By talking almost exclusively about Christ, the argument goes, the church would be preaching a spiritual hero whom even non-believers can admire. Yale's Protestant Chaplain William Sloane Coffin reports that "a girl said to me the other day, 'I don't know whether I'll ever believe in God, but Jesus is my kind of guy.'"

In a sense, no Christian doctrine of God is possible without Jesus, since the suffering redeemer of Calvary is the only certain glimpse of the

---

* Probably the most famous proofs for God's existence are the five ways of St. Thomas Aquinas, all drawn from the nature of the universe, that he sets out in his *Summa Theologiae*. Aquinas' first proof, for example, is that certain things in the world are seen to be in a state of motion or change. But something cannot be changed or moved except by another, and yet there cannot be an infinite series of movers. Therefore, there must be a first, or prime mover that is not moved or changed by anything else—and this is God.

divine that churches have. But a Christ-centered theology that skirts the question of God raises more questions than it answers. Does it not run the risk of slipping into a variety of ethical humanism? And if Jesus is not clearly related in some way to God, why is he a better focus of faith than Buddha, Socrates or even Albert Camus? Rather than accept this alternative, a majority of Christians would presumably prefer to stay with the traditional language of revelation at any cost. And it is not merely conservative evangelists who believe that the words and ideas of Scripture have lost neither relevance nor meaning. Such a modern novelist as John Updike begins his poem *Seven Stanzas at Easter:*

> *Make no mistake: if He rose at all*
> *it was as His body;*
> *if the cells' dissolution did not reverse,*
> *the molecules reknit, the amino*
> *acids rekindle,*
> *the Church will fall.*

The century's greatest Protestant theologian, Karl Barth of Switzerland, has consistently warned his fellow churchmen that God is a "wholly other" being, whom man can only know by God's self-revelation in the person of Christ, as witnessed by Scripture. Any search for God that starts with human experience, Barth warns, is a vain quest that will discover only an idol, not the true God at all.

 249

Holy Being. The word of God, naked and unadorned, may be fine for the true believer, but some theologians argue that Biblical terminology has ceased to be part of the world's vocabulary, and is in danger of becoming a special jargon as incomprehensible to some as the equations of physicists. To bridge this communications gap, they have tried to reinterpret the concept of God into contemporary philosophical terms. Union Seminary's John Macquarrie, for example, proposes a description of God based on Martin Heidegger's existential philosophy, which is primarily concerned with explaining the nature of "being" as such. To Heidegger, "being" is an incomparable, transcendental mystery, something that confers existence on individual, particular beings. Macquarrie calls Heidegger's mystery "Holy Being," since it represents what Christians have traditionally considered God.

Other philosophical theologians, such as Schubert Ogden of Southern Methodist University and John Cobb of the Southern California School of Theology, have been working out a theism based on the process thinking of Alfred North Whitehead. In their view, God is changing with the universe. Instead of thinking of God as the immutable Prime Mover of the universe, argues Ogden, it makes more sense to describe him as "the ultimate effect" and as "the eminently relative One, whose openness to change contingently on the actions of others is literally boundless." In brief, the world is creating God as much as he is creating it.

Perhaps the most enthusiastic propagandists for a new image of God are the Tweedledum and Tweedledee of Anglican theology, Bishop Robinson of Woolwich, England, and Bishop James A. Pike of California. Both endorse the late Paul Tillich's concept of God as "the ground of being." Pike, who thinks that the church should have fewer but better dogmas, also suggests that the church should abandon the Trinity, on the ground that it really seems to be preaching three Gods instead of one. Christianity, in his view, should stop attributing specific actions to persons of the Trinity— creation to the Father, redemption to the Son, inspiration to the Holy Spirit—and just say that they were all the work of God.

Discernment Situations. The contemporary world appears so biased against metaphysics that any attempt to find philosophical equivalents for God may well be doomed to failure. "God," says Jerry Handspicker of the World Council of Churches, "has suffered from too many attempts to define the indefinable." Leaving unanswered the question of what to say God is, some theologians are instead concentrating on an exploration of the ultimate and unconditional in modern life. Their basic point is that while modern men have rejected God as a solution to life, they cannot evade a questioning anxiety about its meaning. The apparent eclipse of God is merely a sign that the world is experiencing what Jesuit Theologian Karl Rahner calls "the anonymous presence" of God, whose word comes to man not on tablets of stone but in the inner murmurings of the heart.

Following Tillich, Langdon Gilkey argues that the area of life dealing with the ultimate and with mystery points the way toward God. "When we ask, 'Why am I', 'What should I become and be?', 'What is the meaning of my life?'—then we are exploring or encountering that region of experience where language about the ultimate becomes useful and intelligible." That is not to say that God is necessarily found in the depths of anxiety. "Rather we are in the region of our experience where God *may* be known, and so where the meaningful usage of this word can be found." To Ian Ramsey of Oxford, this area of ultimate concern offers what he calls "discernment situations"—events that can be the occasion for insight, for awareness of something beyond man. It is during these insight situations, Ramsey says, that the universe "comes alive, declares some transcendence, and to which we respond by ourselves coming alive and finding another dimension."

A discernment situation could be falling in love, suffering cancer, reading a book. But it need not be a private experience. The Rev. Stephen Rose, editor of Chicago's *Renewal* magazine, argues that "whenever the prophetic word breaks in, either as judgment or as premise, that's when the historical God acts." One such situation, he suggests, was Watts—an outburst of violence that served to chide men for lack of brotherhood. Harvard's Harvey Cox sees God's hand in history, but in a different way. The one area where empirical man is open to transcendence, he argues, is the future: man can be defined as the creature who hopes, who has taken responsibility for the world. Cox proposes a new theology based on the premise that God is the source and ground of this hope—a God "ahead" of man in history rather than "out there" in space.

German Theologian Gerhard Ebeling of Tübingen University finds an arrow pointing the way to God in the problem in language. A word, he suggests, is not merely a means of conveying information; it is also a symbol of man's power over nature and of his basic impotence: one man cannot speak except to another, and language itself possesses a power that eludes his mastery of it. God, he proposes, is the source of the mystery hidden in language, or, as he obscurely puts it, "the basic situation of man as word-situation."

"The Kingdom Within You." For those with a faith that can move mountains, all this tentative groping for God in human experience may seem unnecessary. The man-centered approach to God runs against Barth's warning that a "God" found in human depths may be an imagined idol—or a neurosis that could be dissolved on the psychiatrist's couch. Rudolf Bultmann answers that these human situations of anxiety and discernment represent "transformations of God," and are the only way that secular man is likely to experience any sense of the eternal and unconditional.

This theological approach is not without scriptural roots. A God who writes straight with crooked lines in human history is highly Biblical in outlook. The quest for God in the depths of experience echoes Jesus' words to his Apostles, "The kingdom of God is within you." And the idea of God's anonymous presence suggests Matthew's account of the Last Judgment, when Jesus will separate the nations, telling those on his right: "I was hungry and you gave me food, I was thirsty and you gave me drink." But when? they ask. "And the King will answer them, 'Truly, I say to you, as you did it to one of the least of these my brethren, you did it to me.'"

The theological conviction that God is acting anonymously in human history is not likely to turn many atheists toward him. Secular man may be anxious, but he is also convinced that anxiety can be explained away. As always, faith is something of an irrational leap in the dark, a gift of God. And unlike in earlier centuries, there is no way today for churches to threaten or compel men to face that leap; after Dachau's mass sadism and Hiroshima's instant death, there are all too many real possibilities of hell on earth.

The new approaches to the problem of God, then, will have their greatest impact within the church community. They may help shore up the faith of many believers and, possibly, weaken that of others. They may also lead to a more realistic, and somewhat more abstract, conception of God. "God will be seen as the order in which life takes on meaning, as being, as the source of creativity," suggests Langdon Gilkey. "The old-fashioned personal God who merely judges, gives grace and speaks to us in prayer, is, after all, a pretty feeble God." Gilkey does not deny the omnipotence of God, nor undervalue personal language about God as a means of prayer and worship.

But he argues that Christianity must go on escaping from its too-strictly anthropomorphic past, and still needs to learn that talk of God is largely symbolic.

No More Infallibilities. The new quest for God, which respects no church boundaries, should also contribute to ecumenism. "These changes make many of the old disputes seem pointless, or at least secondary," says Jesuit Theologian Avery Dulles. The churches, moreover, will also have to accept the empiricism of the modern outlook and become more secular themselves, recognizing that God is not the property of the church, and is acting in history as he wills, in encounters for which man is forever unprepared.

To some, this suggests that the church might well need to take a position of reverent agnosticism regarding some doctrines that it had previously proclaimed with excessive conviction. Many of the theologians attempting to work out a new doctrine of God admit that they are uncertain as to the impact of their ultimate findings on other Christian truths; but they agree that such God-related issues as personal salvation in the afterlife and immortality will need considerable re-study. But Christian history allows the possibility of development in doctrine, and even an admission of ignorance in the face of the divine mystery is part of tradition. St. Thomas Aquinas declared that "we cannot know what God is, but rather what he is not."

Gabriel Vahanian suggests that there may well be no true faith without a measure of doubt, and thus contemporary Christian worry about God could be a necessary and healthy antidote to centuries in which faith was too confident and sure. Perhaps today, the Christian can do no better than echo the prayer of the worried father who pleaded with Christ to heal his spirit-possessed son: "I believe; help my unbelief."

TIME, April 8, 1966

from

A Coney Island of the Mind

5

Sometime during eternity
some guys show up
and one of them
who shows up real late
is a kind of carpenter
from some square-type place
like Galilee
and he starts wailing
and claiming he is hep
to who made heaven
and earth
and that the cat
who really laid it on us
is his Dad

And moreover
he adds
It's all writ down
on some scroll-type parchments
which some henchmen
leave lying around the Dead Sea somewheres
a long time ago
and which you won't even find
for a coupla thousand years or so
or at least for
nineteen hundred and fortyseven
of them
to be exact
and even then
nobody really believes them
or me
for that matter

You're hot
          they tell him

And they cool him

They stretch him on the Tree to cool

     And everybody after that
                         is always making models
               of this Tree
                    with Him hung up
and always crooning His name
                    and calling Him to come down
               and sit in
                    on their combo
          as if he is <u>the</u> king cat
                         who's got to blow
or they can't quite make it

Only he don't come down
                    from His Tree

Him just hang there
               on His Tree
                         looking real Petered out
               and real cool
                         and also
          according to a roundup
                         of late world news
     from the usual unreliable sources
                         real dead

Lawrence Ferlinghetti

This century of woe and rebellion!

Our women depose us.

Our children defy us.

The communists would liquidate us.

And dark-skinned people all over the world
want to further humiliate us.

What did we adult,
white, protestant,
male businessmen ever
do to deserve such a world?

At least He is one of us.

♠ 258

Christ on the Cross

"New Christ Cardiac Hero"

I'd like to say before singing this controversial song that this isn't about anybody's god specific on account of some of my best friends are gods. This about New Christ Cardiac Hero who is the latest hero and the latest leader of the younger generation.

Yesterday's preacher, today's bikini beacher
They've stolen your clerical robes and your bible's been thrown.
Your virgin red crown of thorns has turned to ivory horns,
And your corner throne it has become a corner stone.
Your crucifix you prayed on turned to jailhouse bars.
Still the chain you left out in the rain's aglow with dust
And turned to seaweed tangled in your heart.
Now how does it feel to pull out the nails and find you still can walk?
Oh you can't feel at all
From your self imposed rack on the wall.
The tighter you drive the nails the harder you fall.
So come on down, come off it sir,
You're gonna get hurt.

Oh the holy water you bathe in mingles with the sewer.
All your disciples have reclaimed their rifles and taken the cure.
Your lectures of ways are only today's poolroom jokes,
Remaining scrawls on the walls of tenement halls and bathroom bowls.
As jingle bells cry pay us well or you'll go to hell.
Freedom's chains they bind your pains and tie you well.
But how could you know the gallows you hold weigh you down?
Now isn't it boss you don't need a cross to get around?
Oh, you can't feel at all from your self-imposed rack on the wall,
And the tighter you drive the nails the harder you fall.
So come on down, come off it sir,
You're gonna get hurt.

Oh your eyes that cried for mankind's pride are covered with shades
As the children of God trample unshod past your grave.
New Christ, hipster, cardiac hero of 2,000 years past, you're mine.
He spits at your feet crying we have no need of a God.
Each of us is his own.
Yesterday's preacher, today's bikini beacher
They've stolen your clerical robes and your bible's been thrown.
Oh you must have a cross, but they've taken you God and shot you filled with lead.
So following new Christ, pick up a cycle instead.
Oh you can't feel at all from your self-imposed rack on the wall,
And the tighter you drive the nails, the harder you fall.
So come on down, come off it sir,
Before you get hurt.

Janis Ian

259 ♠

THE ART

I WAS traveling in Mexico when I found myself suddenly hustled, clutching at my side and yelling, through the iron-grated doors of this hospital. I remember the shadowing of the trees against the whiteness of the stuccoed walls and the blue window casements, though when I arrived here I was in torment and merely glanced at what in health I would have enjoyed. In fact, my recall of the exterior is already dim, but I grow increasingly aware of what the stuccoed walls enclosed.

I might best express it by saying that, at night especially, the interior seems to come to pieces. I realize this observation is irrational, because in the morning there the hospital is again, complete in the sun. Perhaps the illusion of the hospital's disintegration is created because sickness flourishes under cover of darkness. It is night that draws the horror forth, like a poultice on our wounds. Within the pre-dawn hours there is a particularly intense suspension of all we acknowledge as real, a release from the usual restrictions, a reaching out and a falling apart.

I find this bearable due to the ironic fact that I never see the blackness of the night itself, because those of us who are troublesome—meaning that we might vomit, have noisy nightmares or urinate in bed—are haloed throughout the night by an indirect lamp that lights our hair, the tips of our noses, and faintly glows the ceiling. I amuse myself by raising my hand and seeing, there on the opposite wall, its shadow. What else is there for me to do? I sleep little, because I am uncomfortably weak and newly frightened by my own body.

But I hold the noises equally responsible for bolstering me against the disintegration. Often during the night it is like a zoo where each animal with his special sound vies for attention. Up the hall is a skinny man who has been retching. In the day he lies quietly, even innocently, with long fingers curled upon the sheet, with only the big holes in his nose noticeable because they are so black with hair. But at night he grows vicious and revengeful. I think

OF PAIN

he's somewhat better, for his retching has increased in vigor, and he has begun to yell hoarsely with each spasm of the throat.

I have learned it is expected that on most nights a person will die. And, to my surprise, I notice that some try very hard to end, as hard as most of us struggle to continue. But being of a liberal turn, I have brought myself, even in so short a time, to tentatively accept their position, to even wish to congratulate them should they succeed. Goals are what we make them, and I cannot see that death is not a proper one, particularly in Mexico where it is familiar enough to be specialized into entertainment of the grandest sort, to the accompaniment of trumpets and obeisance to *El Presidente*. For instance, I would like to have said something of a congratulatory nature to the girl whose room was next to mine. But then, so magnificent were her final moments that I would not have had the words.

A new noise has begun. It is a low scream unusually suited to the echoing qualities of the walls. It comes from a man who, during the sunlit hours when neighbors and relatives scurry in, laden with gladiolas and smuggled candy, manages to lie sanely calm. I have looked in upon him at these festive times and seen that he does look weak and pathetic and drools pitiably out of the side of his mouth. I have noticed, too, that his thoughts and agonies seem turned inward, his spirit restive, his pain controlled to the point of apathy. He is old and hollow-looking like a winter-hatched fly.

This man is surrounded by bottles turned upside down, hanging gem-like from steel pipes near the ceiling. Yesterday, when he wasn't looking, I watched the liquid ooze into him. It is like having parts of one's body disconnected and suspended about the room. Apparently the fluids are energizing, for, as evening encroaches, the old man's screaming starts at the bottom of the scale and climbs in semi-tones until his throat is so wide he must finally cease with a gurgling.

But now that I have grown used to such performances, I think that those who suffer delicately are the real artists. A genius in this genre died in the hospital with a refined candor that leads one to shout 'bravo' and stand breathless with admiration. She was a master. There is an absurd rumor circulating among the nuns and nurses that we were in love. This is not true. There was, rather, admiration on my part and a certain acceptance of that admiration on hers. Hateful to me have been the nuns today who, stiffly starched and smelling damp like basements, confided they have prayed for her soul. What is her soul to me?

Yet, because her door was next to mine, I am intimately acquainted with the particulars of her case. My sense of isolation while here has become intense, as was hers, and this, as well as the closeness of our rooms, drew us together. Though in fairness to her memory I must admit that my loneliness was the more extreme.

In spite of the fact that it was but a few days after the peak of my illness and the operation which ensued, I was prodded into activity, literally forced to take toddling walks up and down the corridors. It was my first ambulatory effort that brought me, staggering, faint, to lean against the door-frame of her room. My eyes dizzily watched the floor, and she must have sensed my embarrassment for she said to me in Spanish, "Come in and rest. You've come a long way, from several rooms up the corridor?" Her voice seemed to smile though her face was motionless, even stolid. Then she said, "I don't remember how to walk any more," lending to my efforts a nobility, a kind of approbation for which I was grateful.

"Yes," I answered and then, "Yes" again as I settled myself unsteadily in the white chair which faced her bed. Though I was not certain what I was saying, a weakness laved me. But I sensed I was drawn to her knowing what it was; I thought I could tell her about it without feeling that I was complaining or having to explain what only the initiate can know. Besides, there was a helpfulness in her manner which her own weakened body made pure of pity. I turned slightly my chair. I found I had placed my hand, allowing it to lie lightly across the sheets near the foot of her bed. I began watching her, mutely claiming exhaustion as the excuse for my almost insolent friendliness.

I saw she was wasted, yet there was an aura of beauty as well as a certain ascetic quality nature had thoroughly explored through her. She must have been part Indian; her face against the pillow was not sallow, nor was it pinkish and veined like a thinly peeled radish as the bedridden members of the white race usually are. Her skin was darkly luminescent and seemed to glow from within as though lighted by a subcutaneous flame.

I leaned toward her, catching my breath again, for through the now familiar odor of disinfectants I detected a far more penetrating and disturbing smell that seemed to float like a fine yeast in the air about the bed. I said to her, perhaps too quickly to cover my embarrassment at this discovery, before, in fact, my chest had stopped its obvious panting, that I wanted to wish her a pleasant morning. I spoke in a kind of breathless camaraderie, letting my words suggest we were in this mess together and that friendship need not be taboo, even in a place for the moribund. Everyone is moribund from birth, after all; our lives are what our friendships are. My mind was a whirl of excuses for breaking in upon her privacy, when she suddenly murmured:

"It's good to see someone, someone besides mama again."

And she smiled faintly and blinked her preoccupied eyes in a way that indicated she had expressed what her illness would allow in the way of external warmth. She spoke each Spanish word slowly, but whether in deference to my obvious difficulty with the language or because of the pain which seemed to flow like an ichor through her body, I could not be certain.

I tried to keep my eyes from watching her face where anguish danced on the delicate muscles about the mouth. So I watched out the window a palm whirl like a propeller in the wind. It was more polite to do that. And before I knew what I was about, I found myself humming, forcing air through my throat in a disordered monotone.

"Well, well," I cried, straightening myself in the chair, trying not to see or smell the darkness that seemed to emanate from her skin. "It's a fine day. This Mexico of yours—it's a fine place."

"Oh yes," she said, brightening a little.

I felt she was indulging, not my presence, but my pain. In hospitals pain is one's distinction, winning indulgences in proportion. Piqued by my inferiority in this area—after all I had only had a simple appendectomy—I bluntly inquired, "And who are you, I mean, what is your name?" But before the sentence was out I noticed my voice becoming hushed, filled with trepidation, as though I already knew, sensed at least, that I questioned an undisputable identity.

To which she answered amusedly, "I'm not sure that I know. I've been here so long. . . ."

And then the ichor seemed to flow with a gigantic force all through her. She did not whimper or cry out; her eyes watched inward. It was as though she were too concerned with what she might be seeing.

I hastily whispered, "Goodbye for now."

Because she said nothing as I struggled out of her room, leaning with my hands first on the white chair back, then on the dresser top, and finally lurching into the hall, I began, even before reaching my room, to grow curious about the impression I had made upon her. I fought against the idea that I was to be but a brief interruption, a momentary breath upon the glass of her existence. Her existence that I was forced to admit was made perfect, not clouded, by the cancerous horror which ravaged it. How could I have hoped to significantly interfere with the machinations of so deadly a grappling?

Now, though her death was only a matter of hours ago, I find it difficult to recall her appearance. Her hair always seemed to have a bit of the night caught up about it. It was long hair, loose, shining, and several strands of it lay against her forehead, partially hiding the sweat which the pain always caused to be there. Her nose, though much too long, curved slightly upward at the tip, allowing the nostrils great prominence. How fortunate this was because, though the nose is usually considered a receptor, in the expression of pain it plays a role only secondary to that of the mouth. There was an over-all beauty the agony had wrought in her; it had placed its sullen paw upon her being. From the brilliant hair to the feverish glow of the skin bathed to shining, she lay as one chosen for more than the ecstasy of human love. My interest in her was her ability to channel pain into death, just as it is the art-work and not the artist that is the proper concern of the aesthete.

I recall our second meeting with reluctance. There are things we should not know about people of significance. It is better to sacrifice them to the symbol we have prescribed than to expose their essence, bourgeois and bleeding. Her biography was no exception; it made her human in the vulgar sense.

On our second meeting I said to her that I thought her face beautiful. I was not prepared for the tears my comment inspired. I was sitting close to her bed, my face near to hers, our eyes in pleasant rapport.

"Señor," she said, blinking rapidly and turning her black eyes from mine and fingering the bed clothes, "so what good, what good, I ask, has beauty been to me?"

"Yes?" I questioned, realizing her loneliness was going to drive her to confession, hoping for this chance to peer, yet dreading our mutual response to so premature an intimacy.

"He left me . . . when I loved him most. Is there anything, anything worse than that? It would be better if he had died!"

There was a soft choking sound in her throat as she paused, apparently in an effort to compose herself, and, though the pause and the throat sound were overdone, I could not help but respond with a feeble raising of my hand to steady her.

"We had been married," she continued, "at my insistence. And of course that was wrong. He seemed willing enough at the time but I know now he was hesitant. So damned hesitant. And you know why? Because I loved him more! Oh, God, was that my crime? Yes, it's a crime of indiscretion. . . ."

She pulled at her bed clothes. Sometimes her back would arch as though she were curving herself to fit the pain. But her attention was not focused upon her art. Then she glanced at me sidelong, even lingeringly.

"He was a good man. He did so much for me . . . he did nice things so he wouldn't hate me out loud! I remember his face when he was leaving for good, I remember him looking down at me. 'What have I done?' I said to that face. But there is nothing really to ask a face like that, a face whose eyes open wide, that stare from a long way off. . . ."

Her thin right hand went near her eyes. She touched at the tears without wiping them away. But for the first time her voice came strong.

"I have no trust. Our Father is as nothing, and Our Mother is as less. I believe in Our Saviour's hate, not in His love. The world is a pen for pigs!"

And to my surprise she laughed, drowsily, for her emotions had exhausted her, but with a bitterness I had somehow presumed she would be beyond. But I reminded myself that this was not the triumph of man over adversity, this was adversity itself, merciless, ridiculous.

"Now I am dying!" she cried out at me as I started to rise from my chair shaken, for I felt I had seen too much of what was weak. She had raised the upper portion of her body with one thin arm as support, the bed clothes falling away, exposing the startling whiteness of her hospital gown. Her shoulders shook like the wings of a white moth stunned. I felt a cold wind upon the back of my neck. We watched each other intently, caught by the thing we saw in each other's eyes. And then with a soft flutter of breath she lowered herself to the bed.

I returned to my room. I knew she was not talking to me. I returned with the burden of admiration oppressing my heart. Not admiration for the way of her life, but for that other, nobler aspect of her character. There was a controlled, rational quality about her endurance of physical suffering, a

265 ♠

restraint in the tone of her voice and the attitudes of her body when dealing with that phenomenon that seemed to subtilize her insight to wisdom. Her sentimental view of herself was to be expected and then dismissed. I refuse to let it color what I sensed was the inner power of that discipline.

Whereas I had no visitors, she had one, her mother, who came to cry over her bed at exactly four every afternoon. She had explained to me that her mother, being Indian, was simpler-minded than her Spanish father. Her father, she had said with a sigh, avoided even the fact of her extreme illness, referring to her always as tainted and viewing her pain as a retribution with which he would not interfere. Once her mother brought flowers, but usually only tears. Tears are the poor people's fruit and harvest and, as I presumed their poverty, my sympathy for them grew.

Several days ago I had managed to hobble out of my room at exactly four to lean against the wall as the mother arrived. She passed by me, slightly bent, with a blue-black *rebozo* thrown over her head and wound about her chest. Her face was buried deep inside.

I entered the room after her, directly upon her footsteps in fact, and stood swaying, for I was weak and my head felt high and detached like a circus balloon. The girl glanced up, touched me lightly on the arm, ignored her mother as though she were pretending she was somehow not important, and began to gaze with a finite fixedness at the ceiling. Her eyes were not glazed but alert to the depth of her pain. As the mother crept closer, the girl's eyes began to sweep the ceiling and walls of her room with an intensity that was like fury.

To me the mother was more a force than a person. Standing as she did, she possessed the room, seeming to hold the walls, the furniture at her command. Short, her tiny legs carrying her with more of a scuttle than a walk, she approached her daughter's bed with the quick assurance of a small, strong bird of prey.

"So it's you," the girl said, her lips restrained, her eyes not daring the scrutiny of what I could not help but think was death itself in the shoddy disguise of a mother. Because when I walked near enough to view the face tucked in the shadow of the *rebozo*, I saw there was hair on it, and I felt uncomfortable and unmistakably challenged beyond what my present health might accept.

Folds of blue-black cloth unwound and dropped straight from her stomach to the floor as she bent obsequiously to her knees, her now uncovered head laid upon the bed, her fingers alternately clawing and plucking at the ridge of covering under which the sick girl's legs lay hidden.

"*Mi querida*. My darling one," she crooned, "my baby."

From her spotted dress she withdrew a small wood crucifix and kissed it with wet lips. When she pleaded with the girl to do the same, and as she carried it up over the bed clothes, I could see small bubbles of saliva on our Saviour's hair. The girl refused, sniffing it like a hound, and threw it across the room.

"Ah," rasped the mother, leaning backward while still upon her knees, her tiny arms showing dark and thin where her *rebozo* had fallen back. "Little wretch, look here!" And she indicated the mighty symbol of Christianity which she had rescued from the floor and now held like a trident in her hand, the four-pointed emblem with the agonized Christ, the crucifix with hands convulsed against the inevitability of the suffering itself.

"*I* am suffering," the girl whispered harshly. "*I* have pain."

Was this, I wondered, paralyzed from action, cut off from the very world that seemed to hurl me forward—was this the artist denying a former artist's work in the effort to go beyond? But she didn't plead 'I Thirst' like a pitiable child unable to contain the loneliness of darkness. Nor did she cry 'Forgive Them' in one last melodramatic burst.

She said rather, "I accept," as though pain were the inevitable and not to be fought or avoided but to be explored like a dark sea cave.

As a medical student peering with feigned casualness down upon the glaringly lighted operating amphitheatre, or like an *aficionado* at the bull ring awed by the garishly bedecked animal that sways, rayed like a star and dying, I stared without embarrassment, with undisguised fascination at the triumphant performance that was before me.

Suddenly, the mother turned to watch me with piercing eyes. Still on her knees, she tipped her head back like a drinking bird and, shaking her head in alarm, she spat at me. I flattened myself against the wall.

No lizard has stared lidless through the sun at the hawk with more intensity than I at that woman. She held the crucifix high in the air before her, warding me off. She had remained upon her knees as though she were a supplicant with the power of some horrific god behind her. I skulked toward the door like the evil she thought me.

She shouted, "Go. You will not take my child from me as other men have before." And then she shut her eyes and swayed with the crucifix still clutched in her two outstretched hands, moaning, "May God be with us and remain with us forever. Forever and Amen. Jesus, come to us now at the hour of our death. Come to us, come to us now at the hour."

I paused with my arms straight out from my body, my fingers holding the molding of the door frame, my head lolling with a sorrow I could not possibly grasp. Had I known I would never see the girl again, I would have spoken some farewell to her, I would have acknowledged my admiration and would have said, 'Yes, I understand,' I would have whispered this lie over and over to her as if it were a holy incantation; I would have pressed my lips to her ear and whisperingly lied, 'Yes, I understand,' until from her eyes there shone no awareness and I would have known her ears were deaf.

But as it was, I unceremoniously left. And the next afternoon, at four with the afternoon rain, mama came again to drench the inside with her tears and supplications. I was amused by her punctuality and grinned, snuggled beneath my coverlet. But when she left she passed my door just as she was rearranging her dark *rebozo*. It flapped in that second like wings in the air and she was like a soul escaping from blackness to nothing.

"My God," I cried, and hid my head and listened to the rain for a long time.

Evening is coming on, the showers here always dwindle into darkness. Everything is beginning to look very blue. The hospital has started to tremor in preparation for the night's pulling apart. Already the thin man is vomiting. Already the halls are taking on his echo. Earlier, there was much vigorous scrubbing and fumigating of the room next door, her room. The nurse whistled briskly at the task and everything seemed as it should be. But of course it's not, because the artistry is gone.

Like her predecessors, her glory must be either ignored or distorted. I am pleased notoriety shall not sweep her on to the gall-drinker's maudlin defeat.

In her instance, I am the only one who saw . . . her essence so soon to be reduced to a mere slant of my head and eyes when, in some future moment, I nod off to sleep late at night on the subway, leaning in weariness against the shivering window glass.

♠ 268

ROBERT BURDETTE SWEET

from
The Devil's Dictionary

ZEUS, n.   The chief of Grecian gods,
adored by the Romans as Jupiter and by
the modern Americans as God, Gold, Mob and Dog.
Some explorers who have touched upon
the shores of America, and one who professes
to have penetrated a considerable distance
into the interior, have thought that
these four names stand for
as many distinct deities, but in his monumental
work on Surviving Faiths, Frumpp
insists that the natives are monotheists,
each having no other god
than himself, whom he worships
under many sacred names.

Ambrose Bierce

ACTOR SHOT

LOS ANGELES—Actor Lance Fuller was shot and critically wounded by a policeman yesterday when the actor allegedly attacked the officer. The policeman, who was treated for a broken right hand, said Fuller was beating on parked cars with a piece of pipe and yelling, "I am Jesus Christ—I am God." Police said Fuller was shot when he turned on the lawman.

CRUCIFIXION

The night comes again to the circle-studded sky.
The stars settle slowly, in loneliness they lie,
Till the universe explodes as a falling star is raised.
Planets are paralyzed, the mountains are amazed,
But they all glow brighter from the brilliance of the blaze
With the speed of insanity. Then he dies.
In the green fields a-turning a baby is born.
His cries freeze the wind and mingle with the morn.
Assault upon the order, the changing of the guard,
Chosen for a challenge that is hopelessly hard.
And the only single sigh is the sighing of the stars,
But to the silence of distance they are sworn.
So dance, dance, dance,
Teach us to be true.
Come dance, dance, dance,
'Cause we love you.

 270

Images of innocence charging to go on,
But the decadence of history is looking for a pawn.
To a nightmare of knowledge he opens up the gate
A blinding revelation is served upon his plate:
That beneath the greatest love is a hurricane of hate,
And God help the critic of the dawn.
So he stands on the sea and he shouts to the shore.
But the louder that he screams the longer he's ignored,
For the wine of oblivion is drunk to the dregs
And the merchants of the masses always have to be repaid.
Till the giant is aware someone's pulling at his leg,
And someone is tapping at the door.
So dance, dance, dance,
Teach us to be true.
Come dance, dance, dance,
'Cause we love you.

Then his message gathers meaning and it spreads across the land.
The rewarding of the fame is the falling of the man,
But ignorance is everywhere and people have their way.
Success is an enemy to the losers of the day.
In the shadows of the churches, who knows what they pray.
And God is the language of the band.
The Spanish bulls are beaten.
The crowd is soon beguiled.
The matador is beautiful a symphony of style.
Excitement is ecstatic; passion places bets,
Gracefully he bows to ovations that he gets,
But the hands that are applauding are slippery with sweat,
And saliva is falling from their smiles.
So dance, dance, dance,
Teach us to be true.
Come dance, dance, dance,
'Cause we love you.

Then this overflow of life is crushed into a lyre.
The gentle soul is ripped apart and tossed into a fire.
Death of beauty, the victory of night.
Truth becomes a tragedy limping from the light.
The heavens are horrified. They stagger at the sight,
And the cross is trembling with desire.
They say they can't believe it. It's a sacrilegious shame.
Now who would want to hurt such a hero of the game?
But you know I predicted it.
I knew he had to fall.
How did it happen? I hope his suffering was small.
Tell me every detail. I've got to know it all.
And do you have a picture of the pain?
So dance, dance, dance,
Teach us to be true.
Come dance, dance, dance,
'Cause we love you.

Time takes a toll and the memory fades.
But his glory is growing in the magic that he made.
Reality is ruined, there's nothing more to fear.
The drama is distorted to what they want to hear.
Swimming in their sorrow in the twisting of a tear
As they wait for the new thrill parade.
The eyes of the rebel have been branded by the blind.
To the safety of sterility, the threat has been refined.
The child was created. To the slaughter house he's led.
So good to be alive when the eulogies are read.
The climax of emotion, the worship of the dead
As the cycle of sacrifice unwinds.
So dance, dance, dance,
Teach us to be true.
Come dance, dance, dance,
'Cause we love you.

Night comes again to the circle-studded sky.
The stars that go slowly, in loneliness they lie.
Till the universe explodes as a falling star is raised.
Planets are paralyzed, the mountains are amazed.
For they all glow brighter from the brilliance of the blaze
With the speed of insanity—then he dies.

Phil Ochs

Welded wire and burlap create a study in texture and form in tree shown at the East Bay Children's Hospital Festival of Trees. Welded wire hoop (reinforced by wire spokes) with pieces extending upward to form cone shape, resembles a partially opened umbrella. Half-inch metal dowel tree shaft fits into weighted metal base. Red burlap weaves in and out of wire frame with exposed portions of wire wrapped by gold braid. Weaving begins at bottom using 54″ wide burlap for three circles, packing down hard, cutting and securing with stitches. Process is repeated with 27″ wide burlap, followed by 13½″ wide material. Tree top has four tassels tipped by bells. Designed by Mrs. Robert White.

CHRIST CLIMBED DOWN

Christ climbed down
from His bare Tree
this year
and ran away to where
there were no rootless Christmas trees
hung with candycanes and breakable stars

Christ climbed down
from His bare Tree
this year
and ran away to where
there were no gilded Christmas trees
and no tinsel Christmas trees
and no tinfoil Christmas trees
and no pink plastic Christmas trees
and no gold Christmas trees
and no black Christmas trees
and no powderblue Christmas trees
hung with electric candles
and encircled by tin electric trains
and clever cornball relatives

Christ climbed down
from His bare Tree
this year
and ran away to where
no intrepid Bible salesmen
covered the territory
in two-tone cadillacs
and where no Sears Roebuck creches
complete with plastic babe in manger
arrived by parcel post
the babe by special delivery
and where no televised Wise Men
praised the Lord Calvert Whiskey

Christ climbed down
from His bare Tree
this year
and ran away to where
no fat handshaking stranger
in a red flannel suit
and a fake white beard
went around passing himself off
as some sort of North Pole saint
crossing the desert to Bethlehem
Pennsylvania
in a Volkswagen sled
drawn by rollicking Adirondack reindeer
with German names
and bearing sacks of Humble Gifts
from Saks Fifth Avenue
for everybody's imagined Christ child

Christ climbed down
from His bare Tree
this year
and ran away to where
no Bing Crosby carollers
groaned of a tight Christmas
and where no Radio City angels
iceskated wingless
thru a winter wonderland
into a jinglebell heaven
daily at 8:30
with Midnight Mass matinees

Christ climbed down
from His bare Tree
this year
and softly stole away into
some anonymous Mary's womb again
where in the darkest night
of everybody's anonymous soul
He awaits again
an unimaginable
and impossibly
Immaculate Reconception
the very craziest
of Second Comings

Lawrence Ferlinghetti

273 ♠

from OPUS 21

Philip Wylie

It could have been morning; it could have been night; the light on the airfield was such as seeps across the northern pole in winter. Engines hiccupped and caught fire within themselves. Gouts of blue fire streamed from their steel nostrils and human figures warily aimed extinguishers as they crouched under the great wings. One B-29—a special craft—sucked up its ladder.

"Good luck!" a thin voice called.

The slam of a hatch replied. The plane snorted, bellowed, vibrated against its chocks, and lurched about. Like a house on casters—like a house-sized aluminum insect, it moved in the opalescent murk.

There was a pause.

At Flight Control, the ground officers of the Twentieth Air Force made a last check. It was not sergeant's work, or lieutenant's. Brass looked at the weather maps—high brass read the bulletins, squinted into the instruments, followed the meteorological balloons, talked through telephones. Anxious brass at the hangar interrogated the mechs—studied the quadruple checks, the four-colored V's ranged after a list of thirteen hundred and eleven critical parts of a very heavy bomber. In the officers' mess, captains, young majors, young lieutenant colonels filled their trays, walked to the tables, sat, listened while the juke box sang—

My mammy done tole me—

Listened not to the song but to the quartet of motors on the gloomy, loud field.

Above the coughing and the clamor, the roar and thump of other engines—came the long run, tightening nerves.

"There she goes!"

"War's over."

"Shut up! And who told you, lieutenant, anyhow? And what?"

The ship—wider than she was long and just under a hundred feet from tailfin to bombardier's glass snout—gained altitude. Below, the island sank in the sea of air—palms, runways, warm, damp tropical odor of mold, hangars and administration buildings, flags.

There was now only the sky and the Pacific. . . .

They would—someday—laugh at the B-29 even while they admired her, and more especially, the men who flew her. Schoolkids in a museum of the far centuries—walking along plush ropes—examining the early aeronautical exhibits. "What a clumsy contraption! How dangerous! They used to explode in the air, you know. They could only fly about five thousand miles—bumped along at three hundred an hour. Hour, mind you! What on earth did they do to pass the time in such tight quarters? They fought with guns—yeah—those tubes. Central fire control, they called it—they could shoot eleven pairs at once. Shoot? A chemical explosion that pushed streamlined bits of metal from the tubes at low velocities—fast enough, though, to kill a man—or bring down such a crazy craft. Who'd think—one just like that—took the first real missile—?"

The bright kids-to-be, perhaps. Their galleons and triremes.

She took off—the then-perfect air-frame, slick and silver—a multiplicity of engineering feats. She climbed. Five thousand. Eight.

"Okay. Pressurize."

The ears, hearts, lungs of sixteen men lost the feel of altitude and swiftly accepted the bubble of air that now flew in a metal skin.

Colonel Calm turned over the controls to Major Waite. The colonel's famous fighting smile flashed upon the proud navigator, the flight engineer, the idle bombardier, and the co-pilot. "You know the course, major."

The course, he meant, to the enemy.

The major had set plenty of cities on fire in his time. His brief time; he was twenty-six. Twenty-six years old and he'd flown courses that had burned out, smothered, smashed, and otherwise eliminated something on the order (he figured, being a man of mathematical bent) of three billion hours of human life. Expunged on that milk run. (You take the average life expectancy in enemy cities, multiply by days in a year and hours in a day, and multiply that by two further factors: average fatalities in a raid and number of raids led by Major Waite. Three billion man-woman-child hours, conservatively).

Colonel Calm glanced at Mr. Learned, the lone journalist permitted to go along—to write the eyewitness account. Mr. Learned sat on a parachute, his spectacles aslant, his hair awry, lost sleep whitewashed on his sharp countenance. His knees made a desk for an aluminum hospital chart board and on this, on yellow paper, using a pencil of a soft sort with which his pockets bulged, he scribbled. Once, he hitched at the collar of his unfamiliar uniform. A moment later, he glanced up. He smiled.

Colonel Calm nodded and scrambled into the tunnel that ran to the rear of his ship.

It was a journey he detested.

The passageway—a straight, metal intestine lined with cloth—traversed the bomb bay and was of a diameter sufficient to contain one crawling man. If a pressurized B-29 were hit badly—or if it blew a blister—a man in the tunnel would be rammed through it by compressed air like a projectile and hurled against a bulkhead—head first, or feet first—at the speed of a hundred and sixty miles an hour.

The colonel crawled—gnawed by claustrophobia. He pushed his chute ahead in the dim tube—because that was regulations. He wished he had chosen to drag it, instead. The thing stuck. He lunged up over it and his ribs came in contact with the curved top of the tunnel. He was half-jammed there. Sweat broke out on him—he tried to breathe—his ribs hurt. He could yell—they could get a rope around his foot and haul him back. He inched clear of the chute—pushed it forward, and went on more slowly, struggling now with the afreets of panic—putting them down like mutineers, savagely.

Now he thought of the bomb bay—the oblong maw atop which he fought his way. Big as a freight car. Big as two garages set end to end. Big enough to hold—how many horses? A dozen? And what did it contain?

His sweat dried up. His skin pimpled. Coldness seemed to flush the tube as coldness flushes a belly into which ice water has been gulped. Was the air here invisibly alive? Did uranium exude invisible, lethal rays—like radium? Or did it lie inert—in uncritical masses of unknown sizes (but not big)—waiting for union?

He went on.

When at last his head appeared at the far end of the tunnel he wore, again, his placid fighting smile.

The top CFC man dawdled in his swivel chair. The two blister gunners nodded and looked back into the neutral nothing of their provinces. The third chap smiled softly.

Colonel Calm came down the ladder,

stretched, picked up his chute familiarly, and went on to the radar room. It was, he thought, glancing back at the tunnel opening, hardly bigger than a torpedo tube. The craft in many ways resembled a submarine, when you thought about it.

There were four men in the radar room. Two at tables. One squatting, rocking with the plane's slight motion; and one stretched on the Army cot. He saw the colonel.

"'Shun!" he bawled.

"At ease, for God's sake!" Colonel Calm went to an old man who stared into the hood of a scope with the fascinated pleasure of a child seeing his first stereopticon slides. "Well, doctor? How is it going?"

Sopho glanced up—and he smiled, too. That was the thing about the colonel's mouth and eyes: you saw and you also smiled. Even when the kamikaze had connected, when Number 3 engine was on fire—pluming smoke and the CO_2 wasn't making headway, when flak splashed black flowers on the morning, when tracers rose like tennis balls, the deck was slick with gunners' blood, and when the inadequate, high, freezing air whistled through the ship—scaling fast, bits of plexiglass. Even then, he smiled—and you smiled back—and went on.

"Wonderful gadget," Dr. Sopho said, pointing to the hood, within which the colonel could see a scanning lightstreak and the radiant wake, following and fading perpetually. "After this trip," the scientist went on, "maybe we can go back to work. Real work. Maybe—" he pointed at the scope—"use that for saving a few lives, instead."

"Hope so." The colonel thought of his tedious wife—of weary years in Washington—desiccated military establishments in Texas—the drain and drag of peacetime. "Hope so," he lied. "Everything set?"

Sopho grinned. "Hope so."

"There's a chance of a dud—?"

"Some. Partial dud, anyhow."

The colonel seemed agitated. "In that case, wouldn't they get the secret?"

The old man had a goatee. He reached for it. "Yes. Yes, they might. And spend the next twenty years trying to put one together."

Colonel Calm continued down a narrow passage and opened a small door. Freckles Mahoney was taking his ease at the breeches of his tail guns—rocked back—staring at the vault where the powdery light was least. Daydreaming of a gum-chewing, short-haired, underbreasted Kalamazoo High School babe—and keeping his eyes peeled.

The door shut.

The colonel nerved himself for the return passage. Worse than being born—so far as he could remember. Dragging a placenta of parachute and harness through an aluminum canal with an atomic bomb beneath. He gave the three gunners his smile and they did not know it was—this time—a smile of fighting himself. At any rate, he thought, after one more crawl through eternity he could stay in the control compartment, forward. Unless Sopho wanted him.

He took hold of the ladder, sighted through the black tube to freedom's eye at the far end—and his blood turned to water.

Three men besides the gunners?

He felt horror between his shoulder blades—gun, knife, and worse. He checked crew and passengers.

He pretended to be untangling his chute straps, preparing to go through the round-eyed hell. Jordan on the top blister. Smith left, here. White right—and the unknown man beside him. No visible rank. Coveralls—insignia worn or torn off. Bearded like a submariner or the men he had relieved on Guadal. Hawk nose, brown eyes—extraordinarily intelligent, too—firm mouth, a gentle, definitely civilian look. Never saw him before.

This, the colonel realized, was obviously impossible.

He'd trained the crew, himself—picked each man, with special help from Headquarters—and met all the passengers weeks ago—old Sopho last—but, still—weeks ago.

Each member of the company—cleared,

checked, quadruple-checked, traced by G2 back through every childhood peccadillo, back through generations. Truman himself couldn't have got a man on board without the colonel's okay—his invitation and acquaintance.

He felt sick and feeble; he clung to the ladder under the tunnel mouth and staggered as the B-29 dived ponderously through a downdraft. Some last-minute thing, he decided; certainly the impossible passenger did not appear to be dangerous. One could not look at him and think of sabotage at the same time. These bloody, accursed, God-damned scientists! Very Important Person—he looked every inch a VIP—a VIP in science, not military affairs. No bearing to speak of—and that kindly smile at the corners of that mouth.

Last-minute stuff.

It would be assumed the colonel knew—but his four-way check had slipped.

When he returned to base—chevrons would fall. Lieutenants, captains, majors would drop back a grade.

See who he is.

The colonel went over to Smith, squatted.

"Skipper!" Smith said, returning the smile, the Air Force treasure.

The ship thrummed. Buzzed. Hummed. Ate air. Hurried toward the enemy islands.

Colonel Calm feigned to look from the blister. He supposed he saw, in the gray below, the corrugations of the Pacific, and above, the pearly heavens, the solid stretch of wing, the streamlined engine-housing. They were there, at least.

"The man with White. His name. Can't think of it."

"Chris."

"Chris what?"

Smith seemed embarrassed. "All I know. He came through the tunnel half an hour ago. 'Call me Chris,' he said. And he said, 'Mind if I sit?' "

The smile was a mask. He could keep it on his face even now. Eyes lighted up by the battery of will, corners crinkled, lips relaxed, a human twitch of the nose—man-loving, disdainful of blood and death, enemy and calamity. He could.

Came through the tunnel.

The man had not been in the control cabin, to begin with.

No bearded man.

No—Chris.

The colonel turned on his bent toes, the stranger watching.

Should he jump the guy?

Tell Smith to dive in with him?

Go back for a pistol and shoot from the tunnel?

The man smiled pleasantly.

Colonel Calm stood up, went round the post and track—the high barber's chair—and the gear and machinery that subtended the gunner in the top blister.

"Hi," the colonel said.

"Wonderful—a ship like this!"

"I've forgotten your last name."

"Chris."

"Oh, I don't believe I've had the pleasure—?"

The man held out his hand. "We've met. It was long ago, though,"

Colonel Calm had the momentary sensation of remembering. Seen him somewhere—that's a fact.

Chris was smiling. "My being along was arranged late."

"I see."

"You'll want to look over my papers, perhaps? My orders, I should say."

"Yeah. White House stuff?"

The man shrugged. "Pretty high up, I'll admit." He began unbuttoning his coveralls.

The colonel wished the man would stop looking so directly at him. Powerful eyes—like a lot of those scientific birds. They could, with a glance, give you an impotent sensation—a feeling that you weren't in command at all. A feeling that they commanded a force which could outlast you and would defeat you in the end. They made you feel—Christ bite them!—like a tin soldier, sometimes. And yet—high up. VIP. This was a trick mission—the trickiest of the war. You couldn't afford to make a fool of yourself. "Never mind," the colonel said. "My major probably checked you in—and forgot to mention it. The strain—"

"I know your major, yes. Sad."

"Sad? Greatest flying officer who ever took a plane off a base!"

"Cold-blooded."

"Right! Veins full of liquid helium. Have to be!"

"Have to be? Perhaps. I always hesitated—though—to think of men as numbers."

The colonel felt relieved. Major Waite's discussion of flight plans—his harangues in the briefing rooms—sometimes left the colonel a little chilled. Emptied out. Obviously this Chris knew the major. He wasn't—fantastically—impossibly—an agent of the enemy. Now the colonel gestured toward the bomb bay—the radioactive uterus of the plane. "You—helped put it together?"

The man seemed to grow pale. His smile disappeared. "No."

"Then what—? In God's name what—?"

"I am here," Chris said in so low a tone his voice scarcely carried through the pulsing air, "because I promised."

"Promised? Promised who—when—?"

"Because I said it. Lo, I shall be with you always, even unto the end of the world."

The colonel stared—and remembered. He turned the color of ashes. His right hand, ungoverned, made upon brow, shoulders and chest the sign of the Cross. His knees bent tremblingly.

But before he could genuflect the man called Chris touched his arm. "Don't, colonel!"

The officer, in his distraction, was muttering a woman's name, over and over.

Chris smiled painfully. "I am here." He glanced, then, at the watching gunners.

The colonel looked that way, too, and recovered something of his fighting smile. They were—after all—his command. It wouldn't do to let them see him prostrate. The gunners responded to the direct glance—and the return of the smile—

by a brightening of their eyes and a faint curving of the corners of their mouths; their attention went back to duty—the duty of scanning the void outside the domes of plexiglass.

"My Lord—" the colonel all but whispered—"what shall we do?"

"Return."

The soldier's eyes faltered. "Abort the mission!"

"I hoped I might persuade you."

"Another would merely follow—!"

"And them."

"But—duty!"

"To whom is duty?"

A head appeared in the round mouth of the tunnel. Learned, the journalist, grinned like an imp. "Nasty crawl," he yelled. "Hope they've got that thing well insulated. Otherwise—I'm unsexed—or hotter than radium myself!" He saw the stranger, and halfway down on the ladder stood still. His eyes, ordinarily shrewd and compassionate, showed first a little amazement—and then twinkled. "A ringer! You would pull one like that, colonel! The American press wants to know who he is!" Learned chuckled and dropped to the metal floor. Strode the two steps forward. Gave his name. Held out his hand. Explained himself. "You're a physicist, I take it?"

"My name is Chris." The dark eyes were luminous and kind.

"Chris who?"

The colonel took the journalist's arm in a hand like steel and whispered.

Learned, also, grew pale. He stared first at the colonel and then, uneasily, he eyed the stranger. Twice, the gleam of sardonic doubt shone. And twice, with all his will and concentration, he endeavored to make some satirical reply: to say, skeptically, that this would be the greatest interview in two millenniums.

Or to ask how things were in the Blue Up Yonder.

He failed. He—too—abruptly knew. The resources of his training abandoned him—left but the residue of naked personality. His tongue circled his lips. He gave the stranger another uncertain glance, a hopeful glance—and suddenly, on the impulse, took out his cigarettes and offered them.

Chris shook his head. "Thanks, Learned."

"Do you mind—"

"Of course not."

Now the journalist and the colonel shakily fumbled with cigarettes and the wavering flame of a match.

Chris had turned. He was looking expectantly toward the narrow door that led to the radar room and from it, presently, Sopho came. "Thought I'd run a counter through the tunnel," he began. "Check things." He saw Chris. "Hello! Didn't realize I hadn't met the ship's full complement."

The colonel and the reporter watched.

"My name is Chris, doctor."

"Can't place you. The Chicago Group, perhaps. I didn't meet them all."

"No."

"Army, then? White House? OSS? I'm a physicist. Sopho's the name."

"This man," said Learned, in a hoarse, uneven voice his ears had never heard before, "comes from—another place." He told the physicist.

Dr. Sopho's right thumb and forefinger touched his small beard. Across the back of his hand—tanned to leather by his long residence in the desert—skin pimpled and the reddish hairs rose. The tiny phenomenon passed—passed like the eddy of air that dimples still water and disappears. His great head with the thin nose and the straight, exaggerate brow bent forward attentively. He was searching the stranger for obvious signs of madness. It became apparent that he found none.

"Incredible," he murmured.

"You do not believe me?"

The scientist shook his head. "My dear fellow—I do not even believe *in* you. So—naturally—" He turned with abruptness to the colonel. "How did he get aboard? His papers?" He now saw the colonel's frantic, imploring eyes. "Great God, man—you don't accept—?"

"It's the truth," Colonel Calm responded.

Sopho looked quickly at Learned—who glanced away.

The scientist seemed, for the first time, alarmed. Not alarmed at the statement made by the man but at its effect upon two persons whom he had considered impervious to wild suggestion. Obviously, it was up to him to break the lunatic's spell. Some fabulous stowaway—and the journalist and the soldier—drawn overfine by the magnitude of this mission—had become prey to imagination.

One humors the mad—at any rate, to begin with. "I see," said Sopho.

He now faced the stranger—who stood in their midst. "Tell me. Just why did you decide to accompany this particular raid?"

Chris, still smiling, repeated his words about his promise—and after that, the promise.

"End of the world, eh?" Sopho chuckled. "You sure?"

"Your world—perhaps."

"You want us to give it up? The mission?" Sopho pointed at the bomb bay. "That?"

Chris looked steadily at him. "If I remember rightly, doctor, you began the preparation of—that—" he, also, pointed—"not to use against men, but to have on hand if your other enemy employed such instruments. He did not. He lies defeated."

Sopho nodded. "Right. Now we are using it to shorten the war. Save lives."

"*Save lives?*"

"By shortening the war, man! Simple arithmetic—!"

"What about—the next war? And the next? The wars beyond that?"

"This weapon should—and in my opinion will—put an end to war."

Slowly, Chris shook his head. "Strange reasoning. A *weapon* will put an end to war."

"An absolute weapon, man! The world will never again risk going to war. Never again dare take the risk!"

"It will fear too much, you think?"

"Precisely."

"But isn't it fear, doctor, that has always caused men to wage war? Fear in this form today—tomorrow in that form—?"

"Can you think of a better means of ending wars—foolish wastes!—than an absolute weapon? We have changed the whole picture of war!"

"But not changed men!"

There ensued a moment without talk.

Chris presently said, "This weapon. Where it falls, the genes of men will be broken. Perhaps their children—perhaps their grandchildren—will carry the heritage. Headless bodies. Eyeless faces. There—teeth everywhere. And yonder—no voice. Generation after generation, for a thousand years—this great invention will go on waging your present war, doctor, against the unborn."

The colonel grabbed the scientist's arm. "Is that true?"

Sopho shrugged. "In a certain per cent of cases, where radiation is extreme but not fatal—naturally, the reproductive capacity will display unpredictable, permanent damage. Recessive damage. When, however, two persons mate who exhibit matching gene deterioration—then—as this man says—"

The colonel's hand dropped. "I didn't know," he murmured. "Not certainly. I didn't even know that you men were sure."

Learned spoke. "War against the generations! Good—!" He checked himself.

Chris said, "Have you that right?"

Sopho replied angrily, "That's a right implicit in any war! If you kill a soldier—you destroy *all* his potential progeny—not simply endanger a few of them. The same fact applies to civilians."

"You do not," Chris answered, "corrupt the children of the survivors for centuries to come. No." He meditated a moment. "If the salt of the earth shall lose its savor, wherewith shall ye resavor it?"

Sopho said, "If changing man's environment will not change the evil of war—"

"Evil?" Chris repeated questioningly. "But does not man always believe his wars are just? Whatever cause—whichever side?"

Sopho ignored the inquiry. "—how do we change man?"

"Love one another," Chris said.

A slow smile came upon the physicist's face. "We should have loved the Nazis? And love the Jap who lies ahead?"

"Of course." Chris nodded soberly. "If you had loved them, you would never have let them sink into the pit of their despair—arm—turn upon yourselves. Had you loved them, you would have assisted them—before you were compelled to restrain them by such violence."

"The rights of nations—" Sopho began.

"—exist in the minds of men. You did not love them. You loved yourselves. You saw torment born in them all, and saw it grow, and feared it—and stood, like any Pharisee, reciting your virtues but not lifting a finger to assist them."

"He's right." Learned shook his head ruefully. "How right he is!"

"Love!" Sopho said the word scornfully. "Little you know of Nature. Little of love you'll see there!"

"It's strange," Chris answered, "that I see in Nature nothing *else* but love. Pain—yes. Sorrow—yes. Tragedy—yes. To every individual. Yet—in the sum of Nature—only love."

Sopho's eyebrows arched skeptically. "Do you really believe that the primitive phrases of a man who possibly existed—some two thousand years ago—could fix the attention of a modern scientist?"

"Evidently they do not." Chris bent and peered through the round, bowed window of the ship as if he could orient himself even among the traceless clouds. He looked at them again. "I talked in very simple words, doctor, to very simple people. The extreme simplicity of the formulations should—I thought—make the concepts increasingly understandable, as men pursued truth. I advised them, remember, to know the truth. I meant all of truth. I warned them that an excessive fascination with worldly goods—to the exclusion of inner goodness—would undo all peace of mind—"

Sopho chuckled. "Surely—we've pursued truth? What we carry today represents a great accumulation of truth! And I'll also agree that most men who merely amass worldly goods—the rich—aren't greatly interested in science. In truth. In anything but money. Still—"

Chris had raised his hand. "This ship—the bomb it carries—all the equipment and paraphernalia of the universities which lie behind it—the projects undertaken and achieved there—what are they, too, doctor—if not worldly goods?"

"Then you would have us put science aside? Stop seeking such truth—?"

"Seek truth in two ways, doctor. Within—and without." He drew a breath, frowned and spoke again. "Love—in man—takes various forms. Love of self. Love of woman. Love of other men. Love of cosmos. Each is an altruism so designed that, through love, man shall preserve himself in dignity, procreate, and preserve all others even at the cost of his own life. Greater love hath no man than this last. Not one of these altruisms can be peacefully maintained unless the others also are given their proportionate due. The conscience of a man rises from the relatedness of these loves and is his power to interpret how valuable, relatively, each one is—not to him alone, but to all men, as each man is beholden to all. To reason only in the mind is to express the love of worldly goods, alone. Have you ever reasoned in your heart, doctor?"

"Irrational emotions! Reason has no place there!"

"But it has. As a man thinketh in his heart, so is he. You scientists refuse to study how your hearts think. Repent, I said. Confess, the churches say—and worldliness encompasses them! Join, they say. But I say, when you have yielded up your vanity you will contain the immortal love. My time is short, gentlemen. I thought to remind you."

"I remember—!" the colonel's lips pronounced the inaudible words.

Learned looked at the floor. "How do you tell them—now?"

Sopho said disgustedly, "Metaphysics!"

"Light was the symbol I tried to give them," Chris went on gently. "The Cross was the symbol they adopted. The pain of self-sacrifice was obvious to them. The subjective reward—incomprehensible. Thus they changed it all. I told them of many mansions. They chose this mansion or that—and scoured each other off the earth, to set one heaven in place of the heaven of those they defeated. Holy wars! Is such a thing conceivable to God as a holy war? Alas. The words—the images—the effort is still uncomprehended. I said Light. I said Truth. I said Freedom. I meant enlightenment. Yet nearly every church that uses my name is a wall against light and a rampart against enlightenment, using fear, not love, to chain the generations in terror and pain and ignorance." He pointed again. "And now—this is called civilization, and in my name, also! Enlightenment! Knowledge!" He fell silent; but at last, smiled a little. "A few knew. A few will always know. Francis of Assisi—he guessed. Thomas à Kempis. Most who knew were church heretics in their day—as I was in mine. And what I say is still heresy."

He became silent again. He looked from face to face. "Colonel. You are a soldier. You are ready by your profession to die for other men. It is a noble readiness. Will you turn back?"

The colonel retreated a step and leaned against the riveted bulkhead. Sweat once more broke upon his countenance, poured down; he crossed himself again and Chris sadly shook his head.

Finally the colonel could speak. "You ask me to be disloyal."

"I ask you—only to decide in your own self—what loyalty is."

"I cannot turn, then."

"Learned?"

The journalist's eyes were steady—and tragic. "Nothing would be gained. Others would merely follow in place of us."

"I but asked you to decide for yourself—not for them."

The journalist flushed. "In my profession we

do not even agree to stand ready to die for other men. I am here not to determine, but merely to report."

"Sopho?"

The physicist's eyes blazed suddenly. "Yes," he said. "I'll go back! I was never certain. I am always ready to restudy a problem!"

Chris put his arm around the old man. "You!"

But the scientist pulled away. "On one condition."

"And that?"

"Prove yourself!"

"But, doctor, it is you who must provide the testimony—!"

"Empirical evidence is my condition. Something measurable. Suspend, for one moment, one natural principle—"

Ruefully, Chris laughed. "To simple men—fishermen, farmers, tax collectors—the power of any genuine conviction seemed miraculous because of its accomplishments. I healed the neurotics of my day. By suggestion, I added to the innocent gaiety of many a gathering. But even that poor, positive procedure is inverted now; many churches find their miracles in the hysterics of their own sick—bleeding, stigmata, fits!" He sighed. "Surely you, doctor, a miracle-maker in reality—are not naïve enough to ask that the very heart of truth be magically violated so you may *accept* truth? The evidence is—*within you*. I never said more. Find it there, man!"

"I thought so," the doctor replied in a cold voice.

Chris spoke persuasively. "*You* could work a miracle of transformation within *yourself*. But—even if I should suspend the very forces upon which that possibility depends—you would exert the last resource of your ingenuity to find out by what mechanical trick I achieved your illusion, as you'd call it! Prove, doctor, that you would not!"

"Let's see the experiment." Sopho's eyes were hard.

The stranger thought a moment and presently chuckled to himself. "The unsolved riddle of

the *cause*—the *source*—the nature—of the energy in your atoms, doctor! Would you like to understand that next step in your science?"

"Impossible!"

Chris looked ardently at the old man.

A moment later, the scientist's eyes shut. An expression of immense concentration came upon his features. Perspiration welled and trickled on his countenance—as on the colonel's. Suddenly his eyes opened again. He grabbed the colonel's arm. "Great God, man! I've cracked the toughest problem in physics! The thing just came to me this moment! Why! With this equation—we'll be able to make bombs that will assure American domination for a century! I'll win my second Nobel Prize! Every nuclear physicist's head will swim with envy! The financial possibilities—billions!—trillions! I'll just get it on paper—!" He broke off. "Wasn't there—somebody else—standing here?" he said perplexedly. "Never mind! Lend me a pencil, Learned!"

"Somebody else?" The colonel shook his head. "Nobody but the three of us. And the gunners. Jesus, I wish this mission was ended! I've been having a terrible struggle in my conscience about it!"

Learned said, "Have you? Me—too. I kind of hate humanity today. I kept wishing—something would break down, and stop the whole thing. I get a choked-up feeling when I think of those people."

The scientist was crouching, now—gazing at the streaming gray desolation beyond the windows. "Funny," he said to the gunner at his side. "A minute ago—I was sure I'd got a new insight into a very complex problem. Now—I can't even remember my approach."

The gunner, who held palaver of the brass and all VIPs to be but one more nuisance of war, said, "Yeah?"

The B-29 flew on toward its as yet unspecified destination.

The City of Horror and Shame.

Back at the base, the brass was laying plans for a second run—to the City of Naked Sorrow.

283 ♠

"Tell me more about this Christianity of yours. I'm terribly interested."

NAIL
A COMMIE
FOR CHRIST

♠ 284

REMEMBRANCE TRIBUTE

Today we pay, as individuals, the gentle tribute of remembrance, in humble gratitude, to all the dead who have served America on fields and seas around the world in wars to preserve the nation and our liberties.

We mark their graves with flags. We honor them with the firing of salutes and with the bugle's bitter-sweet song of requiem.

In their lifetime these dead defenders of America kept the heritage of freedom intact and passed it on to us. It is our duty to keep it intact in our time and hand it on to generations coming after us. We living Américans can make sure those who have given their lives in the nation's defense shall not have died in vain. Many of the young men marching away to battle and perhaps to die for us in foreign lands may never come back; but those who do return will march, year after year, in solemn Memorial Day parades in honor of their fallen comrades and of those who, in other wars, gave the last full measure of devotion to our country and the flag.

May 5 marked the centennial of General Logan's General Orders No. 11 in which he asked that May 30 be set aside as the day on which the surviving veterans of the Civil War should visit the graves of their fallen comrades and decorate them in memory of the service they had rendered. May 30, marks the centennial of Memorial Day. This is also the 90th Annual Memorial Day parade, or what we usually call a memorial procession.

For the honored war dead, we say: "To Almighty God, O dear departed comrades, we now commend you. May the bright company of the angels come and seek you. May the Lord appear to you with a mild and cheerful smile, and give you a place in His presence forever."

Mrs. Evelyn L. Gill,
Adjutant, Grand Army Of
The Republic Memorial
Assn. of Cook County

17 ¶ And when he was gone forth into the way, there came one running, and kneeled to him, and asked him, Good Master, what shall I do that I may inherit eternal life?

18 And Jesus said unto him, Why callest thou me good? *there is* none good but one, *that is,* God.

19 Thou knowest the commandments, Do not commit adultery, Do not kill, Do not steal, Do not bear false witness, Defraud not, Honor thy father and mother.

20 And he answered and said unto him, Master, all these have I observed from my youth.

21 Then Jesus beholding him loved him, and said unto him, One thing thou lackest: go thy way, sell whatsoever thou hast, and give to the poor, and thou shalt have treasure in heaven: and come, take up the cross, and follow me.

22 And he was sad at that saying, and went away grieved: for he had great possessions.

23 ¶ And Jesus looked round about, and saith unto his disciples, How hardly shall they that have riches enter into the kingdom of God!

24 And the disciples were astonished at his words. But Jesus answereth again, and saith unto them, Children, how hard is it for them that trust in riches to enter into the kingdom of God!

25 It is easier for a camel to go through the eye of a needle, than for a rich man to enter into the kingdom of God.

26 And they were astonished out of measure, saying among themselves, Who then can be saved?

27 And Jesus looking upon them saith, With men *it is* impossible, but not with God: for with God all things are possible.

28 ¶ Then Peter began to say unto him, Lo, we have left all, and have followed thee.

29 And Jesus answered and said, Verily I say unto you, There is no man that hath left house, or brethren, or sisters, or father, or mother, or wife, or children, or lands, for my sake, and the gospel's,

30 But he shall receive a hundredfold now in this time, houses, and brethren, and sisters, and mothers, and children, and lands, with persecutions; and in the world to come eternal life.

31 But many *that are* first shall be last; and the last first.

THE RICH CREEP HAS IT HARD

The Story of the Rich Young Man (Mark 10:17-31)

One day a rich creep
   Came fast lamming it up to Jesus.

He said,
   "Hey, good man,
     What I gotta do to live forever?"

Jesus says,
   "Why ya call me 'good,' man?
     Only God's good.
      You know
        You're not supposed to steal
        Or rub out or lie."

"Ya, I know," says the rich creep,
   "But I still ain't got it."

But Jesus still likes the creep
   So he tells him,
     "Get rid of all your apartment houses
      And 'rent-a-trucks'
       And give lots of money to the poor.

"Then you will be happy
   And come on back
     And join my gang."

The rich creep says,
   "Ah, no, ya don't,"
     And does a slow lam out of there.

Jesus was not happy
   And said, "It ain't easy for a rich creep to get in heaven."

He liked what he could see better than God
   And he would always feel empty inside.

It's like the feeling you have when you skip school
   Or when you ride in a stolen car
     Or stay out late.

No, it's more like always wishing
   You had done the other thing.

Carl F. Burke

EXODUS 20: 1–17

And God spake all these words, saying,

2 I *am* the LORD thy God, which have brought thee out of the land of Egypt, out of the house of bondage.

3 Thou shalt have no other gods before me.

4 Thou shalt not make unto thee any graven image, or any likeness *of any thing* that *is* in heaven above, or that *is* in the earth beneath, or that *is* in the water under the earth:

5 Thou shalt not bow down thyself to them, nor serve them: for I the LORD thy God *am* a jealous God, visiting the iniquity of the fathers upon the children unto the third and fourth *generation* of them that hate me;

6 And showing mercy unto thousands of them that love me, and keep my commandments.

7 Thou shalt not take the name of the LORD thy God in vain: for the LORD will not hold him guiltless that taketh his name in vain.

8 Remember the sabbath day, to keep it holy.

9 Six days shalt thou labor, and do all thy work:

10 But the seventh day *is* the sabbath of the LORD thy God: *in it* thou shalt not do any work, thou, nor thy son, nor thy daughter, thy manservant, nor thy maidservant, nor thy cattle, nor thy stranger that *is* within thy gates:

11 For *in* six days the LORD made heaven and earth, the sea, and all that in them *is,* and rested the seventh day: wherefore the LORD blessed the sabbath day, and hallowed it.

12 ¶ Honor thy father and thy mother: that thy days may be long upon the land which the LORD thy God giveth thee.

13 Thou shalt not kill.

14 Thou shalt not commit adultery.

15 Thou shalt not steal.

16 Thou shalt not bear false witness against thy neighbor.

17 Thou shalt not covet thy neighbor's house, thou shalt not covet thy neighbor's wife, nor his manservant, nor his maidservant, nor his ox, nor his ass, nor any thing that *is* thy neighbor's.

God Is Mr. Big, Real Big

Interpretations of The Ten Commandments (Exodus 20:3—17)

1. *You shall have no other gods before me. . . .*
   Means God's the leader—nobody, but nobody, man, gets in the way. This is the top. He is Mr. Big, real big.

2. *You shall not make for yourself a graven image. . . .*
   This means no making things that look like God in the craftshop at the settlement house. No worship things like rabbits' foots and lucky dice and, damn it, dolls.

3. *You shall not take the name of the Lord your God in vain. . . .*
   It means knock off the swearing, or you better watch out.

4. *Observe the Sabbath day, to keep it holy. . . .*
   a. It means going to church on Sunday and listen to people who don't know much about what they are talking about.
   b. Keeping holy means no snatching purses on Sunday.
   c. Means: Taking a rest on Sunday—like my old man not feeling bad 'cause he can't find a job and loafing around at the gin mill.

5. *Honor your father and your mother.*
    a. It means no calling your father a wino or your mother the old lady, even if they are.
    b. It means to love your mother, even if she hollers at you, and try to understand she is tired from working all day. It means to try to love your father, even if you don't know him or where he is.
    c. Maybe the others are OK, but this one is a real gasser—honor my father and mother—to hell with that, man!

6. *You shall not kill. . . .*
    a. No holding up people with switch blades.
    b. No playing chicken in the freight yards.
    c. No real rough fighting.

7. *Neither shall you commit adultery. . . .*
    a. No messing around with the girls in the park.
    b. No whoring around.

8. *Neither shall you steal. . . .*
    That's it, don't need to say more.
    Why not? Everybody does it.

9. *Neither shall you bear false witness. . . .*
    No telling lies to the cops or in court, no matter how many breaks they say they'll give you.

10. *Neither shall you covet. . . .*
    a. Stop being so sorry for yourself and always wanting something you ain't got. (Feeling sorry only takes up time when you could be shining shoes to earn money to get the things you covet.)
    b. You ain't supposed to do it—but it's not so bad if it makes you try hard to get something you ain't got—if you don't get it by shoplifting.

Carl F. Burke

TIGERS

Photograph by Sid Avery.

Wild! is the word for the uninhibited jungle beat of Tigress Parfum Extraordinaire...made in France by Fabergé

295

Maneater.

Don't ask for "a martini." Ask for "a maneater."
Bengal Gin. Imported (and undomesticated). Grrrr! 94 proof.

IMPORTED FROM THE UNITED KINGDOM, IN THE BOTTLE, BY GENERAL WINE & SPIRITS COMPANY, N.Y.
DISTILLED FROM 100% GRAIN NEUTRAL SPIRITS.

Grrrr! 94 Proof.

Bengal Gin. Imported (and undomesticated).
Makes a ferocious martini

IMPORTED FROM THE UNITED KINGDOM, IN THE BOTTLE, BY GENERAL WINE & SPIRITS COMPANY, N.Y.
DISTILLED FROM 100% GRAIN NEUTRAL SPIRITS.

How to turn on a tiger.

Get him one of these smart new Man-Time Watches. Fine time-pieces in brushed-chrome, slide-shut cases for playboys, sports-men, guys who go for the smart, sharp, and different. $8.98*
Shock-resistant, anti-magnetic movement. Grrreat gift idea. $9.98*

*SUGGESTED RETAIL PRICE

WESTCLOX
WESTCLOX DIVISION **GENERAL TIME**
Progress in the World of Time

How does a little bug survive in the automotive jungle?

Inconspicuously.

It's rarely observed around gas stations. Because it doesn't often need gas (it gets around 27 miles to a gallon). It doesn't often need tires (it gets around 40,000 miles to a set). And it never goes near the water (its engine is cooled by air instead of water, which means it doesn't need anti-freeze either).

As you can see, the care and feeding of a bug doesn't amount to much. So even though it isn't one of those real wild jungle animals, it makes an ideal house pet.

That explains how 2 little bugs who came to America in 1949 multiplied into 2,000,000.

THE TIGER

Tiger! Tiger! burning bright
In the forests of the night,
What immortal hand or eye
Could frame thy fearful symmetry?

In what distant deeps or skies
Burnt the fire of thine eyes?
On what wings dare he aspire?
What the hand dare seize the fire?

And what shoulder, and what art,
Could twist the sinews of thy heart?
And when thy heart began to beat,
What dread hand? and what dread feet?

What the hammer? what the chain?
In what furnace was thy brain?
What the anvil? what dread grasp
Dare its deadly terrors clasp?

When the stars threw down their spears,
And water'd heaven with their tears,
Did he smile his work to see?
Did he who made the Lamb make thee?

Tiger! Tiger! burning bright
In the forests of the night,
What immortal hand or eye,
Dare frame thy fearful symmetry?

William Blake

"Still, did you ever stop to think
where you and I would be if it <u>weren't</u> for evil?"

300

For the One Who Would Take Man's Life in His Hands

Tiger Christ unsheathed his sword,
Threw it down, became a lamb.
Swift spat upon the species, but
Took two women to his heart.
Samson who was strong as death
Paid his strength to kiss a slut.
Othello that stiff warrior
Was broken by a woman's heart.
Troy burned for a sea-tax, also for
Possession of a charming whore.
What do all examples show?
What must the finished murderer know?

You cannot sit on bayonets,
Nor can you eat among the dead.
When all are killed, you are alone,
A vacuum comes where hate has fed.
Murder's fruit is silent stone,
The gun increases poverty.
With what do these examples shine?
The soldier turned to girls and wine.
Love is the tact of every good,
The only warmth, the only peace.

"What have I said?" asked Socrates,
"Affirmed extremes, cried yes and no,
Taken all parts, denied myself,
Praised the caress, extolled the blow,
Soldier and lover quite deranged
Until their motions are exchanged.
—What do all examples show?
What can any actor know?
The contradiction in every act,
The infinite task of the human heart."

Delmore Schwartz

Triumph of Sensibility

"Tiger, strolling at my side,
Why have you unbound the zone
Of your individual pride?
Why so meek did you come sneaking
After me as I walked alone?

"Since the goat and since the deer
Wait the shattering death you wield
In a constancy of fear,
By your stripes, my strange disciple,
Am I also to be healed?"

"Woman, it was your tender heart
Did my bloody heart compel.
Master-mistress of my art,
Past my wit of wrath your pity,
Ruthless and inexorable.

"I hunt flesh by fallible sense;
You a more exquisite prey pursue
With a finer prescience,
And lap up another's unhappiness:
Woman, let me learn of you."

Sylvia Townsend Warner

MY YEAR WITH THE TIGERS

My wife Kay and I were sitting on the veranda of our bungalow looking out over the forests and meadows to the hills of central India shimmering in the heat of the early afternoon. Several axis deer grazed a hundred feet away and peafowl rustled among the leaves of the forest floor. Suddenly a doe and her small fawn ran, barking in alarm, from the undergrowth. Thirty seconds later a tigress appeared in their tracks. She looked at the doe, then at the fawn which had strayed off to one side. All three froze, oblivious of our presence. At last the fawn broke and attempted to rejoin its mother by dashing past the tigress. In a fraction of a second the tigress had uncoiled her 300 pounds in flashing, bounding pursuit. She pounced on the fawn, muffling its dying bleats, and carried it into the brush. Casually, the doe began to forage.

I had come to India under the auspices of Johns Hopkins University to study big game, in particular the tiger and its relation to the deer, antelope, and other prey species. Until then, the tiger had been studied mostly along the sights of a rifle. The lore that emerged from these necessarily brief encounters attributed to the tiger fearsome characteristics of ferocity, speed, cunning and invincibility. Sporting teams and military units unhesitatingly choose the tiger as the symbol of their prowess. And so too, lately, has the American advertising industry seized on the tiger to sell everything from automobiles to hair dressing. But this lore, while entertaining, provided very little detailed information on the animal's habits.

My hope was to learn about the tiger's true nature, to become acquainted with the animal as it lived undisturbed in its jungle realm. To do this, I roamed the forests alone and unarmed, observing tigers on their hunts, and watching them on moonlight nights from the cover of tree trunks and blinds as they feasted on their kills.

The area I had picked, after much searching for a suitable study area, was Kanha National Park in the state of Madhya Pradesh. It is a small park—not much more than 100 square miles—but quite remote and unspoiled. In the forests of this sanctuary it is still possible to recapture India's past, when wildlife was abundant almost everywhere, when domestic livestock had not overgrazed the range, and when tigers were not the rare creatures they have become elsewhere in the country as the result of decades of ruthless slaughter. Here, too, the tiger lives under optimum conditions, with its three necessities of life—food, water and cover—all in good supply.

The tiger, an adaptable animal, is found in many of the forested parts of India, Burma, Thailand, Laos, Malaya, Sumatra and in Siberia, as well as in a variety of habitats from hot, humid mangrove swamps, reed beds and rain forest, to dry semi-desert shrub and cold coniferous forests where the snow may lie several feet deep during the winter. Naturally it varies somewhat in its behavior from area to area. However, I feel that my observations in Kanha Park are fairly typical of those tigers in India which have not been constantly persecuted by man.

The method I had chosen for studying tigers was not always easy. Tigers are of a shy and retiring nature, and they prefer to go about their daily routines inconspicuously. They travel largely by themselves and tend to stay in cover. They avoid man by stealing away or by hiding in the grass. Sometimes when a tiger resented my intrusion, it growled a warning or gave a coughing roar to indicate its anger. However, there was usually peace between us, even when I once inadvertently approached a sleeping tiger on a rock and we locked eyes at a distance of just three feet.

But the compensations in my method outweighed such disadvantages. I found that tigers are easy to recognize individually at close range by the distinctive patterns of black markings above each eye. I soon learned to distinguish the individual tigers in my study area, and some of these in turn probably knew me on sight. In particular, one tigress with four cubs provided me with endless hours of pleasure, for as the weeks and months passed they grew quite used to my presence.

The quest for food fills much of the tiger's life. It usually hunts alone, padding steadily along at two to three miles per hour, over forest paths, up ravines and through tall grass, eyes and ears alert, trying to sense some unsuspecting victim. Much of the hunting is done between dusk and dawn, when wild pigs, deer and other hoofed animals are out feeding and can be stalked most readily. But when hungry, or when a female has cubs to feed, a tiger may hunt at any time of the day.

The tiger's seemingly unbeatable array of weapons—its acute senses, great speed (but over short distance only), strength and size, and formidable claws and teeth—has given many naturalists the impression that the tiger can kill at will, that it lives in a sort of animal Eden with nothing to do but pluck, so to speak, the fruits of the forest. My experience shows quite the contrary—a tiger has to work quite hard for its meals. During the hot season at Kanha Park, when some 800 head of big game concentrate in less than 5 square miles in order to be near the few remaining waterholes, I observed tigers who sometimes hunted for several nights in a row without being able to kill a single animal. Conditions for the tiger must be just so. It must have some cover to be able to creep close enough to its victim before trying to surprise it during the final rush of about 30 to 80 feet. The prey species also have their own defenses, particularly an acute sense of smell and a speed greater than that of a tiger. I estimate that, for every wild prey killed, the tiger makes 20 to 30 unsuccessful attempts.

Take this example of a frustrating morning in the life of a tigress: I first became aware of her when a jackal yipped and raced along, closely followed by the tiger. She chased this scavenger for a full quarter of a mile, but was easily outdistanced. She then retraced her steps, spotted three swamp deer along the forest edge, and stalked them. However, the deer scented her and barked shrilly, facing the direction of their hidden enemy. Knowing herself discovered, the tigress rose and walked away, moaning softly as tigers often do after an unsuccessful stalk. Seeing seven swamp deer in the distance, the tigress anticipated their movements and hid at the edge of some high grass. When only 40 feet separated the hunter from the hunted, the lead doe gave a shrill bark and the herd wheeled and scattered. The tigress rushed out, swiping the air with her forepaws in a futile attempt to reach one of the animals. She then strode off, while the deer trotted contemptuously some 70 feet behind her, knowing that the tiger, deprived of the factor of surprise, could do them no harm.

By carefully checking the age of nearly 200 remains of deer killed by tigers, I found that many were either young or old. Proportionally few were in the prime of life—and natural selection tends to save those deer with the sharpest senses and swiftest feet. Exceptions are females that are about to fawn, as their bulging abdomen robs them of agility.

In the case of the gaur, a huge type of wild cattle in which the bulls may reach a weight of over 1500 pounds, tigers prey mostly on the calves, taking as many as half of the young born in any one year. But once the gaur are grown, tigers tackle them only infrequently, showing great respect for the sweep of their horns. The tiger cannot afford to make the slightest mistake in attacking a potentially dangerous animal. There are records of gaur and buffalo goring tigers and of wild boars disemboweling them with their tusks.

With so many factors arrayed against them, it is not surprising that tigers may go hungry for several days. Sometimes they are reduced to eating langur monkeys, frogs, bird eggs, crabs, even berries. Once I watched a tigress pounce into a thicket in an attempt to catch jungle fowl, five of which flushed cackling around her. Any meat, including carrion no matter how decomposed, will do. And they are not above robbing a leopard of its prey. In one instance, a leopard killed an axis deer fawn near me, but that night a tigress with one small cub appropriated the carcass.

Taking India as a whole, domestic cattle and domestic buffalo are the most important items in the tiger's diet. With the wildlife in most forests decimated or eliminated, the tiger has taken partly or wholly to living on livestock, which is easy to kill and readily available. At least 10 per cent of the cattle grazing in Kanha Park and on its fringes are killed by tigers each year.

Once a tiger has made a kill, its life revolves around the carcass until all meat, viscera and soft bones have been eaten. The tiger sleeps nearby, perhaps under a shady clump of bamboo or partially submerged in a forest pool. At intervals throughout the day it returns to the remains, sometimes for a snack and at other times to charge with a roar at any imprudent crows or vultures that may have descended to the kill. The tiger often hides the carcass in a ravine or paws grass and dirt over it to prevent the scavengers from stripping the meat off the bones. The number of days spent beside a kill depends, of course, on the size of the victim. An axis deer weighing 125 pounds may last two to three days, a 300-pound swamp deer five or six days, before the last rotting scrap has been devoured.

I estimate that the average adult tiger needs about 15 to 20 pounds of meat per day, or roughly $3\frac{1}{2}$ tons per year, to remain in prime condition. However, as only about 60 to 70 per cent of each prey animal is edible, the rest being bones and stomach contents, each tiger has to kill about $4\frac{1}{2}$ tons of animal every year. Thus, the annual needs of a tiger would be satisfied by some 30 of India's scrubby cattle or by about 70 adult axis deer. Actually, tigers have to kill more than this in most areas, because they are frequently chased from the remains by man, especially if they have attacked a domestic animal. Where tigers are persistently shot at over their kills, they have learned never to return for a second meal.

When all the meat has been devoured, the tiger again begins its nightly rounds, probably covering about 15 to 20 miles of terrain between dusk and dawn. Most adults hunt within a definite range using certain routes and resting places more frequently than others. One tigress I came to know at Kanha roamed over about 25 square miles of forest, but most of her hunting was done in about eight square miles. However, the ranges of some tigers, especially in areas where game is scarce, may be considerably larger.

A tigress will readily share all or part of her jungle beat with other females and with a male. However, an adult male probably will not tolerate for long the presence of another male within the boundaries of his range. At least at Kanha, I noted that only one male was resident in the whole central part of the park, and another was once a casual visitor, whereas I knew of three resident and at least six transient tigresses. Such transients appeared to be tigresses in heat who had abandoned their range in some distant forest to wander widely in search of a mate. They passed through my study area, particularly from December to February, stayed perhaps a day or two, then disappeared. A male probably mates with any female in heat, resident or transient, found within the boundaries of its territory. The territory thus functions as a spacing mechanism, decreasing competition between males for the females.

Perhaps no aspect of the tiger's behavior has been as misunderstood as its social life. They are often said to be totally solitary, except during mating. It is true that tigers generally hunt alone, but it is also quite common for them to meet briefly during the night. Tigers possess quite efficient means of long-distance communication. The main one is a call signifying, "Here I am"—a roaring *aa-uuu, aa-uuu*, repeated again and again with emphasis on the first vowel. In the stillness of the night this sound carries for well over a mile. Both male and female tigers raise their tails at intervals when walking along and spray a mixture of scent and urine on trees and bushes, leaving a powerful odor which in some instances I could discern for as long as three months. The odor undoubtedly helps tigers to track and find each other in the forest, in addition to serving as calling cards.

Tigers also share kills. Once, for example, a tigress loudly called her distant cubs to dinner by sending her *aa-uuu* rolling over the forest. From afar came an answer. More than an hour later another tigress joined the family in their feast. On another occasion a tigress with four cubs and a tigress with one cub remained together for at least two days at a kill.

The male tiger who presided over the section of Kanha Park that I was studying was a huge, amiable fellow with a scraggly ruff surrounding his face. He was a gentleman in the true sense of the word when it came to dealing with the females and cubs that shared his range. The tigresses in turn appeared to trust and like him, and they made no effort to keep him away from their cubs, even fairly small ones. Once a total of seven tigers—two tigresses, four cubs, and the male—shared a bullock. On another occasion the male visited the female with four cubs at their kill. Although he was obviously hungry and the meat must have been tempting, he lay down 20 feet away and waited patiently until everyone had finished before taking his first bite. Intermittently the cubs rubbed their faces against his and sinuously moved their bodies along his head and neck—the typical friendly greeting between tigers. He remained with the family until morning, then resumed his rounds—solitary but certainly not unsociable.

The most lasting social bond is between a tigress and her cubs. After a gestation period of about 105 days the cubs—there may be only one or as many as seven, but the average is two to three—are born blind and helpless under some rocky ledge or fallen tree. There the mother suckles them and perhaps brings them meat. By the age of 6 weeks they leave their shelter to accompany the tigress to the kill for the first time. From that day on they never again have a permanent home, but live like nomads, moving from covert to covert and from kill to kill. Their life is spent waiting quietly for hours and days in some hidden spot for the tigress to return to lead them to a meal.

I first encountered the tiger family I was to become particularly well acquainted with when the four cubs were about 4 months old and the size of setter dogs. The mother had killed a bull gaur in a shallow ravine and I watched the family throughout the night from behind a tree at a distance of 100 feet. During the hours of darkness the cubs mostly ate the carcass and slept, but when the sun replaced the moon they began to play. They raced in a single file, stalked each other through the grass and wrestled vigorously. They explored their surroundings, sniffing at leaves, looking into holes, occasionally pouncing on something—perhaps an insect. As the cool of the morning gave way to the searing heat of the day, the tigress arose, emitted a series of low grunts—evidently meaning "Follow me"—and led her brood to a shady bower nearby. For five days the family camped by the dead gaur until it was gone. Then they disappeared. Eleven days later I again saw the tigress, walking across the meadow at mid-afternoon dragging a freshly killed gaur calf by the neck. The calf's mother paced nervously back and forth at the edge of the forest but lacked the courage to attack the tigress. Stopping now and then to adjust her grip, the tigress hauled her kill out of sight into a grassy ravine. There she apparently ate a little and then rested. An hour and a half later, she reappeared and padded steadily off into the forest. When darkness fell, several swamp deer barked hysterically as the tigress returned, bringing her cubs to the feast. Then came the sounds of tigers at a kill: the crunch of bones, the grating of teeth cutting skin, the occasional growl or cough of a minor dispute between the cubs. The cubs had their own pecking order, with the largest taking the choicest feeding spot and the smallest sometimes having to wait for its meal until a place was vacated. (When food is scarce, the weaklings probably die. It appears uncommon for a tigress to raise as many as four cubs to adulthood. But mine seemed to be making it.) By next morning the family had totally finished the gaur calf, and, led by the tigress, they filed away to a copse of trees near a waterhole about half a mile distant. I had weighed the calf earlier, when the mother first went to fetch her cubs, and now I checked the few remaining scraps of bone. The tigers had eaten a total of 85 pounds during the night.

While the cubs are small, the tigress sometimes takes a respite from her hunting duties and rests even though the larder is empty. The family I watched once ate an axis deer during the night, but on the following evening, instead of going out to hunt again, the female just lay in the grass on her back, legs up in the air, while the cubs wrestled with each other all around her. One of the cubs climbed over her stomach, another followed and she cuffed it lightly, then a third draped itself over her face and gnawed on an ear. All the next day the animals lolled indolently in the deep grass, but at dusk the tigress set off alone on a hunt. Only a little over an hour later she was able to kill a buffalo that had strayed from the village—a lucky find which provided the family with meat for another two days.

As the cubs grew older, nights of leisure were a thing of the past for the tigress. She had great difficulty in securing enough food to satisfy her ravenous brood. When the cubs had reached the age of one year—and were as large as a St. Bernard—they required the equivalent of one axis deer per day and it was almost too much for the tigress to handle. Repeatedly she invaded the cattle enclosure in the nearest village at night until, in desperation, the villagers removed all their livestock from the area. She also stole a lamb we were fattening for our Christmas dinner by clawing her way into our shed. And unable to obtain enough food at home, the male cub—by then considerably larger than his female siblings—set off on his own. He was inexperienced but determined. One day he entered the village and secured a pig; and on another night he demolished our chickenhouse and ate all five occupants. However, he remained in contact with the rest of the family and usually showed up when there was something to eat.

Until the age of one year the cubs seemed to have no actual experience in hunting big game. But now one or more sometimes accompanied their mother on her nightly prowl. She in turn appeared to make a definite effort to provide them with experience in the art of killing. On one occasion she felled a buffalo without injuring it, then stepped back while three of her cubs attempted to kill it. They were so inept that the buffalo shook them off. Once again the tigress pulled the animal down for the cubs, and finally, biting almost at random, they managed to dispatch it. Obviously the cubs had much to learn before they could survive on their own. Even at the age of 16 months the female cubs were not proficient at killing. However, the male cub, which weighed well over 200 pounds and by trial and error had gathered experience on his own, had become quite adept. Soon the bond between the cubs and their mother grew tenuous. Every two or so days she dropped by to see them, and undoubtedly provided an occasional kill—just enough to tide them over from partial independence to the complete independence they would reach by the age of two years. By that time she would probably have a new litter of cubs.

This then is the life of the tiger. To kill to live is its main concern, and much of its energy and time is devoted to the task of securing a meal. Like all cats the tiger presents a violent contrast between action and indolence, gentleness and courage, shyness and persistence, and like all cats it possesses a certain exalted indifference that makes any attempt by man to enter the world of the tiger both difficult and challenging.

Yet it is worth the effort to try. Partly—perhaps mostly—there is the beauty of the beast. To see a tiger striding on velvety paws across a meadow of yellow grass, with the fading rays of the setting sun harmonizing with its tawny, black-striped coat—self-assured, a picture of barely contained power yet lithe grace, the very symbol of physical beauty, strength and dignity—is surely one of the greatest aesthetic experiences in nature.

George B. Schaller

The Lion

The Lion, the Lion, he dwells in the waste,
He has a big head and a very small waist;
But his shoulders are stark, and his jaws they are grim,
And a good little child will not play with him.

The Tiger

The Tiger, on the other hand, is kittenish and mild,
He makes a pretty playfellow for any little child;
And mothers of large families (who claim to common sense)
Will find a Tiger well repays the trouble and expense.

Hilaire Belloc

The Lady, or The Tiger?

Frank Stockton

In the very olden time, there lived a semi-barbaric king, whose ideas, though somewhat polished and sharpened by the progressiveness of distant Latin neighbors, were still large, florid, and untrammelled, as became the half of him which was barbaric. He was a man of exuberant fancy, and, withal, of an authority so irresistible that, at his will, he turned his varied fancies into facts. He was greatly given to self-communing; and, when he and himself agreed upon any thing, the thing was done. When every member of his domestic and political systems moved smoothly in its appointed course, his nature was bland and genial; but whenever there was a little hitch, and some of his orbs got out of their orbits, he was blander and more genial still, for nothing pleased him so much as to make the crooked straight, and crush down uneven places.

Among the borrowed notions by which his barbarism had become semified was that of the public arena, in which, by exhibitions of manly and beastly valor, the minds of his subjects were refined and cultured.

But even here the exuberant and barbaric fancy asserted itself. The arena of the king was built, not to give the people an opportunity of hearing the rhapsodies of dying gladiators, nor to enable them to view the inevitable conclusion of a conflict between religious opinions and hungry jaws, but for purposes far better adapted to widen and develop the mental energies of the people. This vast amphitheatre, with its encircling galleries, its mysterious vaults, and its unseen passages, was an agent of poetic justice, in which crime was punished, or virtue rewarded, by the decrees of an impartial and incorruptible chance.

When a subject was accused of a crime of sufficient importance to interest the king, public notice was given that on an appointed day the fate of the accused person would be decided in the king's arena,—a structure which well deserved its name; for, although its form and plan were borrowed from afar, its purpose emanated solely from the brain of this man, who, every barleycorn a king, knew no tradition to which he owed more allegiance than pleased his fancy, and who ingrafted on every adopted form of human thought and action the rich growth of his barbaric idealism.

When all the people had assembled in the galleries, and the king, surrounded by his court, sat high up on his throne of royal state on one side of the arena, he gave a signal, a door beneath him opened, and the accused subject stepped out into the amphitheatre. Directly opposite him, on the other side of the enclosed space, were two doors, exactly alike and side by side. It was the duty and the privilege of the person on trial to walk directly to these doors and open one of them. He could open either door he pleased: he was subject to no guidance or influence but that of the aforementioned impartial and incorruptible chance. If he opened the one, there came out of it a hungry tiger, the fiercest and most cruel that could be procured, which immediately sprang upon him, and tore him to pieces, as a punishment for his guilt. The moment that the case of the criminal was thus decided, doleful iron bells were clanged, great wails went up from the hired mourners posted on the outer rim of the arena, and the vast audience, with bowed heads and downcast hearts, wended slowly their homeward way, mourning greatly that one so young and fair, or so old and respected, should have merited so dire a fate.

But, if the accused person opened the other door, there came forth from it a lady, the most suitable to his years and station that his majesty could select among his fair subjects; and to this lady he was immediately married, as a reward of his innocence. It mattered not that he might already possess a wife and family, or that his affections might be engaged upon an object of his own selection: the king allowed no such subordinate arrangements to interfere with his great scheme of retribution and reward. The exercises, as in the other instance, took place immediately, and in the arena. Another door opened beneath the king, and a priest, followed by a band of choristers, and dancing maidens blowing joyous airs on golden horns and treading an epithalamic measure, advanced to where the pair stood, side by side; and the wedding was promptly and cheerily solemnized. Then the gay brass bells rang forth their merry peals, the people shouted glad hurrahs, and the innocent man, preceded by children strewing flowers on his path, led his bride to his home.

This was the king's semi-barbaric method of administering justice. Its perfect fairness is obvious. The criminal could not know out of which door would come the lady: he opened either he pleased, without having the slightest idea whether, in the next instant, he was to be devoured or married. On some occasions the tiger came out of one door, and on some out of the other. The decisions of this tribunal were not only fair, they were positively determinate: the accused person was instantly punished if he found himself guilty; and, if innocent, he was rewarded on the spot, whether he liked it or not. There was no escape from the judgments of the king's arena.

313

The institution was a very popular one. When the people gathered together on one of the great trial days, they never knew whether they were to witness a bloody slaughter or a hilarious wedding. This element of uncertainty lent an interest to the occasion which it could not otherwise have attained. Thus, the masses were entertained and pleased, and the thinking part of the community could bring no charge of unfairness against this plan; for did not the accused person have the whole matter in his own hands?

This semi-barbaric king had a daughter as blooming as his most florid fancies, and with a soul as fervent and imperious as his own. As is usual in such cases, she was the apple of his eye, and was loved by him above all humanity. Among his courtiers was a young man of that fineness of blood and lowness of station common to the conventional heroes of romance who love royal maidens. This royal maiden was well satisfied with her lover, for he was handsome and brave to a degree unsurpassed in all this kingdom; and she loved him with an ardor that had enough of barbarism in it to make it exceedingly warm and strong. This love affair moved on happily for many months, until one day the king happened to discover its existence. He did not hesitate nor waver in regard to his duty in the premises. The youth was immediately cast into prison, and a day was appointed for his trial in the king's arena. This, of course, was an especially important occasion; and his majesty, as well as all the people, was greatly interested in the workings and development of this trial. Never before had such a case occurred; never before had a subject dared to love the daughter of a king. In after-years such things became commonplace enough; but then they were, in no slight degree, novel and startling.

The tiger-cages of the kingdom were searched for the most savage and relentless beasts, from which the fiercest monster might be selected for the arena; and the ranks of maiden youth and beauty throughout the land were carefully surveyed by competent judges, in order that the young man might have a fitting bride in case fate did not determine for him a different destiny. Of course, everybody knew that the deed with which the accused was charged had been done. He had loved the princess, and neither he, she, nor any one else thought of denying the fact; but the king would not think of allowing any fact of this kind to interfere with the workings of the tribunal, in which he took such great delight and satisfaction. No matter how the affair turned out, the youth would be disposed of; and the king would take an aesthetic pleasure in watching the course of events, which would determine whether or not the young man had done wrong in allowing himself to love the princess.

The appointed day arrived. From far and near the people gathered, and thronged the great galleries of the arena; and crowds, unable to gain admittance, massed themselves against its outside walls. The king and his court were in their places, opposite the twin doors,—those fateful portals, so terrible in their similarity.

All was ready. The signal was given. A door beneath the royal party opened, and the lover of the princess walked into the arena. Tall, beautiful, fair, his appearance was greeted with a low hum of admiration and anxiety. Half the audience had not known so grand a youth had lived among them. No wonder the princess loved him! What a terrible thing for him to be there!

As the youth advanced into the arena, he turned, as the custom was, to bow to the king: but he did not think at all of that royal personage; his eyes were fixed upon the princess, who sat to the right of her father. Had it not been for the moiety of barbarism in her nature, it is probable that lady would not have been there; but her intense and fervid soul would not allow her to be absent on an occasion in which she was so terribly interested. From the moment that the decree had gone forth, that her lover should decide his fate in the king's arena, she had thought of nothing, night or day, but this great event and the various subjects connected with it. Possessed of more power, influence, and force of character than any one who had ever before been interested in such a case, she had done what no other person had done,—she had possessed herself of the secret of the doors. She knew in which of the two rooms, that lay behind those doors, stood the cage of the tiger, with its open front, and in which waited the lady. Through these thick doors, heavily curtained with skins on the inside, it was impossible that any noise or suggestion should come from within to the person who should approach to raise the latch of one of them; but gold, and the power of a woman's will, had brought the secret to the princess.

315

And not only did she know in which room stood the lady ready to emerge, all blushing and radiant, should her door be opened, but she knew who the lady was. It was one of the fairest and loveliest of the damsels of the court who had been selected as the reward of the accused youth, should he be proved innocent of the crime of aspiring to one so far above him; and the princess hated her. Often had she seen, or imagined that she had seen, this fair creature throwing glances of admiration upon the person of her lover, and sometimes she thought these glances were perceived and even returned. Now and then she had seen them talking together; it was but for a moment or two, but much can be said in a brief space; it may have been on most unimportant topics, but how could she know that? The girl was lovely, but she had dared to raise her eyes to the loved one of the princess; and, with all the intensity of the savage blood transmitted to her through long lines of wholly barbaric ancestors, she hated the woman who blushed and trembled behind that silent door.

When her lover turned and looked at her, and his eye met hers as she sat there paler and whiter than any one in the vast ocean of anxious faces about her, he saw, by that power of quick perception which is given to those whose souls are one, that she knew behind which door crouched the tiger, and behind which stood the lady. He had expected her to know it. He understood her nature, and his soul was assured that she would never rest until she had made plain to herself this thing, hidden to all other lookers-on, even to the king. The only hope for the youth in which there was any element of certainty was based upon the success of the princess in discovering this mystery; and the moment he looked upon her, he saw she had succeeded, as in his soul he knew she would succeed.

Then it was that his quick and anxious glance asked the question: "Which?" It was as plain to her as if he shouted it from where he stood. There was not an instant to be lost. The question was asked in a flash; it must be answered in another.

Her right arm lay on the cushioned parapet before her. She raised her hand, and made a slight, quick movement toward the right. No one but her lover saw her. Every eye but his was fixed on the man in the arena.

He turned, and with a firm and rapid step he walked across the empty space. Every heart stopped beating, every breath was held, every eye was fixed immovably upon that man. Without the slightest hesitation, he went to the door on the right, and opened it.

Now, the point of the story is this: Did the tiger come out of that door, or did the lady?

The more we reflect upon this question, the harder it is to answer. It involves a study of the human heart which leads us through devious mazes of passion, out of which it is difficult to find our way. Think of it, fair reader, not as if the decision of the question depended upon yourself, but upon that hot-blooded, semi-barbaric princess, her soul at a white heat beneath the combined fires of despair and jealousy. She had lost him, but who should have him?

How often, in her waking hours and in her dreams, had she started in wild horror, and covered her face with her hands as she thought of her lover opening the door on the other side of which waited the cruel fangs of the tiger!

But how much oftener had she seen him at the other door! How in her grievous reveries had she gnashed her teeth, and torn her hair, when she saw his start of rapturous delight as he opened the door of the lady! How her soul had burned in agony when she had seen him rush to meet that woman, with her flushing cheek and sparkling eye of triumph; when she had seen him lead her forth, his whole frame kindled with the joy of recovered life; when she had heard the glad shouts from the multitude, and the wild ringing of the happy bells; when she had seen the priest, with his joyous followers, advance to the couple, and make them man and wife before her very eyes; and when she had seen them walk away together upon their path of flowers, followed by the tremendous shouts of the hilarious multitude, in which her one despairing shriek was lost and drowned!

Would it not be better for him to die at once, and go to wait for her in the blessed regions of semi-barbaric futurity?

And yet, that awful tiger, those shrieks, that blood!

Her decision had been indicated in an instant, but it had been made after days and nights of anguished deliberation. She had known she would be asked, she had decided what she would answer, and, without the slightest hesitation, she had moved her hand to the right.

The question of her decision is one not to be lightly considered, and it is not for me to presume to set myself up as the one person able to answer it. And so I leave it with all of you: Which came out of the opened door,—the lady, or the tiger?

317

TOMBSTONES ARE ERECTED IN INDO-CHINA OVER THE GRAVES OF **WILD TIGERS** *!* NATIVES HOPE TO ESCAPE THE VENGEANCE OF THE SLAIN ANIMAL'S SPIRIT

tiger Tigers are sensitive and easily insulted. In Malaya, Sumatra, Assam, the Bengal, and southern China where tigers are native, they are notable for their bravery, and are man-killers, and shapeshifters. In a central Chinese version of the Red Riding Hood story, the tiger takes the place of the west European wolf and eats the old woman. The people of this area also believe that having eaten a man, the tiger can force the man's physical ghost to walk before him through the jungle and entice other victims. When the next victim has been devoured, the ghost of the first is liberated.

Propitiation ceremonies are frequent and often concern the sensitiveness of tigers. In some of the Sumatran villages, people will not speak disrespectfully of tigers. If a trail has been unused for some time the villagers will not use it because they fear they might be trespassing. If they travel bareheaded the tiger might take this as a mark of disrespect; when traveling at night they will not look behind them because the tiger might think they are afraid of him and this too would offend him. At night they will not knock out a firebrand because the sparks are the tiger's eyes. They will kill a tiger only in self-defense or after a tiger has killed a near relative. When strange hunters set traps villagers have been known to go to the place and explain to the tiger that *they* did not do it. Normally they try to catch killer-tigers alive and before killing them explain why it is necessary to perform the execution and ask forgiveness for what they are about to do. The Battas, who kill only killer-tigers, bring the carcass back to the village, pray its soul into an incense pot, burn incense, and ask the spirits to explain to the tiger why it was necessary to execute it. They then dance around the carcass until they are exhausted. They believe that human souls may have migrated into the tiger's body. A priest offers food and drink and asks the soul not to be angry. The hill folk of Bengal believe that if a man kills a tiger without divine orders he or a near relative will in turn be killed by a tiger. Having killed, the hunter lays his weapons on the tiger's carcass, reports to his god that this was a just punishment for the tiger's crimes, and promises not to kill again unless provoked. The Cochin Chinese trap tigers and then lament over them.

Certain peoples of the Malay Peninsula believe that tigers live in houses in cities of their own, and describe a fabulous Tiger Village where the roofs are thatched with human hair. A young boy who was "given many stripes" by his teacher ran away into the forest and became the first tiger, and he knows the secret of certain magic leaves to heal his wounds. All over the Peninsula tiger claws and tiger whiskers are valued as potent charms. One tiger whisker knotted into a man's facial hair will terrify his enemies. Quite generally also the tiger is regarded as the familiar of the medicine man or magician, and is said to be immortal.

The Miris of Assam think that tiger meat when eaten will give strength and courage to men but should not be eaten by women because it would make them too strong-minded. In Korean belief, tiger bones when ground to a powder and taken with wine will give strength and are more potent than leopard's bones which serve the same purpose. A Chinese in Seoul is reported to have bought and eaten a whole tiger in order to become brave and fierce. The gallbladder is considered particularly potent.

In south and central China the tiger is as notable a shapeshifter as the fox in north China. The stories are much the same but the protagonist differs. [RDJ]

Standard Dictionary of Folklore and Mythology (New York: Funk & Wagnalls, 1950).

318

THE JUNGLE: TIGER ATTACKING A BUFFALO

Henri Rousseau: *THE JUNGLE: TIGER ATTACKING A BUFFALO*
The Cleveland Museum of Art, Gift of Hanna Fund.

A Note on the Type

This book has been set in a variety of type
faces, some of which are noted below:

p.1	title type 48 pt. Bank Script
2	text type 10/12 Melior
5	title type 14/18 Laurel Bold
7	title type 30 pt. Bodoni Modern; text type 9/10 Imperial
10	title type 14 pt. Fraktur
17	text type 11/12 Helvetica Medium
20	title type 18 pt. Davida Bold
22	caption type 12 pt. Kismet
23	title type 24 pt. Smoke; text type 10/12 Baskerville Roman; author name type 12 pt. Smoke
35	title type 8 pt. and up Gothic Shaded Condensed
37	title type 24 pt. Alfereta
40	title type 18 pt. Michelangelo with facing R's
43	title type 48 pt. Caslon; initial cap 48 pt. Excelsior Script
44	title type 18 pt. Profil
45	title type 18 pt. Bernard Fashion
51	title type 36 pt. Ringlet; author name type 18 pt. Ringlet
70	title type 14 pt. P. T. Barnum
87	title type 36 pt. Libra Italic; author name type 12 pt. Helvetica Light Italic
94	title type 18 pt. Buxom
96	title type 36 pt. Ad Lib
104	title type 24 pt. Garamond Italic
105	title type 30 pt. Grotesque Bold Titling No. 1
117	title type 20 pt. Futura Black
123	title type 30 pt. Cubist Bold; text type 10 pt. Standard Bold
126	title type 36 pt. Fairlane
131	title type Folio Bold Italic
134	text type 10/12 Times Bold Italic
138	title type 48 pt. Futura Ultra Bold Antique
141	title type 48 pt. Phosphor; author name type 12 pt. Standard Bold
144	title type 30 pt. Recherche; author name type 18 pt. Recherche
148	title type 24 pt. Permanent Massiv; author name type 16 pt. Permanent Headline Solid
154	title type 72 pt. Clear Face Heavy; author name type 18 pt. Clear Face Heavy
156	title type 30 pt. Concerto; author name type 18 pt. Concerto
159	title type 24 pt. Pistilli Roman Outline
162	title type 24 pt. Comstock
186	title type 60 pt. Gold Rush
189	title type 48 pt. Caslon Antique
190	title type 30 pt. Arriola Caslon Swash; text type 10/11 Bodoni Bold Italic
191	title type 24 pt. Regina Titling; text type 10/11 Folio
192	title type 36 pt. Intrigue; text type 10/11 Optima; author name type 18 pt. Intrigue
196	title type 30 pt. Cooper Contour; author name type 18 pt. Augusta Inline
198	title type 24 pt. Cooper Italic Swash
199	title type 10 pt. Plantin Bold
200	title type 30 pt. Caslon Openface
202	title type (Rubaiyat) 30 pt. Khayyam; text type 11/12 Times Roman Italic; title type (Ozymandias) 24 pt. Egyptian Bold Expanded; text type 10/12 Century Schoolbook
203	title type 12 pt. Windsor Light Italic
205	title type 18 pt. Roman No. 1
206	title type 24 pt. Epic Shaded Caps; text type 10/12 Palatino
208	title type 18/22 Aurora Bold Condensed
210	title type 36 pt. Stradivarius
211	title type 30 pt. Gazette No. 24; text type 10/11 Futura Medium
212	title type 42 pt. Stripes; text type 11/12 Garamond; author name type 24 pt. Stripes

219 title type 12 pt. Toga Bold Swash
220 title type 18 pt. Crayon; text type
11/12 Laurel
221 title type 48 pt. Twogar Caps; text
type 10/11 Century Expanded; author
name type 18 pt. Matador
241 title type 36 pt. Roman No. 1 Outline
254 title type 25 pt. Karnac
255 author name type 18 pt. Karnac
258 title type 12 pt. Bookman Bold
259 title type 18 pt. Bookman Italic Swash;
author name type 14 pt. Bookman
Italic Swash
260 title type 72 pt. Dodge Ornate; author
name type 18 pt. Dodge Caps

269 title type 18 pt. City Bold; text type
10/13 News Gothic; author name type
14 pt. City Light (Bierce selection)
270 title type 30 pt. New Times Black
273 title type 24 pt. Victory
274 title type 72 pt. Antiqua Bold; author
name type 24 pt. Antiqua Bold
287 title type 30 pt. Rome; author name
type 24 pt. Menlor Lined
289 title type Arriola Caslon
293 title type Futura Black Open
299 14 pt. Eurostyle Bold
301 text type 11/12 Futura Book
311 title type 36 pt. Sign
319 caption type 10 pt. Manor Caps

The book was designed by John Reuter-Pacyna.
The compositors were Graphic Services, Inc., York, Pennsylvania,
and Frederic Ryder Co., Chicago, Illinois.
The engravers were Graphic Services, Inc., and
Kieffer-Nolde, Chicago, Illinois.
The printer and binder was Rand-McNally, Chicago, Illinois.